Who Are You, and Who Am I?

In this book, Hannes Wiher, a renowned evangelical missiologist in the French-speaking world, has developed an in-depth study of culture with the aim of equipping the body of Christ with an understanding of societies, religions and worldviews, in order to communicate the gospel to different communities in a way that is faithful to Scripture and relevant to multiple cultures. Based on an interdisciplinary study that navigates through cultural anthropology, psychology, philosophy, theology and Bible translation, Wiher develops five models of cross-cultural communication that help the missionary to share the good news with a deeper understanding of people's identities so as to win the world for Christ with effectiveness, conscience and love. Based on an accurate scholarship in missiology, practical theology and linguistics, the book is highly recommended for intercultural studies and ministries to the unreached communities.

George P. Atido, PhD
Rector and Professor of Missiology and World Christianity,
Shalom University of Bunia, Democratic Republic of the Congo

Veteran missiologist and author Hannes Wiher provides the global church with a text that is interdisciplinary, drawing on communication theory, philosophy, anthropology, theology and missiology. The text is not merely about anthropological theory and cultural description – it has as its stated purpose the goal of improving relationships that enable faithful gospel transmission. One outstanding feature that separates this work from others like it is how Wiher consistently brings to the forefront the critical global issues of honour and shame. This work is biblically grounded and would serve as an excellent introductory text for the study of culture and mission, especially for those who wish to pursue an approach that focusses on worldview.

Christopher L. Flanders, PhD
Professor of Missions, Graduate School of Theology,
Abilene Christian University, Texas, USA

A must for all those who teach cross-cultural workers. A book that I myself as a lecturer wish I had known much earlier. Why? Because the so-called short-cuts, simplifications and generalizations, at first glance hard to accept (for myself), are not arbitrary but the result of decades of teaching. They lead to concise and practicable grids, which can be used in various teaching and ministry contexts. At the same time, they help teachers to not get lost in the virtually infinite realities of cultures, religions and worldviews.

The clear structure of the book is impressive. The well-chosen and precise case studies exemplify its practical use. Important elements are repeated, partly in helpful summaries. The cyclic structure of the book itself serves as a teaching model for teachers; cultures, religions and worldviews can be taught only as living and whole entities. The appendixes provide comprehensive and compact teaching aids. The concluding index makes the work an indispensable compendium.

Martin Heißwolf, ThD
Dean of Missiology,
BibelStudienKolleg, Germany
Chairman of missiotop

This book presents an introduction to the modern understanding of culture in the comprehensive sense, as understood by cultural anthropology and ethnology, as a primarily mental system of rules, attributions, understanding of the world, instructions for action, etc. The author works strictly according to the layered model of mental deep structure adopted from linguistics in recent anthropological research. The deep structures generate then surface structures of human behaviour accessible to the senses. The author conclusively proves that knowledge of this connection is essential for understanding people of other cultures. The consequences that result for the task of evangelization, and for other fields, are presented systematically and didactically. As an introduction to this topic, the textbook is a novelty. It is intended for ethnological and anthropological lay people.

Lothar Käser, PhD
Emeritus Professor of Ethnology,
University of Freiburg, Germany

Communicating effectively requires a better understanding of a person beyond appearances, as several dynamics come into play, including personality, culture and religion. Hannes Wiher's book, although conceived through a theoretical framework of Western literature, is a goldmine for researchers and communicators of any doctrinal tendencies and sociological contexts for a transformational engagement and a contextual theological discourse. The complexity of such a requirement is meticulously demonstrated, unraveled and resolved in this highly informative book, thanks to the author's international and multicultural experience. Theologians of any discipline and missionaries of various ministries are particularly encouraged to make use of this valuable tool, but with regard for their own context or the context of their working environment.

Fohle Lygunda li-M, PhD
Professor of Missiology and Contextual Theology,
North-West University, South Africa

As a teacher of missiology in the theological seminaries of French-speaking Africa, I often have difficulties finding an adequate work for the preparatory readings of the courses in cultural anthropology and models of cultural analysis. The book, *Who Are You, and Who Am I?*, by Hannes Wiher, fills the void and brings functional clarity to the central question, how to communicate the gospel in a way that is faithful to Scripture and relevant to peoples and their cultures. As the author so aptly put it, reaching people with our biblical message implies that our communication takes place at the deep level of peoples, cultures and religions. This book represents a rare blend of solid scholarship and practical experience. If you are scholars, Bible college students, theology students, or missionaries, pastors, church leaders and Christians interested in cross-cultural gospel communication, this book is for you!

Djimalngar Madjibaye, PhD
Professor of Missiology,
Bangui Evangelical School of Theology (FATEB),
Bangui, Central African Republic, and Yaoundé, Cameroon,
Shalom Evangelical School of Theology (FATES), N'Djamena, Chad

Who Are You, and Who Am I?

Biblical and Anthropological Models for Understanding Each Other

Hannes Wiher

© 2024 Hannes Wiher

Translation from German by Derek Cheeseman.
Title of the German version (forthcoming): *Wer bist du, und wer bin ich? Wie man Menschen und Kulturen verstehen lernt, damit Begegnungen und das Teilen der guten Nachricht gelingen können.*

English version published 2024 by Langham Global Library
An imprint of Langham Publishing
www.langhampublishing.org

Langham Publishing and its imprints are a ministry of Langham Partnership

Langham Partnership
PO Box 296, Carlisle, Cumbria, CA3 9WZ, UK
www.langham.org

ISBNs:
978-1-78641-025-2 Print
978-1-78641-088-7 ePub
978-1-78641-089-4 PDF

Hannes Wiher has asserted his right under the Copyright, Designs and Patents Act, 1988 to be identified as the Author of this work.

All rights reserved. No part of this publication may be reproduced, stored in a retrieval system or transmitted, in any form or by any means, electronic, mechanical, photocopying, recording or otherwise, without the prior written permission of the publisher or the Copyright Licensing Agency.

Requests to reuse content from Langham Publishing are processed through PLSclear. Please visit www.plsclear.com to complete your request.

Unless otherwise stated, Scripture quotations are from the New Revised Standard Version Bible, copyright © 1989 National Council of the Churches of Christ in the United States of America. Used by permission. All rights reserved.

Scripture quotations marked (NIV) are taken from the Holy Bible, New International Version®, NIV®. Copyright © 1973, 1978, 1984, 2011 by Biblica, Inc.™ Used by permission of Zondervan.

Scripture quotations marked (NLT) are taken from the Holy Bible, New Living Translation, copyright © 1996, 2004, 2007, 2013, 2015 by Tyndale House Foundation. Used by permission of Tyndale House Publishers, Inc., Carol Stream, Illinois 60188. All rights reserved.

Scripture quotations marked (NKJV) are taken from New King James Version (NKJV). Copyright © 1982 by Thomas Nelson, Inc. Used by permission. All rights reserved.

Scripture quotations marked (NJB) are taken from *The New Jerusalem Bible*, published and copyright 1985 by Darton, Longman & Todd Ltd and *Les Editions du Cerf*, and used by permission of the publishers.

The Koran is cited according to *The Holy Quran*, Text, Translation and Commentary by Abdullah Yusuf Ali (Doha: Publications of Presidency of Islamic Courts & Affairs, State of Qatar, 1946).

British Library Cataloguing-in-Publication Data
A catalogue record for this book is available from the British Library

ISBN: 978-1-78641-025-2

Cover & Book Design: projectluz.com

Langham Partnership actively supports theological dialogue and an author's right to publish but does not necessarily endorse the views and opinions set forth here or in works referenced within this publication, nor can we guarantee technical and grammatical correctness. Langham Partnership does not accept any responsibility or liability to persons or property as a consequence of the reading, use or interpretation of its published content.

Contents

1 Introduction 1
    1.1 Learning to Understand Peoples and Their Cultures   2
    1.2 Integrating Biblical and Scientific Data   3
    1.3 Structure of the Book   5
    1.4 Hint for the Reader   5

2 Basic Concepts: Personality, Culture and Religion 7
    2.1 Socio-Anthropological Theories Underlying the Basic Concepts   7
    2.2 Personality   9
        2.2.1 Brief History of the Development of the Concept   9
        2.2.2 Biblical-Theological Approach to Personality   10
        2.2.3 Anthropological Approach to Personality   11
        2.2.4 Synthesis   13
    2.3 Culture   14
        2.3.1 Brief History of the Development of the Concept   14
        2.3.2 Biblical-Theological Approach to Culture   15
        2.3.3 Anthropological Approach to Culture   17
        2.3.4 Theories of Culture   19
        2.3.5 Synthesis   21
    2.4 Religion   22
        2.4.1 Brief History of the Development of the Concept   22
        2.4.2 Biblical-Theological Approach to Religion   23
        2.4.3 Religious Studies' Approach to Religion   24
        2.4.4 Synthesis   27
    2.5 Summary   27
    For Further Reading   28

3 Accessing the Deep Structures: Worldview and Identity 29
    3.1 The Deep Structures of the Person in the Bible and in the Sciences   29
        3.1.1 The Deep Structures of the Person in the Bible   29
        3.1.2 The Deep Structures of the Person in the Sciences   31
    3.2 The Concept of Worldview   31
        3.2.1 Brief History of the Concept   32
        3.2.2 Definition of Worldview   33
        3.2.3 Adoption of the Worldview Concept by Evangelicals   35

  3.2.4 Synthesis   38
 3.3 Five Models to Make Worldview Practical   39
  3.3.1 The Layers Model of the Order of Creation   40
  3.3.2 The Five Soteriological Concepts   45
  3.3.3 The Orientation of the Conscience   47
  3.3.4 Time Orientation   59
  3.3.5 Mana   62
 3.4 Identity   66
  3.4.1 Biblical-Theological Approach to Identity   67
  3.4.2 Psychological Approach to Identity   67
  3.4.3 Philosophical Approach to Identity   69
  3.4.4 Kwame Bediako and the Search for Identity in Theology   69
 3.5 Otherness   70
 3.6 Transformation of Worldview and Identity   72
  3.6.1 Transformation in Practice   73
  3.6.2 Transformation of the Core of Personality and of the Cultural Skin Layers   73
  3.6.3 Conversion Alters One's Worldview and Identity   74
  3.6.4 Conversion Does Not Alter Worldview and Identity   75
  3.6.5 Pre-Christian and "Christian" Worldview Side by Side   76
 3.7 Summary   77
 For Further Reading   78

4 In-Depth Analysis of Scripture, Theology and Church Life   79
 4.1 Scripture   79
  4.1.1 The Creation   80
  4.1.2 The Fall   81
  4.1.3 The Relational Conscience in Genesis   82
  4.1.4 The Formation of a New Worldview in Exodus   86
  4.1.5 Jesus Christ, the Answer to Human Need   91
  4.1.6 Four Case Studies   93
  4.1.7 Analysis of Cultures in Scripture   96
  4.1.8 Scripture and Multiculturalism   100
  4.1.9 The Biblical or "Christian" Worldview   102
 4.2 Theology   104
  4.2.1 Brief History of Theological Study   104
  4.2.2 Conscience and Theology   105
  4.2.3 Conscience and Soteriology   107
  4.2.4 Conscience and Ethics   111

	4.3 Church Life	115
	4.3.1 Interpretation and Translation of the Bible	115
	4.3.2 Church Leadership	124
	4.3.3 Counselling	125
	4.3.4 Communicating the Gospel	127
	4.4 Summary	132
	For Further Reading	133
5	In-Depth Analysis of Personality, Culture and Religion	135
	5.1 Persons	135
	5.1.1 Typology of Personality	135
	5.1.2 Typical Behaviour Patterns of Rules-Based and Relational Persons	138
	5.1.3 Preference for Functioning Orally, Audio-Visually or through Written Text	139
	5.1.4 The Bimodal Functioning of the Brain	141
	5.2 Communication	143
	5.2.1 Communication Models	143
	5.2.2 Communication as a Function of the Conscience	145
	5.2.3 Examples of Communication in the Bible	146
	5.2.4 Examples of Intercultural Communication	147
	5.3 Societies	148
	5.3.1 Typology of Societies According to their Conscience Orientation	149
	5.3.2 Historical Epochs	150
	5.3.3 Modernity and Postmodernity	152
	5.3.4 Globalization and Hybridity	154
	5.3.5 The Generations of the Twentieth and Twenty-First Centuries in the West	156
	5.3.6 An Encounter on the Bus	162
	5.3.7 Being a Single Woman in Egypt	163
	5.4 Religions	164
	5.4.1 Animism	164
	5.4.2 Religions and Their Worldviews	169
	5.4.3 An Offering for the Smallpox Goddess	173
	5.5 Analysis of the Cultures and Religions of the World	174
	5.6 Leadership	176
	5.6.1 Leadership and Conscience Orientation	176
	5.6.2 Leadership and Western Generations	177
	5.6.3 Decisions	178

	5.6.4 Attitudes to Planning	178
	5.6.5 Negotiations	178
	5.6.6 The Role of Written Agreements	179
	5.7 Dealing with Conflicts	179
	5.7.1 Perception of Conflicts	179
	5.7.2 Causes of Conflicts	180
	5.7.3 Styles of Conflict Resolution	180
	5.8 Summary	182
	For Further Reading	183
6	Conclusion	185

Appendices

Appendix 1: Individuals and Their "Cultural Skin Layers" 189

Appendix 2: Typologies of Peoples and Cultures 193

Appendix 3: Typology of Personality According to Conscience Orientation 199

Appendix 4: Questionnaire and Personality Profile 203

Appendix 5: The Five Soteriological Concepts and Chronological Bible Teaching 209

Bibliography 213

Index of Names 223

Index of Subjects 227

List of Tables

Table 1: Relationship between Scripture, Theology and Science 4
Table 2: Modern and Postmodern Socio-Anthropological Theories 9
Table 3: Concepts of the Personality throughout History 13
Table 4: Theories of Culture 22
Table 5: Religious Studies' Focus according to the Sciences 25
Table 6: Concepts of Worldview in the Sciences 39
Table 7: Layers Model of the Order of Creation 41
Table 8: The Psychoanalytic Model of the Conscience 55
Table 9: The Cognitive Model of the Conscience 56
Table 10: Time Orientations 60
Table 11: Steps in Approaching the Other 71
Table 12: Operational Level of Worldview Models 77
Table 13: Conscience and Theology 107
Table 14: Strategic Pastoral Counselling According to Green and
  Lawrenz 126
Table 15: Resolution of Feelings of Shame and Guilt 127
Table 16: The Evangelism Model of Jesus Christ 132
Table 17: The Personality as a Function of the Conscience 136
Table 18: Functions of the Two Hemispheres of the Brain 142
Table 19: Communication as a Function of the Conscience 145
Table 20: Typology of Societies According to their Conscience
  Orientation 149
Table 21: Typological Analysis of Modernism and Postmodernism 154
Table 22: Features of Postmodernism by Scientific Discipline 154
Table 23: Chronology of Generations in the West 156
Table 24: Changes in the Western Context 157
Table 25: Spirituality in Western Generations 160

Table 26: Main Features of Western Generations 161
Table 27: Worldviews of Western Generations 162
Table 28: Classification of Terms for Soul in Four Languages........... 168
Table 29: Religions and Their Worldviews........................... 170
Table 30: Leadership Style and Western Generations.................. 178
Table 31: Perception of Conflict According to Conscience Orientation . . 179
Table 32: Styles in Dealing with Conflicts 181
Table 33: Mary Douglas' Typology 193
Table 34: Mary Douglas' Characteristics of Culture Types 193
Table 35: Hofstede's Typology 195
Table 36: Meyer's Typology 196
Table 37: Weber's Typology 196
Table 38: Lingenfelter and Mayers' Typology 197

List of Figures

Figure 1: The Process of the Communication of the Gospel. 3

Figure 2: Personality as a Black Box 12

Figure 3: Onion Model of Culture 18

Figure 4: The Soteriological Model of the Conscience. 58

Figure 5: Formation of a Unified Identity 68

Figure 6: The Cultural Triangle 116

Figure 7: Change from One Language into Another during Translation . . . 119

Figure 8: Convergences and Divergences of the Consciences. 129

Figure 9: Causes of Conflict and Conceptions of Forgiveness 180

1

Introduction

The reader may wonder why we need yet another book about cultures. Don't we have enough available already? And to what extent is the author qualified to add yet another book on this topic? Today, people from other cultures are not only far away from us in other countries. In today's fragmented societies, we most often live alongside people from other cultures and religions. Even if these persons do not visibly practise their culture of origin, it has formed their worldview since early childhood. That is why there are considerable differences in worldview between individuals, even within the same society. Furthermore, one can hardly expect interested Christians, pastors, theologians and students to acquire a comprehensive knowledge of the various disciplines that deal with the study of other people and their cultures and religions: history, philosophy, psychology, sociology, cultural anthropology and religious studies. Instead, we need some kind of simplification.

As for my qualifications, I have been closely involved in exchanges of ideas with the local people and students of theology during my teaching in three continents (Europe, Africa and Asia). These contacts have given me access to the deep layers of the people and their cultures, enabling me to simplify a complex analysis of the various relevant phenomena, in other words, a kind of "short cut." I developed my approach in an earlier study,[1] drawing on the reflections of Lothar Käser and Klaus Müller.[2]

---

1. Hannes Wiher, *Shame and Guilt: A Key to Cross-Cultural Ministry* (Bonn: Culture and Science Publications, 2003).

2. Later published in Lothar Käser, *Foreign Cultures: A Cognitive Approach* (Nuremberg: VTR, 2014); also Lothar Käser, *Animism: A Cognitive Approach* (Nuremberg: VTR, 2014); Klaus W. Müller, *Conscience – The Moral Law Within: Formation and Function of Super-Ego/Ego-Ideal, Shame and Guilt within Society, Culture and Religion. Handbook Elenctics* (Nuremberg: VTR, 2024).

1.1 Learning to Understand Peoples and Their Cultures

To communicate the gospel in a way that is both faithful to Scripture and relevant to people and their cultures, the Bible and its message should in principle be our starting point. Based on that foundation, we should then consider how to convey that message to those we aim to reach, bearing in mind their particular personality, the social and cultural situation they live in, and the religion, if any, that they belong to. The work of missions therefore involves considering three aspects: Scripture, communication, and the nature of the people to be reached. My focus in this book will be the personalities, cultures and religions found in Scripture and in the various contexts of our globe. In conjunction with this, I must also discuss the personalities, cultures and religions through which and within which the Bible, theology and church life have developed and taken shape.

To reach people with our biblical message means that our communication must take place on the deep level of persons, their culture and their religion. It is therefore necessary to carefully analyze both Scripture and cultures, delving deeply into their structures. That is the aim of this book. In this I take Jesus Christ as a model. Of the roughly thirty-three years he lived on this earth, he spent about thirty getting to know and analysing the Hebrew Bible and the Jewish culture of the first century. This should provide enough reason for us to prepare ourselves in the same way for sharing the good news of the gospel with others.

The overall term used by philosophy and the humanities to describe the deep structures of people, cultures and religions is *worldview*, whereas the Bible talks essentially of the *heart* or the *conscience*. In dealing primarily with deep structures, this book focuses on analysing people, cultures and religions through the prism of worldview. Its in-depth approach enables effective sharing of the gospel while also presenting an abbreviated form of cultural analysis. This in-depth approach permits a simplification because on the level of worldview the concepts of personality, culture and religion meet in one concept. This approach also helps us 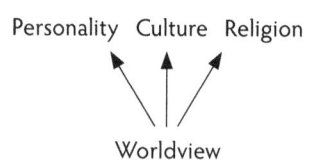 understand how God brings about change in people, cultures and religions. Deep inward change in a person and the formation of a new identity in Christ are indeed the aim of everyone working in God's kingdom.

I understand that communicating the gospel involves a thorough analysis of Scripture using exegetical and theological methods. Second, a consideration of the communication process with the help of insights from communication science is necessary. Third, we want to aim for an in-depth engagement with conversation partners and their contexts. This calls for applying the methods and insights of history, philosophy, the humanities and religious studies. The content of this book is particularly concerned with the whole area of "context" as set out in Figure 1. However, now that the field of biblical studies has discovered the importance of the social sciences in exegesis, the book will also deal with the analysis of people and contexts in Scripture. In addition, attention will be given to the influence of the cultural context on communication style. Hence, all three components of the process of communicating the gospel indicated in Figure 1 will be addressed.

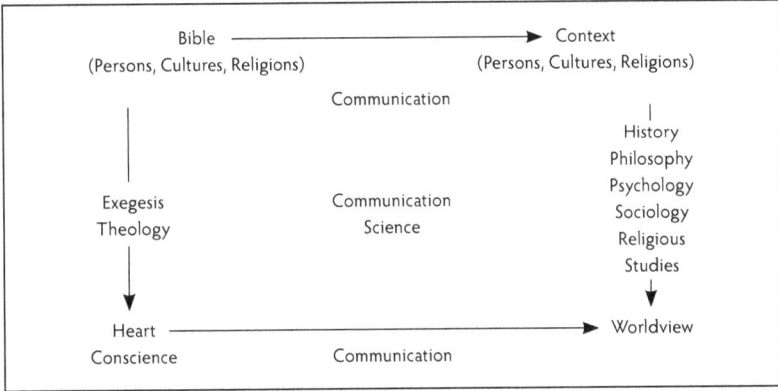

Figure 1: The Process of the Communication of the Gospel

1.2 Integrating Biblical and Scientific Data

Mission studies involve different academic disciplines. It entails study of the Bible using exegetical and theological tools, reflection on the process of communication with the help of communication science, and an analysis of the conversation partners and their environment which includes the methodologies of history, philosophy, psychology, sociology and religious studies. So, one can hardly avoid bringing together the results of biblical analysis and those of the various sciences. Throughout the course of history, evangelicals have been in general very hesitant to do this. But here I follow the example of the great theologian Augustine. Impressed by the great eloquence of the preacher Ambrose of Milan, Augustine was probably the first to systematically integrate classical rhetoric into Christian preaching. He based this move on an event in the book of Exodus, where the Israelites took gold from the idolatrous people of Egypt (Exod 11:2; 12:35–36). From this example, he reasoned by analogy that he could make use of the riches of the rhetorical method.

However, "has not God made foolish the wisdom of the world?" (1 Cor 1:20). Since the creator of the universe is also the God who revealed the Bible, we can proceed on the basis that the facts of science – the data of the universe – also convey the wisdom of God. This means that in the relationship between Scripture, theology and the sciences there should be no conflicts with regards to facts, although there can be conflicts about their perception and interpretation, as presented in Table 1.

In practice, we almost always support our analyses based on perceptions and interpretations of Scripture and on scientific perceptions and theories, the latter being interpretations of scientific facts. Hence, there is always the possibility of conflict between the results of theology and science.

Table 1: Relationship between Scripture, Theology and Science

	Theological Facts (Scripture)	Theological Perceptions	Theological Interpretations
Scientific Facts	No conflict	Possible conflict	Possible conflict
Scientific Perceptions	Possible conflict	Possible conflict	Possible conflict
Scientific Theories	Possible conflict	Possible conflict	Possible conflict

How can these be integrated?[3] I will aim to combine a *critical realist theology*[4] with the results of scientific study gained through a theistic perspective. This is all the more important because Enlightenment scientific thinking and development have been imbued with a secular worldview. So what is meant in practical terms by a critical realist theology? Negatively, this kind of theology dispenses with the presupposition that the systems of thought of the various sciences are uniform, which reveals a *naïve idealist epistemology*.[5] Positively, a critical realist theology recognises that the systems of thought of the various sciences differ. It dismisses any view which trusts in the naïve possibility that the various systems of thought could be harmonized, corresponding to a *naïve*

---

3. Cf. Paul G. Hiebert, *Missiological Implications of Epistemological Shifts: Affirming Truth in a Modern/Postmodern World* (Harrisburg: International Trinity Press, 1999).

4. Critical realism is the theory that some of our sense-data accurately represent external objects (like naïve realism), whereas others do not (as opposed to naïve realism).

5. Epistemology seeks to answer the question of how we can know anything.

realist epistemology. Hence, a critical realist theology has to do with a variety of systems of thought which need to be critically integrated on the foundation of a theistic perspective. In addition, this requires that the diachronic[6] disciplines (biblical and narrative theologies and historical studies) and the synchronic disciplines (systematic theology and the humanities) mutually complement each other.[7] These ideas about integrating biblical material with the sciences seem complex, but in the course of the book I aim to show, with the help of practical examples, how such integration can be successfully constructed.

1.3 Structure of the Book

After the first chapter with the introduction, the second chapter sets out the basic concepts of my research: *personality*, *culture* and *religion*. The third chapter deals with an in-depth approach to the concepts of *worldview* and *identity* and their transformation. The fourth chapter contains an analysis of worldviews in Scripture, theology and church life. Finally, the fifth chapter considers the various forms of personality, societies, cultures and religions that can be observed on our globe.

1.4 Hint for the Reader

Those who prefer not to be delayed by the two preparatory chapters dealing with the basic concepts but would prefer to delve directly into the practical aspects and the analysis of persons, cultures and religions can proceed straight to chapters 4 and 5.

---

6. A diachronic approach (from Greek *dia* "through" and *chronos* "time") considers the development and evolution of something through time. By contrast, a synchronic approach looks at a phenomenon at a specific moment in time.

7. Hiebert, *Missiological Implications of Epistemological Shifts*, 105.

2

Basic Concepts: Personality, Culture and Religion

In this chapter, I shall outline the conceptual basics of personality, culture and religion in view of our study of the socio-cultural environments of the Bible and of our globe. These three concepts were conceived and introduced at particular times in our history. Hence, their correspondence with reality may be high or low. Today they are the object of considerable critique, so that many sociologists and anthropologists propose dropping the terms altogether. Where does the problem lie? To make the issue comprehensible, I present the different scientific theories underlying the three notions in the next section.

2.1 Socio-Anthropological Theories Underlying the Basic Concepts

According to *functionalism*, a theory of sociology and cultural anthropology from the first half of the twentieth century, persons, cultures and religions are basic elements that have the *essential function of giving society structure and stability*. Functionalism provides the foundation for two scientific discourses arising in the mid-twentieth century: structuralism and essentialism. From the perspective of *structuralism*, a direction of thought permeating particularly the humanities and social sciences, *basic structures are the same in all cultures*. Structuralism is closely related to the philosophical discourse of *essentialism*, which draws on Platonism in holding that the nature of all persons and all cultures is the same. This means that both discourses hold the view that what matters is to identify the principal structures and functions which are valid for all peoples, cultures and religions. All three discourses (functionalism, structuralism and essentialism) are products of modernity.[1]

In the second half of the twentieth century, the propositions of these three discourses came up against considerable critique, above all from the representatives of *constructivism*. This scientific approach is an expression of *late modernism*, also known as *postmodernism*. Its premise is that *personalities, cultures and religions are constructed according to power dynamics*. Consequently, these concepts are a function of their setting and are not universal elements. Moreover, these depersonalised concepts (personality, culture or religion) are not the origin of a socio-cultural phenomenon but result from human power plays.[2]

I consider this critique justifiable, but I am of the opinion that both approaches, modern and postmodern, are still valid, while at the same time both have deficiencies. Essentialism ignores the complexity of persons, cultures and religions. It permits the illusion that everything can be understood after one has determined the basic structures and functions of persons and societies. However, there still remain today many mysteries concerning both the surface phenomena and the deep structures in persons, cultures and religions. It is fundamentally an act of love to accept and respect these mysteries. So, after the in-depth analysis of persons, cultures and religions and the development of a general orientation grid, one will study the innumerable details which characterize a person, culture or religion. Later we will see that these two approaches, structuralist and poststructuralist, which also can be termed modern and postmodern, correspond to two different worldviews, and that certain models of worldview, which I will introduce, can combine these two approaches towards a conceptual apprehension of reality (cf. section 4.3.3). Table 2 provides a schematic summary of the discourses presented.

---

1. For the historical periods, I adopt the terms modernity and postmodernity; for the ideological currents, I use modernism and postmodernism. For an in-depth discussion of these two currents and their implications for everyday life, cf. section 5.3.3.

2. Cf. Michael A. Rynkievich, *Soul, Self, and Society: A Postmodern Anthropology for Mission in a Postcolonial World* (Eugene: Cascade, 2011).

Table 2: Modern and Postmodern Socio-Anthropological Theories

"Modern" Theories	"Postmodern" Theories
Functionalism: persons, cultures and religions function rationally. *Structuralism*: the basic structures are the same in all cultures. *Essentialism*: the nature of all persons, cultures and religions is the same.	*Constructivism*: persons, cultures and religions are constructed according to power play and are therefore not necessarily rational. Hence, these concepts are a function of their setting. The source of cultural phenomena is not these de-personalized concepts (personality, culture and religion), but the person who acts.

2.2 Personality

I begin with a brief history of how this concept developed, followed by an examination of the biblical and anthropological approaches to defining what personality is.

2.2.1 Brief History of the Development of the Concept

The term "person" (from Lat. *persona*) originally referred to the mask worn by actors in the ancient theatre. It was through (Lat. *per*) the mask that the sound (*sonus*) came through (*personare*). Two factors in essence denote the personality: it bears the features of the person's behaviour, and also of that which distinguishes one person from another. According to this definition, the personality corresponds to those elements of the person which are visible and audible. This ancient approach reflects a relational and holistic understanding of the person.

During the scholastic period, the personality was also viewed holistically, but based on the structural aspect. For example, Thomas Aquinas (1225–1274) drew a distinction, as regards the person, between the body and the soul. Concerning the soul, Thomas further differentiated:

- The vegetative soul (*anima vegetativa*): concept of the natural and vital needs;
- The sensitive soul (*anima sensitiva*): concept of the emotions and seat of the passions;
- The intelligent soul (*anima intellectiva*): substantive form of the person as a rational being.

Thomas Aquinas regarded the soul as the "form" of the body and applied the hylomorphism[3] of Aristotle to a Christian concept of the person. Thus, the person is an essential unity in two separated parts.

Since the beginning of the twentieth century, personality has been defined as the sum of qualities resulting partly from "temperament" (innate) and partly from "character" (acquired). *Temperament*, a term used by Hippocrates (460–370 BC), and taken up by the German Ernst Kretschmer (1888–1964), describes the bio-psychic aspects of the personality. *Character*, by contrast, is the result of environmental influences. Although at the beginning of the twentieth century, various researchers concentrated on the description or development of character, it seems that the very term has now almost vanished from the vocabulary of psychology as an academic discipline in favour of personality, which is less involved with ideas of morality and value judgements.

> Temperament: bio-psychic aspects of the personality
>
> Personality: unique singularity of each person

Also, at the start of the twentieth century, the psychoanalyst Sigmund Freud (1856–1939) developed a very innovative and influential in-depth model of the soul. It introduced the hypothetical concepts of the ego, the id, the super-ego and the ego-ideal. The last three describe the unconscious aspects of the soul. In turn, the psychoanalyst Carl Gustav Jung (1875–1961) used the term *persona* to pick up on those aspects of the ancient concept which are open to observation. This concept is in contrast with that dimension of the soul (*anima*), which contains partly or completely unconscious aspects. After Jung, the psychology of personality concentrated more on its development and the social influences (socialization). Today, the term "personality" is understood as the unique nature of each person in his or her accustomed mode of being.

2.2.2 Biblical-Theological Approach to Personality

The Bible regards all human beings as persons because, being created in the image of God, we have the potential to develop a relationship with God and with his creation. It follows that human beings are conceived as counterparts to their creator. This is fundamentally a relational concept of the person. As a summary of biblical statements, one can distinguish five aspects of a mature

---

3. Hylomorphism (also hylemorphism, from Greek *hylē* "matter" and *morphē* "form") is a philosophical concept developed by Aristotle, according to which every being (or object) consists of matter and form, which together constitute the substance.

personality capable of being regarded as a counterpart to God.[4] Persons' *rationality* implies that they can say yes or no to impulses, and that they can bring creativity into chaotic situations around them. God will pass judgement on their decisions (Prov 24:12; Jas 2:24; Rev 20:13). The second aspect is *self-awareness*, closely related to the first. Persons are aware of the intentions of their own activities and of being involved in God's historical plan (Isa 1:3). *Mutuality* indicates that persons are social beings, which includes *communication*. The fifth aspect, *self-discipline*, has to do with the integration of body and soul, brain and spirit (2 Tim 1:7).

2.2.3 Anthropological Approach to Personality

The scientific treatment of personality involves many disciplines, combining approaches from philosophy, psychology, sociology (or social psychology) and cultural anthropology (or ethnology).

In psychology personality is *a theoretical construct characterizing an individual, based on observed patterns of behaviour, on dispositions or qualities derived from them, and on actions related to situations.*

Traditionally, four fundamental features are attributed to personality: *individuality*, expressed in the particular profile each individual possesses; *autonomy*, signifying each person's ability to act freely in expressing personality; *stability* over lengthy periods of time and *consistency* in dealing with situations. Personality is determined by a combination of genetic, biological and environmental factors. Various studies indicate that about half of personality features are inherited, the other half coming from environmental influences. The most important psychological approaches to personality today are psychoanalysis, which concentrates on intrapsychic mechanisms; the cognitive-behavioural approach, which examines patterns of behaviour and their possibilities for change; and the systemic approach, which regards the person as a system and as part of several systems in the immediate and wider environment.

> The person as a counterpart to God:
> rationality
> self-awareness
> mutuality
> communication
> self-discipline

Empirical psychology, to which the last two approaches belong, assumes that the personality is a "black box" about which nothing can be said. It limits

---

4. Daniel J. Treier, "Person," in *Evangelical Dictionary of Theology*, eds. Daniel J. Treier and Walter A. Elwell (Grand Rapids: Baker Academic, 2017).

itself to the stimuli to which a person is exposed (*input*) and observes the behavioural responses which they trigger (*output*) (see Figure 2).

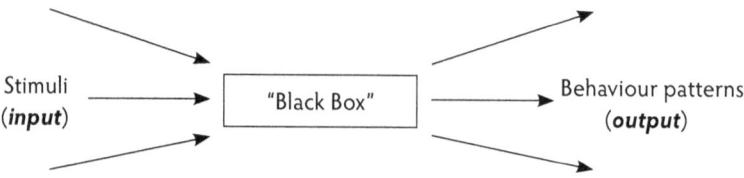

Figure 2: Personality as a Black Box

From the patterns of behaviour ascertained through observation or structured tests, empirical psychology then draws conclusions about personality features. The theory at the basis of most of these tests is the typology of Carl Gustav Jung. Its premise is that the personality operates between two poles on three axes:

- Introversion / extraversion;
- Intuition / sensation;
- Thinking / feeling.

A person's preference for one of these two poles on these three axes determines the psychological type.

The most popular test operating on this basis is the MBTI (*Myers Briggs Type Indicator*). It was developed in 1962 by Isabel Briggs Myers and her mother Katherine Cook Briggs, and it is based on the Jungian typology. The MBTI defines sixteen types of personality according to four main axes: the energizing preference (extraversion or introversion), the attention preference (intuition or sensing), the deciding preference (thinking or feeling) and the living preference (perception or judgement). The test enables a grouping of these features in various ways, leading to a definition of sixteen personality types. Since this test rests on theories relating to the temperament and on Jungian typology, it has come under criticism from some evangelical circles.

In newer approaches, personality is broken down into factors or dimensions, statistically extracted from large questionnaires through factor analysis. Many factor analyses found what is called the *Big Five personality traits*, which are openness to experience, conscientiousness, extraversion, agreeableness, and neuroticism (or emotional stability), known as "OCEAN." These components are generally stable over time, and about half of the variance appears to be attributable to a person's genetics rather than the effects of one's environment.

Many believe that some elements are shared by all cultures and an effort is being made to demonstrate the cross-cultural applicability of the Big Five.

2.2.4 Synthesis

To summarize the various concepts of personality, I have attempted to compile the different historical approaches in Table 3 below. In antiquity, one probed no further than the visible and relational aspects of the person, the *persona*. During the scholastic period, there was an attempt to compile a Christian concept of the surface and deep structure of the person by adapting the Aristotelian model. The person was viewed as a unity of body and soul, the soul being composed of three parts: affective, vegetative and intellectual. Later, psychoanalysis tried to delve deeper, first through a hypothetical approach (Freud), and then by looking again at the concepts of *persona* and *anima* derived from antiquity (Jung). Finally, empirical psychology restricted itself to a secular involvement with personality, avoiding statements about the Black Box of the deep structures of the person.

Table 3: Concepts of the Personality throughout History

	Visible aspects	Invisible and unconscious aspects
Antiquity	*persona*	–
Bible	body	heart, kidneys, bowels, bones, fat, conscience
Scholasticism	body	vegetative, affective, intellectual soulish parts
Freud	body	ego, id, superego, ego-ideal
Jung	*persona*	soul (*anima*)
Empirical Psychology	personality	– (black box)

I will return to these issues in the next chapter when addressing the deep structures of the person in the Bible and in the sciences (cf. section 3.1).

In an attempt to bring together biblical statements, transactional analysis[5] and cultural anthropology, Hans Bürki differentiates a nucleus of the personality and "cultural skin layers." He identifies the nucleus with the use of the "name"

---

5. In psychology, transactional analysis is a theory of the personality, social relationships and communication. It was developed in 1958 by the psychiatrist and psychoanalyst Eric Berne. It postulates "ego states" (parent, adult, child) and investigates intrapsychic phenomena through relationships between people, termed "transactions" (Berne 1968, 1972).

in the Bible (Isa 43:1; 62:2). Transformation during conversion corresponds to the new creation of the nucleus or identity. Concerning the "cultural skin layers," he names the mask (the definition of character in antiquity) and affective, intellectual, physical, linguistic, domestic, sociocultural, cosmic and transcendental skins. According to Bürki, our task is to evaluate our "skin layers" and to let them be changed by the Holy Spirit, which happens during the maturation process of the personality and after conversion (cf. appendix 1).[6]

2.3 Culture

As I did with personality, I will begin this presentation of culture, the second basic concept of my investigation, with a brief history of its development. I then examine the biblical and anthropological approaches to a definition of culture. I conclude with a discussion of the different theories of culture.

2.3.1 Brief History of the Development of the Concept

The word "culture" (from Latin *cultura*, derived from the verb *colere* "to cultivate") suggests that in general culture relates to *human activity in nature*. Cicero was the first to apply the word *cultura* to human activity outside this context. Subsequently, the term culture was often used *in contrast to nature*, indicating that humans alter nature through their culturally determined activities. During modernity this opposition between nature and culture was accentuated. Only late modernity can envisage a harmonious interaction between the two.

- Culture relates to a set of human behaviour patterns, customs and knowledge.
- Society additionally includes economic and political aspects.
- Context incorporates beyond this the geographical dimension.

According to the widespread "modern" usage in cultural anthropology, the term culture indicates a set of patterns of behaviour, customs, knowledge and systems of meaning acquired by an individual or a group of people and handed down in society. In popular terms, culture is also referred to in a limited sense when we talk about literature, architecture and music.

---

6. Hans Bürki, "Évangile et culture," in *Évangile, culture et idéologies*, ed. René Padilla, Hans Bürki and Samuel Escobar (Lausanne: Presses bibliques universitaires, 1977), 13–50.

All this suggests that culture is very close to what we mean by context. The latter embraces not only culture but also the geographical and socio-political dimension. In this book, I refer to culture in its broadest sense as a synonym for context.

It is also important to define the relationship between culture and society more precisely. Culture is a term used in cultural anthropology, whereas society belongs to the sociological discourse. Society covers a wider area than culture, for it denotes not only culture but also other social spheres, such as the economy, politics, associations, clubs, and churches. In summary, widening areas of meaning are included when one moves from culture via society to context.

2.3.2 Biblical-Theological Approach to Culture

The *word* culture, introduced during the so-called "great discoveries" in scientific discourse, is obviously not found in the Bible. On the other hand, culture as a *concept* is by and large present. The Bible emphasizes that culture is part of creation and is a gift from God. It is God's desire for humankind, created in his image, to develop a culture and "cultivate the earth." That is the *cultural mandate* (Gen 1:28; 2:15). After the fall, the incursion of evil into creation, culture was perverted through sin, as was the person who creates it (Gen 3–4). The missiologist Peter Beyerhaus derives from this understanding a *tri-polar perspective on religions*.[7] It proposes that since the fall cultures have had three features: the divine imprint according to the image of God, the human imprint determined by the sinful nature of humankind, and the demonic imprint because of the attempts of the demonic world to manipulate and destroy God's creation. According to the Lausanne Covenant:

> Because men and women are God's creatures, some of their culture is rich in beauty and goodness. Because they are fallen, all of it is tainted with sin and some of it is demonic (§ 10).

One might well expect that after the fall the holy God would abandon this world. Surprisingly, however, he himself became man, indeed a Jew of the first century according to our calendar (John 1:14; Phil 2:5–11). This made the incarnation the standard example of divine and intercultural communication

---

7. Peter Beyerhaus, "Theologisches Verstehen nichtchristlicher Religionen," *Kerygma und Dogma* 35.2 (1989): 106–27.

and of contextualization, or as Dean Gilliland puts it, its "matrix."[8] The apostles, especially Paul, followed this example by becoming "all things to all people" (1 Cor 9:19–22).

From chapters 10 and 11 of Genesis and the book of Revelation, we see that God approves of cultural diversity (Gen 10–11; Rev 5:9; 7:9). Nevertheless, God led Abraham out of his animistic Mesopotamian culture and, together with him, developed an alternative one, reflected in the Hebrew language and way of life. Thus, culture became the context of divine revelation. Subsequently, Israel and the church were called to create and live out a counter-culture, with the aim of providing a model (Deut 4:6–8; Rom 12:1–2; 1 Pet 2:9 quoting Exod 19:5–6). The validity of this model culture is both partial and provisional until God himself begins to create a new culture, a new heaven and earth (Rev 20:4; 21:3, 24; 22:17). The ultimate model culture is the new creation.

When formulated in a trinitarian perspective, this statement leads to a trinitarian theology of culture based on the new creation.[9] Without falling into modalism,[10] we can say that God the Father is the source, the redeemer and the ultimate goal of culture. God the Son became incarnate in human culture, despite the fall. This is a crucial theological declaration. It not only preserves us from a secularization of culture, which would presuppose that it is independent of God; it also preserves us from idolizing any particular form of culture, which would render any criticism – and with it any proposal of change – impossible. God the Son is the model for the new creation, whereas the Holy Spirit is the one who transforms cultures and is therefore the main agent of the new creation. This perspective comprises the following:

> The new creation should become the primary cultural identity of Christians.

- The new creation should become the primary identity of Christians;
- The ultimate meaning of every culture and religion is rooted in the triune God;
- The church in every culture bears witness to the new creation.

---

8. Dean S. Gilliland, "The Incarnation as Matrix for Appropriate Theologies," in *Appropriate Christianity*, ed. Charles H. Kraft (Pasadena: William Carey Library, 2005), 493–520.

9. Cf. Timothy C. Tennent, *Invitation to World Missions: A Trinitarian Missiology for the Twenty-first Century* (Grand Rapids: Kregel, 2010); William Edgar, *Created and Creating: A Biblical Theology of Culture* (Downers Grove: InterVarsity Press, 2017).

10. According to modalism, taught by Sabellius, a third-century theologian, the Father, the Son and the Holy Spirit are three different "modes" of the divine being rather than three different persons. Modalism allocates a "mode" to each of the divine beings: the Father is the creator, the Son the redeemer, and the Spirit the regenerator and the sanctifier.

It must be admitted that all cultures are relative and none can be the source of absolute truth. In the Bible, culture forms the context of revelation (divine communication). In human communication of the gospel, we can, on one hand, look for points of contact within culture for conveying biblical truth so that conversation partners find the message intelligible and meaningful. On the other hand, we can find links with what our conversation partners are interested in. John Stott refers to the Christian's "triple listening": simultaneous listening to God, to the other person, and to the world.[11] In this way, he recommends a trialogue between the Bible, the other person and me. This trialogue takes place in a cultural triangle (cf. section 3.3.1.1).[12]

2.3.3 Anthropological Approach to Culture

What is culture from the perspective of cultural anthropology? The different definitions of culture reflect the different theories which attempt to understand or evaluate human actions. In 1952, the anthropologists Alfred Kroeber and Clyde Kluckhohn compiled a list with over 150 different definitions of culture. A very simple definition from a functionalist perspective regards culture as *a set of strategies which enable a people group to respond to everyday issues and needs.*[13] According to the Willowbank Report (1978) containing the results of a conference of the Lausanne Movement, culture consists of five elements:[14]

> Culture is a set of strategies which enable a people group to respond to everyday issues and needs.

- *Beliefs* (worldview, philosophy and religion);
- *Values* (what is true, good, beautiful, normative);
- *Customs* (behaviour, communication, dress, work, leisure behaviour, trade, eating habits);
- *Institutions* (family, government, justice, religious buildings, schools, hospitals, factories, businesses, trade unions, associations);
- *Artefacts* (technology, art).

---

11. John R. W. Stott, *The Contemporary Christian: Applying God's Word in Today's World* (Leicester: Inter-Varsity Press 1992).

12. Cf. Hannes Wiher, *Sharing the Good News: Evangelism in the Light of Scripture, Mission and Communication Science* (Nuremberg: VTR Publications, 2024).

13. Käser, *Foreign Cultures*, 37.

14. Lausanne Movement. *Willowbank Report: Consultation on Gospel and Culture (1978)*, Lausanne Occasional Paper no. 2, https://lausanne.org/content/lop/lop-2.

Value systems are very central to cultures. Cultures are *culture based judging systems*.[15] Hence, beliefs and values lie at the heart of a culture, and the customs, institutions and artefacts are more on the margin. Thus, one could picture culture as an *onion*, arranging the various elements in concentric circles (cf. Figure 3).

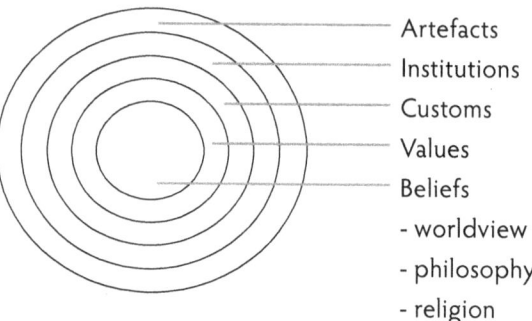

Figure 3: Onion Model of Culture

Whereas certain missiologists recognize in the worldview a central nucleus distinct from the cultural wrappers (the so called "centre-periphery model"), others do not see any possible distinction between kernel and peripheral layers (the "onion model"). David Hesselgrave broadened the definition of culture by adding various dimensions to the elements mentioned in the Willowbank Report. His model of culture also includes *patterns of thinking* (logic), a *language* (with its capacities or lack of them to express certain things), *styles of communication* (verbal or non-verbal, direct or indirect), and *models of decision-making* (individualistic or communal).[16]

From a popular but also anthropological angle, culture can be compared to a *tree*[17]: the roots, the invisible elements (language, worldview, philosophy and religion) are more important than the trunk and foliage, the visible elements (family structures, institutions, customs, technology, art).

---

15. Sheryl Takagi Silzer, *Biblical Multicultural Teams: Applying Biblical Truth to Cultural Differences* (Pasadena: William Carey Library, 2014).

16. David J. Hesselgrave, *Communicating Christ Cross-Culturally* (Grand Rapids: Zondervan, 1980).

17. Tree image: Wikicolorheart, CC BY-SA 4.0 <https://creativecommons.org/licenses/by-sa/4.0>, via Wikimedia Commons.

Culture can also be compared to an *iceberg*: the visible elements are above the surface, the invisible ones below.

The *worldview* is rooted deep within personality, culture and religion. It is like the *BIOS system of the computer*, which determines all the functions of the hard drive. In the image of the computer, the culture corresponds to the operational system – Windows or Mac, for example. The worldview can also be compared to *glasses* or *lenses* through which we view the world and ourselves. It provides a certain perspective or logic. Analogous to the above functionalist definition of culture, it is a *strategy for explaining the world*.

Worldview is the indicator of how each person deals with life, the way each culture defines itself, and that which each religion promotes. Nearly all this is *implicit* and not the result of people carefully thinking it through. In this sense, a worldview does not at all depend on the degree of intelligence or socio-economic level of the people concerned. It is a very useful conceptual tool in mission studies, enabling us to examine the great variety of aspects characterizing the world around us and the people living in it.

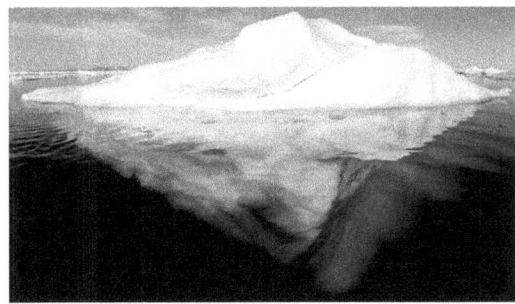

The iceberg analogy: observable elements of the culture above the surface, the invisible elements of the culture below.[18]

In this section, I have presented four analogies of culture: it is a strategy for coping with life; it can be arranged in concentric circles like an onion; it is also constructed like a tree or an iceberg, with observable elements on the surface and invisible aspects deep within. I have also adduced three analogies for worldview: it is a strategy for understanding our environment; it operates like the BIOS, which formats the computer's hard drive, or like lenses through which we consider the world and ourselves. Consequently, to reach deeply into people's souls, we must take account of the culture and especially the worldview of people, cultures and religions in our analysis, and then in our communication of the gospel (cf. sections 3.2 and 3.3).

---

18. Iceberg image: AWeith, CC BY-SA 4.0 <https://creativecommons.org/licenses/by-sa/4.0>, via Wikimedia Commons.

2.3.4 Theories of Culture

One difficulty confronting anthropologists is to explain why there are so many different cultures with so many similarities. Are there common principles underlying all cultures? Various theories have been developed in order to try to understand this mystery.

One logical explanation of the similarities between different cultures could be the theory of an original culture from which various elements have spread. However, this theory, called *diffusionism*, does however not explain why we find similar cultural elements in areas which have never been in contact with each other. By contrast, *functionalism* attributes similarity or analogy between cultures not to a common origin but to the analogous functions which cultures in general carry out. In this way, it is possible for cultures to develop separately from each other and yet demonstrate certain commonalities, since their development depends on the intrinsic demands of human existence. The main contributors to the development of this approach were Émile Durkheim (1858–1917), Bronislaw Malinowski (1884–1942) and Alfred R. Radcliffe-Brown (1881–1955). On the other hand, *evolutionism*, represented among others by Georg Friedrich Hegel (1770–1831) and Auguste Comte (1798–1857), perceives in history a progression from a lower to a higher level and a development from particularities into a condition which achieves the status of general validity. Auguste Comte, for example, distinguishes three successive phases of cultural development: magical, religious, and scientific.

By way of a summary of these three above presented theories, *diffusionism* answers the question of cultural similarities by means of the hypothesis of an original common culture. *Functionalism*, by contrast, represents the notion that social institutions, regarded as constants of human existence, are similar everywhere in terms of function. In turn, *evolutionism* assumes that the similarities stem from an evolutionary process.

Over against all these is the concept of *relativism*, which claims that cultures are completely separate entities the special features of which can be explained through a common leitmotif. The predominant representatives of this current were all from the USA: Franz Boas (1858–1942), Alfred Kroeber (1876–1960), Ruth Benedict (1887–1948) and Margaret Mead (1901–1978).

Alternatively, the *semiotic approach*[19] understands culture as *a text, a system of symbols*. Thus, one of its most well-known proponents, Clifford Geertz (1926–2006), has claimed, "to believe with Max Weber that man is an animal

---

19. Semiotics (from Greek *semeion* "sign") is the theory of signs.

suspended in webs of significance he himself has spun."[20] Hence, Geertz is using the word *web* in the sense of *text*. This represents a holistic approach to the concept of culture, more comprehensive than the functionalist approach.

Finally, *discourse theory* understands culture as a discourse field. This means that culture is no longer regarded as a (semiotic) unit but as a complex field of action characterized by tensions. Lines of separation no longer run between cultures (relativism) but within cultures. The latter are no longer regarded as homogenous, but rather very heterogeneous. Matters are continually negotiated between the various agents of a culture. One of the important representatives of discourse theory is Michel Foucault (1926–1984). From the 1980s onwards, postcolonial research made important contributions to this theory by ascertaining that streams of migrants which are more and more a global feature affecting societies, make those societies more heterogeneous, leading to fragmentation and tensions.[21] Table 4 offers a summary of the theories I have discussed.

Table 4: Theories of Culture

Theory	Hypothesis
Diffusionism	Similarity of cultures through a common original culture
Functionalism	Social institutions, regarded as constants of human existence, have similar functions everywhere
Evolutionism	Evolutionary process which cultures follow
Relativism	Cultures are totally separate and non-comparable entities
Semiotics	Culture is a text, a system of symbols
Discourse theory	Culture is a complex and heterogeneous discourse field, characterized by contradictions and tensions

2.3.5 Synthesis

The Bible says that culture is a creation and gift of God. God wants man to develop a culture. That is the cultural mandate. After the fall, culture has a divine, a human and a demonic imprint. The Bible and cultural anthropology agree that culture is created by people. From the point of view of cultural anthropology, it is a strategy for coping with existence. It can be represented as

---

20. Clifford Geertz, *The Interpretation of Culture* (New York: Basic Books, 1973), 5.
21. Cf. Henning Wrogemann, *Intercultural Theology, vol. 1: Intercultural Hermeneutics* (trans. Karl E. Böhmer; Downers Grove: IVP Academic, 2016), 135–55.

an onion, a tree or an iceberg. The worldview is its core. It works like the BIOS that formats the hard disk of the computer, or like glasses through which we look at ourselves and our environment. The discussion of the most important theories of culture shows that presuppositions largely determine how close to reality one's conceptions of culture are. We can be sure that the debate about the definition and usefulness of the term culture is by no means closed.

2.4 Religion

This third basic term in my investigation also deserves a brief summary of its history. I will then consider how it relates to the Bible and theology and to cultural anthropology.

2.4.1 Brief History of the Development of the Concept

The term religion was first introduced by the Roman philosopher Cicero. It comes from the Latin *religio*, derived either from the verb *religere* "take notice, respect carefully," or from *religare* "bind to, connect to (God)." The first meaning results from carefully observing the magic formulae in the rites of traditional religions, which I will refer to here as animism. The latter meaning was naturally preferred by Christians.

"Religion" as an independent category parallel to culture was developed much later during the Enlightenment, especially during the nineteenth century. However, it was very quickly recognized that the two categories overlapped and were very much interwoven; in reality, religion is part of culture. Religious studies refer to *religious features of a culture that differ from other cultural elements on account of their specific and absolute character*. In the 1950s, Paul Tillich (1886–1965) regarded religion as the *heart of culture on which the identity of its adherents is based*. Religion would therefore be the deep structures of culture. Consequently, the latter would contain the superficial elements. Today, culture and religion are viewed as containing both surface elements and deep structures, the latter constituting their common worldview. As we will see later, in relational contexts, it is often not possible to distinguish between culture and religion, and members of those societies do not perceive them as separated items. Their distinction is obviously a rules-based approach (cf. sections 3.3.3; 5.4).

> Religion is part of culture.

As an illustration, consider the culture of India, which has given birth to two religions, Hinduism and Buddhism. They are both based on the same worldview and hence have many common features (the notions of *karma*, *samsara* and *moksha/nirvana*). On the other hand, they differ considerably in certain features; for example, Hinduism refers to soul (*atman*) and Buddhism to "non-soul" (*anatman/anatta*).

Thus, on one hand, religion is part of culture. On the other hand, religions can be multicultural, particularly the world religions.

2.4.2 Biblical-Theological Approach to Religion

The Bible tells us that adherents of all religions seek a relationship with a supernatural being. This phenomenon is based on the creation of man in the image of God (Gen 1:26–27). As early as the book of Ecclesiastes, the writer is aware that man is created for eternity (Eccl 3:11). The apostle Paul speaks to us of a moral law written in the human heart (Rom 2:15). The reformer John Calvin called this openness of the human conscience to God (Rom 1:19–21) "the sense of the Divine" (*sensus divinitatis*).[22]

The Bible emphasizes that the main struggle for the salvation of man is taking place at the level of the invisible world (Exod 4–15; 1 Kgs 17–18; Eph 6). All religions and the Bible allow for the fact that human actions have outcomes in the here-and-now and in the beyond. This is termed the *principle of retribution* (cf. Prov 14:14; 22:8; Eccl 12:14; Jer 17:10; Rom 2:6, 16; Gal 6:7–9). The analogous concept in the Asian religions is *karma*. In religious wisdom literature, there are many parallels to the Bible. For example, there is an astonishing correlation between Egyptian proverbs and part of the biblical book of Proverbs (22:17–23:14). The Bible comments on wisdom in this way: "O LORD, how manifold are your works! In wisdom you have made them all; the earth is full of your creatures" (Ps 104:24). The tri-polar perspective on religions includes this aspect in the concept of the divine imprint of religions.

Israel's neighbouring tribes belonged to so-called traditional religions (in our terminology, animism). They worshipped the deities Ba'al, Astarte, Nebo and Marduk. The same applied to the religions of the Greeks and Romans, who had mystery cults, worship of the sun-god Zeus-Jupiter, and the cult of the Oracle of Delphi.

If a religion can be defined as a component of a culture, then a theology of religion can be correspondingly understood as one aspect of a theology of culture. A central element of a theology of religion is that God is the source of both creation and revelation (of general and special revelation). According

---

22. John Calvin, *Institutes of the Christian Religion* (Grand Rapids: Eerdmans, 2009), 1.3.1..

to the Bible, religions, like cultures, are "made by human hands" (Pss 115:4–8; 135:15–18; Hab 2:18–19). Both, the Bible and cultural anthropology, are in complete agreement that religions are of human creation. The notion of the *tri-polar perspective on religions* introduced by Peter Beyerhaus and discussed above in connection with culture naturally applies to religion as well. It holds that since the fall cultures and religions share three characteristics: the divine imprint according to the image of God, the human imprint resulting from the sinful nature of humankind who invented them, and the demonic imprint on account of attempts by the demonic world to manipulate and destroy God's creation. This observation is a reminder of what Christopher Wright calls *the two paradoxes*: although to all appearances the deities of the religions exist, they do not as far as the authors of the Bible are concerned, and yet they represent powers that should not be ignored.[23]

The first paradox maintains that idols are "made by human hands." They are part of creation. They have eyes that do not see, ears that do not hear, and mouths that do not speak and have no breath; in other words, they are not really alive. They are a poor comparison with God, the creator of the universe, who is life itself (Ps 115:4–7). Compared with this creator God, they are simply "nothings" (Ps 96:5). Although from an ontological perspective they exist, they do not really. Yet in a visible and material sense, they do exist, both in history and today.

> A theology of religion can be regarded as an aspect of a theology of culture.

The second paradox points out that idols can represent demonic powers, even though they seem not to exist in an ontological sense. Hence, the apostle Paul, for example, warns against the communal meals in the temple of idols, since this could mean fellowship with a demon (1 Cor 10:18–20). He describes the paradox as follows:

> Indeed, even though there may be so-called gods in heaven or on earth – as in fact there are many gods and many lords – yet for us there is one God, the Father, from whom are all things and for whom we exist, and one Lord, Jesus Christ, through whom are all things and through whom we exist. (1 Cor 8:5–6)

---

23. Christopher J. H. Wright, *The Mission of God: Unlocking God's Narrative* (Downers Grove: InterVarsity Press 2006), 136–47.

In summary, deities do indeed exist, both in the Bible and today, but are infinitely subject to the biblical God, the creator of the universe, and at the same time can embody demons.

2.4.3 Religious Studies' Approach to Religion

Religious studies developed according to the logic of the secular thinking of the Enlightenment as a descriptive science, in antithesis to theology, which is prescriptive. Today religious studies are an interdisciplinary undertaking. Every academic discipline follows a particular approach to the human phenomenon of religion, as shown in Table 5.

Table 5: Religious Studies' Focus according to the Sciences

Academic Discipline	Particular Focus
History	Study of holy scriptures as historical documents
Psychology	Study of religious experiences
Sociology	Religion as a social institution
Cultural anthropology	Cultural aspects of religion
Philosophy	Basis of all cultural creation and creativity, working towards ultimate meaning; a positive or negative notion, depending on the author's viewpoint
Theology	Religion as revelation, and the response to it in terms of faith or unbelief

From this, it is apparent that religion is a very complex phenomenon. The field of religious studies has dispensed with a definition and limits itself to considering religion in a pragmatic way. Accordingly, Jacques Waardenburg distinguishes the following dimensions of religion: all religions relate to *"other" realities*. These awaken belief in "supernatural" beings and enable communication with them. The resulting *religious experiences* can be due to paranormal faculties, inspiration (or revelation) or mysticism. Experiences must be interpreted. For this purpose, believers form a *community*, which introduces certain *norms* and *practices* and proposes interpretations (a *thought system*). This gives rise to a distinction between

Dimensions of religion:
"Other" realities
Religious experiences
Community
Norms
Practices
Thought system
Worldview
Identity and meaning

the holy (the absolute norm) and the profane (the relative norm), between the pure and the impure, between the absolute (the religious principles) and the relative (the moral, social and legal principles). In other words, religion provides an interpretation of the world – a *worldview*. Hence, religion and culture are closely connected, with religion providing particularly a sense of *identity and meaning* to life.[24] From an anthropological perspective, religion is an expression of culture. As Lothar Käser puts it, "Religion [next to language] is the second cultural area by which people identify one another as similar or different . . . [It] is one of the most significant auxiliary strategies people employ to shape and master their existence."[25]

One may speak here of the phenomenon of religion in the singular, although religious studies for its part assumes less and less that the manifold religious traditions can be understood as variations on a single theme. It regards this as a perspective of structuralism, for which the basic structures of religions are the same in all cultures. For religious studies, this viewpoint would therefore be superseded. From a poststructuralist and postmodern perspective, one should rather consider particular traditions as independent. John Cobb, for example, represents this position:

> Arguments as to what "religion" truly is are pointless. There is no such thing as "religion." There are only traditions, movements, communities, people, beliefs, and practices that have features that are associated by many people with what they mean by "religion."[26]

In my view, both positions can be justified: the poststructuralist perspective focuses on particular religious phenomena, and the structuralist position investigates the commonalities of different religions on a higher level of generalization.

Along with describing institutional religions, from the second half of the twentieth century on, religious studies have observed *religious features in secularized societies* where formal adherence to a religion is increasingly in decline. An *ideology* can always contain, and a *worldview* always produces religious elements. For example, the rituals preceding a Sunday morning football match can be interpreted as religious elements replacing the church service. The same could be said of some of the rituals at a registry office of

---

24. Jacques Waardenburg, *Classical Approaches to the Study of Religion: Aims, Methods, and Theories of Research. Introduction and Anthology*, 2nd ed. (Berlin and Boston: De Gruyter, 2017).

25. Käser, *Foreign Cultures*, 159.

26. John B. Cobb, Jr., "Beyond Pluralism," in *Christian Uniqueness Reconsidered: The Myth of Pluralistic Theology of Religions*, ed. Gavin D'Costa (Maryknoll: Orbis, 1990), 81–95.

civil weddings in Western culture. In secularized societies, private spirituality is becoming more and more a substitute for formal, public practice of religion. It reflects the same dimensions as institutionalized religions (other realities, religious experiences, giving meaning to life) but often remains at the individual level, without fellowship or norms. Individual spirituality can contain religious elements from several religions, and can remain indistinct and non-committal.

Some clarification is needed here with regard to the relationship between Christianity and religion. Many evangelicals argue that "Christianity is a relationship, not a religion." Certainly, it is true that in Christianity the relationship of the believer to the triune God is of the greatest importance. However, this relationship is comparable to that of a Hindu *bakhti* to Krishna or Shiva and that of a Muslim Sufi to Allah. Moreover, from the point of view of religious studies, Christianity includes all the dimensions of a religion ("other" realities, religious experiences, norms, community, giving meaning to life) just like the other religions.

2.4.4 Synthesis

Religion is a system of beliefs, practices, texts, sanctified places, and organizations that relates humanity to "other" realities. Religion is an expression of worldview and part of culture. There is no consensus on precisely what constitutes a religion. Different religions may or may not contain the various elements mentioned. According to certain researchers, there are an estimated ten thousand distinct religions worldwide. Religion, as one of the central human strategies for coping with life, is an expression of worldview, just like culture and, at the individual level, personality.[27]

2.5 Summary

In this chapter, I have discussed in brief the concepts of personality, culture and religion. These will form the basis of my reflections throughout the book. They are simplifications and abstractions of a very diverse and complex reality, in other words models or concepts. All three are the objects of research of independent disciplines: psychology, sociology, cultural

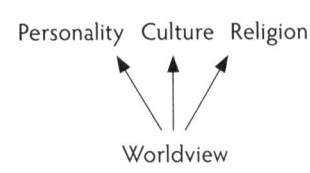

---

27. There will be a more detailed discussion of religions in Hannes Wiher, *What Do You Believe? Learning to Understand Religions* (Carlisle: Langham Global Library, forthcoming).

anthropology, and religious studies. A comprehensive understanding of them would require years of intensive study. As Christians, students, pastors, theologians and missiologists we don't normally have the time for it. That is why I am proposing a "short cut" by means of the concept of "worldview."

We have established that the three concepts of personality, culture and religion are not clearly defined. Hence, many experts have suggested removing them from academic debate. An alternative approach would be to make them practical or, in academic jargon, to *operationalize* them. The MBTI (Myers Briggs Type Indicator) personality test is one such operationalizing of the personality. Similarly, transactional analysis understands the personality as a relational strategy developed from early childhood. An analogous operationalizing of the concepts of culture and religion from the functionalist perspective would view them as strategies for coping with life.

The three concepts entail aspects of both surface and deep structures. The surface dimensions are often more clearly apparent than the deep ones. But the latter ones are in general more important for the daily functioning of persons, cultures and religions. These are two of the three reasons why I have decided on an approach that aims at the deep structures. The third reason is that we desire to touch people with our gospel message in the deep places of their personality. With such an approach, we will not only be more relevant and effective in our communication of the gospel, but will also be using an approach that can serve as a "short cut." On the level of worldview, an encounter with the concepts of personality, culture and religion simplifies all three. This means that by studying worldview we can understand these three concepts more easily and more thoroughly. All three are actually expressions or functions of one's worldview. Hence, in the next chapter, I will examine the deep structures of these three concepts. The Bible calls them heart, kidneys, bones, bowels or conscience; scientific study speaks of worldview and identity.

For Further Reading

Käser, Lothar. *Foreign Cultures: A Cognitive Approach*. Nuremberg: VTR, 2014.
Waardenburg, Jacques. *Classical Approaches to the Study of Religion: Aims, Methods, and Theories of Research. Introduction and Anthology*. 2nd ed. Berlin and Boston: De Gruyter, 2017.

3

Accessing the Deep Structures: Worldview and Identity

In this chapter, I investigate persons, cultures and religions in terms of their underlying deep structures. I begin by studying the deep structures of the person as reflected in the Bible and in the sciences. I then expound the concept of worldview, which is important not only for interpersonal relations but also for understanding cultures and religions. In addition, I explain how I understand the concept of worldview in an everyday sense – how I can apply it in everyday practice (or, in academic jargon, operationalize it). I then tackle identity, the second significant concept along with worldview determining the person's deep structures. As worldview and identity both develop in the tension between self and other, I insert a short presentation of otherness. I will then conclude with a discussion of change of worldview and identity.

3.1 The Deep Structures of the Person in the Bible and in the Sciences
3.1.1 The Deep Structures of the Person in the Bible

The biblical expressions denoting the deep layers of the person are primarily "the innermost being," the "heart," the "kidneys," the "bones," the "bowels" and the "conscience."[1] The three most important of these are the innermost being, the heart and the conscience.

3.1.1.1 The Innermost Being

In the Old Testament, the "innermost being" (*qēréb*, Ps 103:1; Isa 16:11) is located deep within the body. It is often linked to the soul (*nĕfĕsh*), the invisible part of

---

1. Hans Walter Wolff, *Anthropology of the Old Testament*, trans. Margaret Kohl (Mifflintown: Sigler Press, 1996); Herman Ridderbos, *Paul: An Outline of His Theology*, trans. John R. de Witt (Grand Rapids: Eerdmans, 1975), 114–21, 288–93.

the person, with the belly, the bowels and the bosom (*bēthēn*), and with the fat around the diaphragm. The last of these could not be eaten at sacrifices, but had to be burned (Lev 1–7). Finally, the innermost being includes the kidneys, often closely related to the heart (Pss 7:9; 26:2). In the New Testament, the innermost being (*eso anthropos*) is the part of the person which functions according to either the spirit or the flesh and is influenced by them (Rom 7:22; Eph 3:16).

3.1.1.2 The Heart

This is the second significant term used for describing the deep structures of the person, indicating the centre of the personality. Proverbs 4:23 commands us, "Keep your heart with all vigilance, for from it flow the springs of life." The heart reflects our personality: "Just as water reflects the face, so one human heart reflects another" (Prov 27:19). The New Testament also regards the heart as the source of the personality (Matt 12:34; Luke 6:45). The heart reflects the cognitive (Prov 2:10; Rom 1:21), affective (Ps 13:2; Matt 22:37–39), volitional (Prov 16:1; 2 Cor 9:7) and spiritual (Ezek 6:9; 2 Cor 3:3) aspects of the personality. Not only Hebrew culture but also various others identify the heart as the "seat of the emotions, intellect and character" (abbreviated as SEIC, cf. section 5.4.1.4).[2]

3.1.1.3 The Conscience

The conscience (*syneidēsis*), which directs human behaviour, is a third important concept. It was introduced into biblical vocabulary above all by the apostle Paul (e.g. Rom 2:14–15). This is the part of the person which "knows with God." That is the literal meaning of the Greek word *syn-eidēsis* and of the Latin *con-scientia*. But for the Bible, God is an authority over and above the human conscience (2 Cor 4:2; 1 John 3:20).

The Bible uses metaphors to describe the transformation of the deep structures of the person: taking off the old and putting on the new person (Eph 4:22–24; Col 3:9f), birth from above (John 3:3), being born again (*palingenesia*, Tit 3:5), and being a new creation (2 Cor 5:17). This transformation is accomplished through the work of Jesus Christ on the cross and the power of the Holy Spirit.

Thus, the Bible employs numerous expressions in speaking of a person's deep structures, expressions we may often find unusual. Moreover, it makes only very rare use of the term *conscience*, the term which I will employ to describe certain aspects of these deep structures.

---

2. Käser, *Animism*, 145–56.

3.1.2 The Deep Structures of the Person in the Sciences

The deep structures of the person are inaccessible to empirical research. To talk about them, the behavioural sciences have developed the concept of the "black box." Empirical psychology and sociology limit themselves to investigating the influences on the black box (*input*) and their outcomes (*output*). On the other hand, Sigmund Freud developed as part of his hermeneutic psychology the concepts of the ego, the id, the ego-ideal and the super-ego, which, according to him, determine a person's behaviour. The last two are more or less identical to the conscience. An approach with similarities to the conscience introduced by sociologists Peter Berger and Thomas Luckmann is the notion that society comprises a unified structure giving a sense of meaning and direction to people in the midst of a chaotic, meaningless universe.[3] According to Berger, religions function as a "sacred canopy" offering a protective roof below which one can plan one's life in safety.[4] Philosophy, for its part, developed the concept of "worldview" as one of the elements determining human behaviour. As part of the deep structures of the person, worldview is closely bound up with identity, which explains why I am dealing with both concepts in this chapter.

3.2 The Concept of Worldview

According to Clifford Geertz, one's worldview is the way we perceive ourselves and the world around us.[5] It is the image helping members of a culture to see and explain "how things really are." From this definition, we can conclude that we do not perceive reality objectively, but as we view it through the "glasses" formed by our worldview. These "glasses" consist of our unconscious assumptions and our basic values – how we conceive things. Worldview is a simplification of a very complex reality, enabling a better understanding of some of its aspects in order to gain direction for our

> Worldview is the way we perceive ourselves and the world around us. It is a kind of lens or pair of glasses.[6]

---

3. Peter L. Berger and Thomas L. Luckmann, *The Social Construction of Reality: A Treatise in the Sociology of Knowledge* (Oxford: Oxford University Press, 1967).

4. Peter L. Berger, *The Sacred Canopy: Elements of a Sociological Theory of Religion* (Garden City: Doubleday, 1967).

5. Geertz, *The Interpretation of Culture*, 303.

6. Glasses image: Auckland Museum, CC BY 4.0 <https://creativecommons.org/licenses/by/4.0>, via Wikimedia Commons.

actions. Hence, worldviews are abstractions, or rather like models, maps or plans – in Weberian terms, ideal types.[7] We make use of maps according to our needs (political, geographical, street maps). Or we use architectural plans with front or side elevation to show walls, electrical or sanitary installations in a clear and understandable way. Each aspect shows a part of the reality that we are particularly interested in. Worldviews are not only like maps or plans, but are also a bit like scientific models. These are also approximations aiming to simplify a reality which is far too complex for us to deal with in daily life.

To simplify personalities, cultures and religions and make them accessible to lay people, I am treating them in this book as functions of worldview. This approach is part of a trend of growing significance, as evidenced in several important works in recent decades.[8]

3.2.1 Brief History of the Concept

The Prussian philosopher Immanuel Kant (1724–1804) was the first to use the term *Weltanschauung* in his *Kritik der Urteilskraft (Critique of Judgement)* in 1790.[9] In 1858, the term emerged in English as *world view*, defined as understanding of the world, philosophy or concept of existence. Subsequently, the term came to dominate other academic disciplines as well as philosophy. In the natural sciences, through the concept of the "tacit dimension" introduced in 1960 by Michael Polanyi (1891–1976), it attained a rationale and a network of relationships underlying all scientific analysis.[10] In the humanities, the term found great approval. It enables a deeper rapprochement with a person and offers a framework for working towards change. Philosophy thus understands it as a cognitive entity geared to systems of thought. By contrast, psychology regards worldview as an unconscious entity influenced above all by affective forces. It aims to change one's worldview with the help of psychoanalytic methods, cognitive behavioural therapy or systemic therapy. According to

---

7. Ideal types are abstractions and simplifications of social reality, just as models are. See Max Weber, *Gesammelte Aufsätze zur Wissenschaftslehre* (Tübingen: J.C.B. Mohr, 1922), 190ff.

8. Herman Dooyeweerd, *Roots of Western Culture: Pagan, Secular and Christian Options* (Toronto: Wedge, 1979); David K. Naugle, *Worldview: The History of a Concept* (Grand Rapids: Eerdmans, 2001); Philip Graham Ryken, *What Is the Christian Worldview?* (Phillipsburg: P&R Publishing, 2006); Paul G. Hiebert, *Transforming Worldviews: An Anthropological Understanding of How People Change* (Grand Rapids: Baker, 2008); Charles H. Kraft, *Worldview for Christian Witness* (Pasadena: William Carey Library, 2008); Käser, *Foreign Cultures*.

9. Immanuel Kant, *Critique of Judgement* (Indianapolis: Hackett, 1986).

10. Michael Polanyi, *Personal Knowledge: Towards a Post-Critical Philosophy* (Chicago: University of Chicago Press, 1960).

sociology, transformations of worldview are brought about by changes in society, and finally in cultural anthropology by changes in the culture. Thus, philosophy and psychology understand changes from the perspective of conscious cognitive intervention, whereas the behavioural sciences mainly take into account the influence of the context on human behaviour.

One may well ask why the concept of worldview was so influential within the discipline of philosophy. Probably, this was because it corresponded to the desire of philosophers at that time to conceive in terms of a single idea and meaningful concept the deep striving of humankind to comprehend the universe, acquire a general understanding of the world and give meaning to personal life.[11] German idealism and the German romanticism of the nineteenth century, which were protest movements against the "pure reason" of the Enlightenment and its emphasis on the universal essence of things, made use of this new perception to reveal the personal and cultural contingency of all human thought and activity. In so doing they combined the concept of worldview with notions of subjectivism, relativism, perspectivism and historicism.[12] The concept was adopted in the same sense by authors in the postmodern movement of the second half of the twentieth century.

3.2.2 Definition of Worldview

As we attempt to define worldview, we must bear in mind that every definition depends on the person formulating it. One can find all kinds of definitions depending on the academic background and presuppositions of the author.

According to the philosopher David Naugle (1952–2021), "worldview is best understood as a semiotic phenomenon, especially as a system of narrative signs that establishes a powerful framework within which people think (reason), interpret (hermeneutics) and know (epistemology)."[13] This definition by a philosopher focuses particularly on how culture influences one's way of thinking, interpreting and knowing. It implies that there are different styles of thinking and reasoning. One's worldview, with its internalized semiotic structure, can take the form of doctrines and assertions, but it is fundamentally

---

11. One might well link this effort to the search in cosmology for a "grand unified theory" which would explain the universe.

12. Historicism claims that the knowledge, currents of thinking and values of a society are bound up with a contextual historical situation.

13. Naugle, *Worldview*, xix, 253. Hermeneutics is the art of interpretation. Epistemology tries to answer the question of how we can know things.

an interpretation of the world which represents an individual's cultural and religious "bottom line" and "unquestionable truth."[14]

For the anthropologist Charles Kraft (born 1932), worldview comprises *basic assumptions* and *basic values* of a culture.[15] According to Lothar Käser (born 1938), worldview is a *strategy* like culture and religion. From a functionalist perspective, it can also be understood as a set of *interpretations* of the world, society and the self, serving to provide answers to everyday questions and solutions to everyday problems.[16]

Paul Hiebert (1932–2007) defines worldview as the *foundational cognitive, affective and evaluative presuppositions* which a group of people work out for themselves about the nature of reality, and which help them to shape their lives. According to Hiebert's definition, worldview has not only a cognitive dimension as put forward by theologians and philosophers; the affective and evaluative aspects touch on deeper layers of personality and culture than the cognitive aspects.[17]

According to Kraft and Hiebert, the following functions of worldview can therefore be recognized:[18]

1. They are our *plausibility structures*, providing answers to our most profound questions.
2. They grant us emotional security.
3. They confirm our cultural norms.
4. They unite the various elements of our culture into a whole.
5. They keep an eye on cultural change and evaluate it.
6. They provide certainty that the world is indeed as we see it.
7. They give us a sense of peace and well-being.

Thus, worldview represents the basis of personality, culture and religion. This is why we can treat it as a kind of "short cut" towards understanding these three spheres in depth. As a deep structure, worldview is to a large extent part of our subconscious. This means that there is no point in asking someone what

---

14. Naugle, 329.
15. Charles H. Kraft, *Christianity in Culture: A Study in Dynamic Biblical Theologizing in Cross-Cultural Perspective* (Maryknoll: Orbis, 1979), 25–31.
16. Käser, *Foreign Cultures*, 36–37.
17. Hiebert, *Transforming Worldviews*, 25–26.
18. Kraft, *Christianity in Culture*, 54–56; Hiebert, *Transforming Worldviews*, 29–30.

their worldview is. It is part of the "black box" and must therefore be analyzed through indirect ways of measuring.

To put it another way, worldview "formats" a person's behaviour, personality, culture and religion, just as the BIOS[19] determines how the computer's hard drive functions. It is like glasses through which the members of a culture view reality, including the universe, others, and the self. Conversely, cultures and religions influence people's worldview during the socialization process.

3.2.3 Adoption of the Worldview Concept by Evangelicals

The concept of worldview has been very widely adopted by evangelicals, probably because it provides a way to explain reality in its totality and demonstrates the inner consistency of biblical revelation. Here is how David Naugle expresses it:

> Conceiving of Christianity as a worldview has been one of the most significant developments in the recent history of the church . . . [The concept] offers the church a fresh perspective on the holistic nature, cosmic dimensions, and universal applications of the faith. Plus, the explanatory power, intellectual coherence, and pragmatic effectiveness of the Christian worldview not only make it exceedingly relevant for believers personally, but also establish a solid foundation for vigorous cultural and academic engagement.[20]

Among the Reformed churches, the development of a Christian worldview for Christians and students in theological training establishments has become an important task. Their theological institutions and the International Network for Christian Higher Education (INCHE) have produced an impressive number of publications on this topic.[21] In this way, they are continuing the legacy and the apologetic tradition of Augustine (354–430) in his *De civitate Dei* (*City of God*), of Thomas Aquinas (1225–1274) in his *Summa theologiae*, and of John Calvin (1509–1564) in his *Institutes of the Christian Religion*. These authors seek to provide Christians and theologians with a systematic survey of the Bible. Among the representatives of the nineteenth and twentieth centuries,

---

19. BIOS is the abbreviation for "basic input/output system."
20. Naugle, *Worldview*, 4–5.
21. See their website: https://inche.one (heading "Resources"), and their two periodicals: *Christian Higher Education* and *Christian Scholar's Review*.

one should mention the Dutch Calvinist theologian and politician Abraham Kuyper (1837–1920), founder of the Free University of Amsterdam, and Herman Dooyeweerd (1894–1977), student of Abraham Kuyper and professor of jurisprudence at the Free University of Amsterdam from 1926 to 1965, who is regarded as the most creative philosopher among the neo-Calvinists of the twentieth century. Dooyeweerd believed that it is not worldview that has had a predominant influence on human thought and behaviour; rather, in the final analysis, the ultimate conditions and obligations of the human heart, and its acceptance or rejection of God, influence the formation of all philosophy and theory. In this way, Dooyeweerd broadened the concept of worldview to the emotional, evaluative and above all religious dimensions, which are so often neglected in the philosophical approach to worldview. According to Dooyeweerd, every philosophy is based on a worldview.[22] Today, this position is represented by James K. A. Smith (born 1970). In extending this reasoning, he refers to the person as a "liturgical being" (*homo liturgicus*).[23] Nevertheless, it is chiefly David Naugle who continues this approach. It is summed up by a grid of questions relating to worldview: Where are we from? Where are we? What has gone wrong? What is the solution? Where are we going?[24]

Among the well-known evangelical anthropologists and missiologists, Charles Kraft, Lothar Käser, Paul Hiebert and Klaus Müller have produced important studies of the concept of worldview, with a focus on Christian witness and how people can change.[25] Evangelical anthropologists consider the emotional, evaluative and religious dimension particularly important. These dimensions of worldview, as defined by evangelical cultural anthropologists, correspond to the use of the term *heart* in the Bible.

This short survey leads to the question of whether a concept developed by the sciences can be included in the theory (theology) and practice of the Christian faith? If so, how can this be achieved? The apostle Paul offers examples of this approach, taking several notions from the society in which he lives and reshaping them. He applied the titles of the emperor (lord and saviour), and his arrival (*parousia*) to the appearing of our Lord and Saviour Jesus Christ. One might also include terms originating from the mystery cults: *metamorphosis*

---

22. Dooyeweerd, *Roots of Western Culture*.

23. James K. A. Smith, *Desiring the Kingdom: Worship, Worldview, and Cultural Formation* (Cultural Liturgies Series 1; Grand Rapids: Baker Academic, 2009).

24. E.g. Ryken, *What Is the Christian Worldview?*

25. Kraft, *Christianity in Culture* and *Worldview for Christian Witness*; Käser, *Foreign Cultures*; Hiebert, *Transforming Worldviews*; Müller, *Conscience – The Moral Law Within*.

"transformation," which he applied to being born again, the term *mystērion*, signifying the "mystery" of initiation, which he applies to Jesus. The apostle Paul's catch phrase is "take every thought captive to obey Christ" (2 Cor 10:5).

Paul was followed by Augustine, who developed the analogy of the "Egyptian gold," based on the gold the Israelites took with them when leaving Egypt (Exod 11–12). Augustine used this analogy to show how cultural ideas could be integrated into the life of faith.[26] On the other hand, Karl Barth rejected both philosophy and the term "worldview."[27] We have here three of the four approaches regarding the adoption of cultural elements into the Christian faith, as uncovered in the apostle Paul's letters by Dean Flemming: affirming a cultural element (Augustine), opposing it (Karl Barth), modifying it (in the above examples of the apostle Paul) or relativizing it (when Paul relativized the Jewish calendar and food laws).[28]

So how can one transpose a *good integration* of the concept of worldview, which is a product of modernity, into the Christian faith?[29] It is not just about realising that (scientific) systems of thought are subjective and relative, derived from the plurality of languages, cultures and worldviews, but also about acknowledging the objectivity of divine revelation. With regard to the latter, one could consider the following cognitive themes: the trinitarian God of the Bible, monotheistic and personal, reference point of all reality, foundation of the unity and variety of the universe and its personal character; salvation history in relation to creation, fall, redemption and consummation; the sovereignty of God; the reality and activity of the powers of evil; the fallen nature of man; and the goal of making disciples. When it comes to forming a biblical worldview, Paul Hiebert attributes paramount significance to the affective themes (such as those mentioned in Gal 5:22), the evaluative ones (such as the ethical themes) and the diachronic aspects (such as salvation history).

To evaluate worldviews, David Naugle proposes three criteria, corresponding approximately to the criteria of recognition theory: *coherence, agreement* and *practicality*.[30] The rationality test is that of the coherence of

---

26. Augustine, *De Doctrina Christiana*, Corpus Christianorum 1 (Paris: Brepols, 1982), §2, 60.

27. Karl Barth, *Church Dogmatics, vol. 3: The Doctrine of Creation* (London: T&T Clark, 1936/2009), §49, 2.

28. Dean E. Flemming, *Contextualization in the New Testament: Patterns for Theology and Mission* (Leicester: Inter-Varsity Press 2005).

29. Cf. Naugle, *Worldview*, 253–345.

30. Naugle, *Worldview*, 327–28.

a worldview.[31] The second test is empirical, requiring the worldview to be comprehensive and explanatory. The third test is existential and pragmatic, assessing whether a worldview satisfies practical needs. Naugle is convinced that a worldview based on a biblical foundation, with the help of these three criteria, can demonstrate that it possesses a philosophical integrity and a credibility superior to other worldviews and offers a conceptual framework for understanding the all-embracing character of biblical teaching. The spiritual benefit of a Christian faith conceived as a worldview results from its intellectual coherence, its completeness with regard to biblical revelation and real experience, its comprehensive explanatory potential, its practical nature and its personal and cultural power to bring about change. Its biblical character and universal scope remove unnecessary dichotomies and reductionisms such as those between time and eternity, body and soul, faith and reason, the holy and the profane, earth and heaven. "A God-centred conception of a Christian worldview . . . [can impart] a cognitive confidence, an apologetic strategy, a cultural relevance, and a sound, spiritual basis for life."[32]

3.2.4 Synthesis

In an interdisciplinary approach like mine, it is important to understand that the sciences offer widely differing perspectives. The statements of theology, philosophy and history are differentiated and nuanced, whereas the natural sciences and humanities try to simplify the complexity of reality by furnishing them with concepts described as "models." Hence, the former have often reproached the latter for being too simplistic and essentialist.[33] Table 6 summarizes the approaches by the various academic disciplines to the concept of worldview.

---

31. It should be noted that here Naugle is arguing within the logic of modernity. In postmodern thought, the coherence criterion in foundational apologetics is of no effect. Rather it is the desirability of the gospel which carries weight.

32. Naugle, *Worldview*, 341.

33. Essentialism holds that the inward (or essential) nature of all things is the same.

Table 6: Concepts of Worldview in the Sciences

Discipline	Worldview is...
Reformed theology	A cognitive concept explaining the whole of reality and revealing the rational coherence of the biblical revelation; change happens through the work of Jesus Christ on the cross and through the power of the Holy Spirit
Philosophy	A cognitive concept with a focus on systems of thought; change happens through conscious cognitive intervention
Psychology	A subconscious entity influenced by emotional impulses (psychoanalysis) and part of the black box (empirical psychology); change happens through intervention into the sub-conscious (psychoanalysis), or through conscious cognitive intervention (cognitive behavioural therapy)
Sociology	An entity which is part of the black box; change happens through social alterations
Cultural Anthropology	A culturally conditioned entity; change happens through cultural alterations

Multiple approaches are needed to obtain a more complete idea of reality, just as several maps are needed to describe a city or country, or several plans to describe a building. In the same way, several tools are needed to succeed in understanding and changing a worldview.

3.3 Five Models to Make Worldview Practical

The notion of worldview may be well founded, but still remains very vague, just like the notions of personality, culture, religion and identity. That is why many theologians, philosophers and anthropologists have renounced these concepts. I am of the opposite view and suggest a way of enabling the notions of worldview and identity to be of everyday use by means of practical models derived from theology, philosophy and the humanities – operationalizing them, to borrow the current academic jargon. In doing so, I am choosing models where the Bible and the sciences show commonalities, while remaining aware of the problems involved in integrating the concepts selected from those disciplines into the biblical worldview.

The American Marxist anthropologist Michael Kearney (1937-2009) distinguishes five universal dimensions in the various worldviews: 1) the self and the other, 2) relationship between the self and the other, 3) classification of the other, 4) causality, 5) space and time.[34] Reformed philosopher David Naugle considers this model to be the most complete among all the scientific disciplines.[35] Building on these reflections, I suggest five models of worldview which include Kearney's five universal dimensions:

1. The layers model of the order of creation (including the classification of the other and the concept of space);
2. The five soteriological concepts (containing the self and the other and aspects of causality);
3. The orientation of the conscience (representing the self and the other, their relationship and aspects of the classification of the other);
4. Time orientation (including the concept of time);
5. Mana (which also considers aspects of causality): in the animistic conception, mana refers to the extraordinary effect (cf. section 3.3.5).

The layers model of the order of creation, the five soteriological concepts and time orientation represent essentially the cognitive aspects of worldview. The emotional and evaluative aspects are included in the models of the conscience orientation and mana.

For the notion of identity, I propose two models: identity in terms of the tension between the self and the other, and identity as the integration of experiences, values and systems of thought from the past (cf. section 3.4).

3.3.1 The Layers Model of the Order of Creation

A simple way of approaching the concept of worldview is the layers model of the created order. It shows how a worldview arranges the different building blocks of creation such as matter, plants, animals, humans and spirit beings. This answers the worldview question: where are we? We can divide the different worldviews on our globe into four groups, representing Weberian ideal types: the holistic, the Hebrew, the two-tiered and the secular worldview. Table 7 illustrates how different worldviews structure creation and how the layers model of the order of creation is related to the conscience orientation

---

34. Michael Kearney, *Worldview* (Novato: Chandler and Sharp, 1984), 208, based on Robert Redfield, *The Primitive World and its Transformations* (Harmondsworth: Penguin, 1968).
35. Naugle, *Worldview*, 244.

(cf. section 3.3.3). It shows that holistic worldviews are linked to a relational conscience, whereas fragmented worldviews are linked to a rules-based conscience.³⁶

Table 7: Layers Model of the Order of Creation

	Relational Conscience		Rules-Based Conscience	
	Holistic Worldview	Hebrew Worldview	Two-tiered Worldview	Secular Worldview
Layers of Creation		God		"Supernatural" excluded
	Supreme Being		Spirit	
	Spirit beings Ancestral spirits	Spirit beings Angels	"Middle Sphere" excluded	
	Humans Animals Plants Matter	Humans Animals Plants Matter	Humans Animals Plants Matter	Humans Animals Plants Matter

In the *holistic worldview*, the universe is an interrelated whole. The visible and invisible, the material and non-material worlds are not regarded as separate. Man stands at the centre and tries to live in harmony with the universe and persuade spirit beings to serve him. Examples of holistic cultural and religious systems are Animism, Hinduism, Shintoism, Daoism and Chinese Mahayana Buddhism.

The layers model of the order of creation answers the question: "Where are we?"

The *Hebrew worldview* developed from a holistic (animist) worldview. This is particularly attested in the first three books of the Hebrew Bible, Genesis, Exodus and Leviticus.³⁷ They expressly insist that God is the creator of the universe, not part of his

---

36. Propositions for other useful typologies are found in Paul G. Hiebert, *Anthropological Insights for Missionaries* (Grand Rapids: Baker, 1985), 158; Gailyn van Rheenen, "Animism, Secularism and Theism: Developing a Tripartite Model for Understanding World Cultures," *International Journal of Frontier Missions* 10.4 (October 1993): 169–71, 171; Heinzpeter Hempelmann, *Prämodern, Modern, Postmodern* (Neukirchen-Vluyn: Neukirchener Verlagsgesellschaft, 2013).

37. Indications are the new regulations for purity and sacrifices in Leviticus. Cf. sections 4.1.4.4 and 5.4.1.

creation, and that he is "holy" (cf. Gen 1–2; Lev 19:2). God is at the centre of this worldview – it is theocentric. Judaism and Christianity come under this type. Islam, being a reform movement of Judaism and Christianity, orders the elements of creation in the same way as the Hebrew worldview. However, in other aspects of worldview, such as the five soteriological concepts (cf. section 3.3.2), there are considerable differences between the Islamic and the biblical worldview. Within the framework of the layers model, the Hebrew worldview limits itself to arranging the order of the building blocks of creation, thus giving us an understanding of only certain aspects of the biblical worldview.

The *two-tiered worldview* separates the material and visible world from the non-material and invisible world. Plato is a typical example of this way of thinking. Under the influence of Neoplatonism, the Roman Catholic Church, drawing on Thomas Aquinas, adopted this perception of things, a view which would permeate the whole of medieval Europe. In his philosophy, and in philosophy in general, the divine and the human are to be perceived as totally separate categories. However, the incarnation of the Son of God runs totally against this categorization. In Christian expressions of this worldview, God is at the centre, whereas in others it is man who takes centre stage.

The *secular worldview* goes even further than the two-tiered one, excluding not only the middle sphere but all invisible aspects of the world, the so-called "supernatural." It takes account only of what can be observed and measured. At its centre is man. The European philosophy of the Enlightenment with its secular worldview derived its basic ideas from Aristotelian philosophy. Asiatic representatives of a secular worldview reflect the original philosophies of Confucius and the Buddha. The latter corresponds to Theravada Buddhism.

I will now examine some aspects which are clarified in a special way by the layers model of the created order: the concepts of the "spirit double," the "excluded middle" and the "supernatural."

3.3.1.1 The Spirit Double

In the animist (holistic) worldview, according to which the visible world is closely intertwined with the invisible world, every material object or being corresponds to an object or being of spirit nature. This spirit double accompanies its material object or its material life form throughout all its existence. It resembles its material life form or object in shape, colour, taste and smell. Hence, not only are human beings "endowed with a soul," but so are objects of the natural world. This is true of trees, mountains, rivers, waterfalls, and even of rice bowls offered in sacrifice, or a statuette or mask. This notion lies at the heart of Animism and its esoteric knowledge. It can be found, for example, in the Stoic concept of hylozoism, which maintains that matter itself is in some sense alive (Greek *hylē* "matter," *zoē* "life"). By the same token, this notion has been increasingly taken up in the Christianized and secularized West through the concept of the "guardian angel."

In this conception, the visible world is closely bound up with the invisible world. Each exerts influence on the other. According to this notion, masks – as a feature of animist peoples and groups in mountain regions in the West – as well as statues in Hinduism and Buddhism, possess spirit doubles. These latter are of special significance in the rites and worship style of these religions in terms of their influence on the visible world. Among animist peoples, the masks represent beings of spirit nature, e.g. the ancestors, or the so-called "living dead," who exercise influence over the living.[38] On their part, the living attempt to influence the spirit world through offerings. If the bowl of rice, the offering for the ancestors, is still full in the morning after standing in front of the window all night, that is not at all unusual. The ancestor has in a sense "eaten" the spirit double of the rice. I also think of the sorcerer who plunges head-first into the well and shortly afterwards is encountered sitting on a chair in his hut. The way I explain it is that his spirit double plunged into the well. Hence, the way societies with an animist worldview perceive the "beyond" clearly differs from that of the Christianized West.

Spirit doubles and spirit beings in general are not bound by time or space. Malevolent spirit beings can enter into a material being or object and influence it, preferably through available openings. They could get in via the window or door of a house, or the open mouth of a person. Illness could be the result. This is why, in animist cultures, religious experts such as healers are called on to identify the spirit beings which could be causing an illness or calamity.

On a different note, the loss of the spirit double leads to a loss of physical functions. If a person's spirit double is absent for a long period, that person begins to feel tired, becomes ill, then falls into a coma and eventually dies. This process is set in motion if the spirit double is destroyed by a sorcerer through a ritual. In some cultures, important events such as the planting of a sacred tree or the erection of a sacred building are traditionally preceded by human sacrifice, usually a virgin.[39]

---

38. John S. Mbiti, *African Religions and Philosophy* (London: Heinemann, 1969b).
39. Cf. Käser, *Animism*, 88–104, 158–85.

3.3.1.2 The Excluded Middle

In contrast to the holistic worldview, the two-tiered worldview separates the material and visible world from the non-material and invisible world. Between the two lies the "middle sphere" of existence, which the two-tiered worldview ignores.[40] This sphere contains the spirit beings (including the ancestral spirits) who in the animist worldview are the agents of disease and misfortune, among other things. Indeed, this sphere dominates daily life in societies where the animist worldview prevails. If the middle sphere is excluded from the message of the gospel, as was the case with many Western missionaries during the nineteenth and twentieth centuries, the resulting version of Christianity ends up with a two-tiered conception of the world: on one hand, a sphere determined by religion with all the questions involving God, miracles and faith, and on the other hand, a (scientific) sphere determining the natural realm. Such a form of Christianity or Christian mission develops medical, agricultural and educational projects based on a secularized scientific knowledge, independent of religious issues. Moreover, this approach offers no answers to important problems of life such as the cause of disease and misfortune. Hiebert calls this approach *split-level Christianity*.[41]

3.3.1.3 The Supernatural

Finally, in the secular worldview the invisible and non-material world is excluded altogether. It is termed "supernatural" because it is above and beyond the acknowledged valid sphere of the natural. Hence, metaphysics with its questions about God, angels, demons, miracles, the soul and hell are not up for discussion. In Asia, the Buddha adopts such a position: metaphysical questions do not interest him. He is concerned only about the human suffering. Theravada Buddhism takes up this worldview. In Europe, the theologian Rudolf Bultmann (1884–1976) developed a program of demythologizing theology. This endeavour was fundamentally an attempt to contextualize theology for a secular worldview.

It is evident that for a Westerner with a secular worldview the term "supernatural" awakens different associations from those of an African with an animist (holistic) worldview. That which is supernatural for the former seems completely natural for the latter. Theology, psychology, parapsychology,

---

40. Paul G. Hiebert, "The Flaw of the Excluded Middle," *Missiology: An International Review* 10.1 (1982): 35–47.

41. Paul G. Hiebert, R. Daniel Shaw and Tite Tiénou, *Understanding Folk Religion: A Christian Response to Popular Beliefs and Practices* (Grand Rapids: Baker, 1999), 89–91.

the neuroscience and cultural anthropology offer an alternative framework of explanation for analysing phenomena which the secular worldview classifies as supernatural.

3.3.2 The Five Soteriological Concepts

The five key soteriological concepts provide a second cognitive model, encompassing the notions of God, man, evil, sin and salvation. All cultures and religions convey these concepts to their adherents in the course of their socialization, mostly through stories and myths. The Bible has its own. The five soteriological concepts form a worldview, whether on a biblical or another foundation. They provide answers to the following three questions: Where do we come from? What has gone wrong? What is the solution? During the discipleship process, both before and after conversion, these questions must be tackled to transform a cultural worldview into a biblical one. Worldviews will not change unless a chronological Bible teaching on these five concepts and three questions is integrated into the discipleship process. The example of John Calvin in Geneva is significant: within only eighteen years, this Reformer preached between two thousand five hundred and five thousand sermons covering the whole Bible. In this way, he changed the worldview of the population of Geneva.

Traditionally, evangelism began with the proclamation of the good news of Jesus Christ, the heart of the biblical message. But the coming of the kingdom of God through Jesus Christ (Mark 1:15) and the forgiveness of sins (Luke 24:46ff) are not good news where there is no sin to forgive. Jean-Jacques Rousseau (1712–1778) declared that man is born good but is corrupted by society. Western secular education uses the same argument. Also, according to the Koran, man is good but created weak. Therefore, it is normal for him to sin (Sura 2:36; 4:28). In Islam, the notion of a son of God is regarded as polytheism and not as good news (Sura 5:72; 6:100; 9:30). One reason for this may derive from the nightly visits of male and female spirit beings, a popular notion in pre-Islamic Arabic Animism. A further reason probably lies in the teaching of the Marianite sect, according to which the Trinity consists of Father God, Maria and Jesus. Jesus would then have originated from the relationship between Father God and Maria.

> The five soteriological concepts answer the following three questions:
> - Where do we come from?
> - What has gone wrong?
> - What is the solution?

It is pointless to proclaim freedom from sin where sin is not a problem. The concept of sin is closely bound up with that of evil. How did evil enter the world? Is evil bound up with good and bad fate, coming through karma in Hinduism and Buddhism, or from Allah in Islam (Sura 35:15)? Or, as the Bible says, was evil introduced at the initiative of the adversary (Satan) into a thoroughly good creation, which had been brought into being by a thoroughly good God? Moreover, the concept of sin is closely bound up with the concept of man. Is man created in the image of God or is this idea blasphemy (Sura 112)? Is it normal for man to sin, or is it the sin which separates him from fellowship with God?

The way in which man is understood provides insight into the understanding of God. God is our final point of reference. He is the independent source and the transcendent standard for everything. The layers model of the Hebrew worldview of Judaism and Christianity was also adopted by Islam: Allah is conceived as separate from creation; he is holy. This perception contrasts with the monist and pantheist notions of Asian religions, in which the Supreme Being is part of the universe and pervades all things. This means that most of the Asian religions are characterized by a holistic worldview. In the same context, another question arises: what is the moral quality of a deity? The holiness of the biblical God reveals a moral quality which is hard to find in other religions, where deities exhibit the whole spectrum of human character – for example, in Greek mythology or the Hindu pantheon.

In conclusion, the offer of salvation makes sense only where the concepts of sin and evil are taken seriously, based on how man and God are conceived. The Bible teaches these concepts from the first three chapters onwards in reverse order: the concepts of God and man (Gen 1–2), of evil and sin (Gen 3), and of salvation (from Gen 3:15 onwards throughout the whole Bible). Based on these facts, missionaries have begun to teach the Bible chronologically. The Bible itself does this for oral cultures, by employing a narrative style. This can encourage us with regard to how to approach the oral cultures around us.

The model of the five soteriological concepts also sheds light on the question of whether the Old Testament can be replaced by the cultural and religious systems of the different regions of the world as "preparation for the gospel."[42] Were or are, for example, Greek philosophy or African traditional

---

42. The term "preparation for the gospel" was introduced by Eusebius of Caesarea in his work *Praeparatio evangelica*. It probably originated with Origen of Alexandria and forms the foundation of the "anthropological model of contextualization," which starts from the needs of a culture. It was adopted by Matteo Ricci and subsequently by other Catholic and Protestant theologians and missiologists, among them e.g. John Mbiti and Kwame Bediako.

religions a preparation for the gospel? It is apparent that other religious systems create different worldviews from those of the Bible and can therefore not be substituted for the Old Testament with its Hebrew worldview and its very special soteriological concepts. The latter have to be derived and formulated from the stories and concepts recorded in the Bible. On the other hand, cultural and religious elements with a divine imprint can certainly be a "preparation for the gospel" through their proximity to biblical concepts. Appendix 5 provides an example for presenting the five soteriological concepts within the framework of chronological Bible teaching.[43]

3.3.3 The Orientation of the Conscience

Whereas the first two models set forth the cognitive aspects of worldview, the orientation of the conscience presents evaluative and emotional features, thereby touching the deepest layers of personality, culture and religion. It is a particularly fruitful model for cultural analysis from a missiological perspective, since it combines aspects of theology, psychology and cultural anthropology. For this reason, I shall examine it in more detail.

There is also a further reason why the conscience is a good model: it is an important concept in both the Bible and cultural anthropology, which is very rare. In the Bible, the conscience is involved on the pathway from sin to salvation through forgiveness and touches the heart of the biblical message. In cultural anthropology, cultures are examined in terms of feelings of shame and guilt.

3.3.3.1 Defining the Conscience

What is the conscience? I have already presented the biblical perspective briefly at the start of this chapter (cf. section 3.1.1.3). From the perspective of behavioural science and the humanities, it is that which guides the behaviour of individuals and provides them with inner moral navigation. This means that research into the nature of the individual conscience is of great importance for all areas of life, especially with regard to education, psychology and theology. In addition, the conscience has a social function, enabling people to internalize the norms of society and avoid infringing them – in other words, to find their

---

43. For an in-depth study of the five soteriological concepts, which correspond to the main doctrines of theology, the reader is encouraged to consult works of systematic theology. Regarding the divine imprint of cultural and religious elements, see the presentation of the tri-polar perspective on religions (section 2.4.2). For an in-depth rationale of chronological Bible teaching, see Wiher, *Sharing the Good News*.

way within society. One can therefore assert that the conscience is the "organ" that represents a person's cultural, social and religious capabilities.

Because of the complexity of this topic, Protestant theologians disregarded it for a long time. By contrast, Catholic theology has held on to it within the framework of its moral theology. Psychologists and cultural anthropologists no longer refer to the conscience because it is part of the unknown black box of the empirical sciences. They prefer to talk about feelings of shame and guilt. I will therefore in what follows define the conscience in terms of shame and guilt. Both feelings imply an appraisal in connection with personal, cultural or social norms. This means that the model belongs to the level of evaluation, the deepest level of worldview.

3.3.3.2 The Story of John

To illustrate how all this is connected with the orientation of the conscience, here is a story involving myself. During my time as a missionary in Africa, I shared a driver with other missionary colleagues. Since John (not his real name) earned a decent wage, his extended family entrusted children to him for upbringing and education. This increased financial pressure on him, and he began to drink to cope with the stress. On his way to the capital, along with our local agronomist to collect materials, he decided, against official mission regulations and despite the protests of the agronomist, to take fare-paying passengers. At a bend, he unfortunately swerved off the road. The vehicle overturned. One of the passengers was killed, and John was provisionally arrested on suspicion of manslaughter through careless driving.

When our Swiss agronomist arrived at the scene, he discovered that the vehicle was extensively damaged, with a tire flattened by being stabbed with a knife. When John got back home, the missionaries asked him to help with the considerable costs of the accident. His family told the mission they were sorry, but that John must not lose his job because the family depended on it. John never admitted even the slightest thing to do with his actions. He acknowledged only that which his superiors forced him to acknowledge. Pastor Jacob, who had recommended John for this position, came not only to apologize on his behalf for the accident but also to ask for release from having to pay anything towards the costs. Later a second pastor, Josef, whose first child also happens to be called John, came to us along with John to ask us to give him his driving job back.

The missionaries decided to dismiss him forthwith, because during the whole affair he had shown no remorse, nor acknowledged having done anything wrong. Any help with the costs of the accident still completely failed to materialize. His family didn't understand why the mission refused to re-employ him.

In the following sections, I will try to unpack the various elements of the story using the model of conscience orientation.

Restoration of prestige and honour

In this story, the desire to put an end to the loss of honour and to restore respect is very clearly apparent. John has lost face and is looking for ways to remove this disgrace from his life. To restore his honour, a simple apology such as was offered in the scenes of reconciliation, does not suffice. Real forgiveness is demonstrated only through restoring him to his original position as the mission's driver.

How have matters developed for him now that his efforts to be reinstated as the mission's driver have failed? The fact that he is no longer behind the wheel is not only visible to all, and he must also cope with being unable to provide for his family. The whole affair is intolerable. As a result, he leaves town, not only because he can't find a job as a driver, but also because he doesn't want to be exposed to the glances of his friends and the expectations of his immediate and extended family. It is very difficult for him to come to terms with this experience, for the loss of prestige continues remorselessly, with visible outcomes in his daily life.

Restoration of harmony

With rules-based persons the problem is solved through punishment, correction of wrong behaviour, or restitution, whereas with relational persons the problem persists until they are received back into society with their honour restored. Their isolation must be overcome and harmony with the community re-established. John is isolated neither from his extended family nor from his church. Everyone pleads for him at the address of the missionaries. The two pastors even go with him as mediators when he has to appear before the mission. However, even after numerous attempts, the mission maintains its position.

The lack of remorse

The main issue the missionaries charge John with is that they claim that he himself has never made any admission of fault and has entrenched himself behind the excuses of others. A relational person finds it extremely difficult to reveal their failure to others. Such a demand is much harder for John to fulfil than for rules-based persons. Rules-centred persons interpret his refusal to admit guilt as cowardice. For relational persons, the "courage" to admit their guilt is effrontery. A confession would be viewed as a further impropriety.

The mediator

If relational persons are to acknowledge wrongdoing, they require a mediator. Indeed, such persons feel shame before those whom they have offended. It is very painful for them to admit wrongdoing, for it would be effrontery for them to make the confession themselves. Hence, a more esteemed member of the family, such as an older uncle or a church minister, is chosen to make the confession on behalf of the perpetrator and ask for pardon. In John's case, several pastors and the family itself fulfilled this role. However, the missionary society interpreted this as cowardice.

Reparations

For a rules-based person, forgiveness includes punishment for wrongdoing and making reparations. In a relational society, what matters above all is the restoration of harmony, respect and honour. Making reparations is not a matter of priority in their awareness.

In many countries with a relational culture, forgiveness is regarded as complete when the perpetrators or their family members have admitted wrongdoing. The mutual agreement between both family groups is crucial. If things are settled in this way, the decision can mean that reparations are not required. Not until the arrival of modern justice influenced by Western culture were penalties, reparations and fines introduced. According to how forgiveness in 1 John 1:9 is understood, some Christians believe that once forgiveness is assured, there are no further demands. Reparations are no longer required.

In our story, it never occurs to John to pay his share of the costs of the accident. From his perspective, his decision is all the more justifiable because the mission is much richer than he is, and since the accident he hasn't been earning anything. It would be cruel to demand any recompense.

Forgiveness

For John and his family, forgiveness means that he continues to be employed as driver for the mission. The missionaries' claim to have forgiven him while refusing to reinstate him is incomprehensible to the family, which interpret the decision as a refusal to forgive. Deeds convey more than words. In their eyes the missionaries are hypocrites.

John had illegally allowed people to travel with him. For the missionaries the repeated disregard of their rules is sufficient grounds for no longer employing him. For some, the fact that he has never admitted his misbehaviour or shown remorse is another reason. The notion that they don't forgive him, don't accept him as a person and don't love him is very far from the truth. From their perspective, there are only two aspects to the matter: a continued imputation of blame and the personal forgiveness of John. For them these two things are completely separate, but not for the local people. The two positions are not reconcilable, and so misunderstandings and frustrations are inevitable.

Unanswered questions, and what happened later
Several questions come to mind. What would have happened if the employer had been an African untouched by any Western influence? Would John have been rehabilitated? Were not the missionaries afraid of the snowball effect of giving the local people the impression that any and every infringement of the regulations would be forgiven, without any consequences?

Indeed, one could also imagine a different outcome of the story, in which John is employed as a mechanic in the workshop, with part of his wages automatically deducted to gradually pay off part of the cost of the accident. During this period of penalty, he would not be allowed to drive the mission's cars. Although he is subjected to a punishment, he can still care for his family, save face, maintain his honour and stay in the locality.

But now because of his dismissal by the missionaries and his lack of any wage, he was forced to leave town to escape the glances and gossip of the neighbours. Ironically, I encountered him after being transferred to the capital, where he regularly interpreted the sermon at his church. Since he had no money to buy alcohol, he was no longer getting drunk. He had founded a successful taxi firm.

3.3.3.3 Development of the Conscience

The simplest way to understand the conscience and its orientations is to look at how it develops during childhood. Conscience exists in every person in the form of dispositions. Just as a child is born with a disposition to learn a language, in the same way it is born with a disposition for conscience. In the same way as it learns the language of its attachment figures, its conscience also develops during childhood in a way that corresponds to the sociocultural context it is growing up in. Based on this principle, the American anthropologist Melford E. Spiro, drawing on observations he made in an Israeli kibbutz, interpreted them using the methods of psychoanalysis.[44]

---

44. Melford E. Spiro, *Children of the Kibbutz* (Cambridge: Harvard University Press, 1958).

Spiro observed that children reared and socialized by few adults within a nuclear family, e.g. by father and mother, integrated into their consciences not only the norms presented to them, but also the attachment figures responsible for them. They acted according to fixed standards and developed rules-based personalities. They organized their lives according to a plan. They tended to be punctual and set clear objectives for themselves. For them, work was more important than relationships. Since their conscience, with the help of a set of rules, operated autonomously, they were inclined to be individualist. If they infringed a norm, they felt guilty. Hence, Spiro called this kind of imprinting a guilt-oriented conscience. I am adopting a different aspect of this imprinting, referring in more neutral terms to a *rules-based conscience*.

When children are raised by numerous attachment figures, such as in an extended family or a nursery, they do indeed integrate into their conscience the norms presented to them but are unable to do the same with all those responsible for them. As a result, they depend on the attachment figures being present for their conscience to function properly. When mother is present, her norms direct their actions and behaviour; when Grandma is there, hers are the norms which matter. Such children tend to develop a relational personality with a group identity. They prefer relational interaction in the workplace, and when they are working, they prefer to operate as part of a team. Their priority is to achieve status rather than to attain certain goals. If no attachment figure is present, there is no norm to determine their actions, according to the saying: "When the cat is away, the mice will play." This is precisely the basis of the phenomenon of corruption. However, when the violation of the norm is made public, the perpetrator feels ashamed. Hence, Spiro calls this tendency a shame-oriented conscience. Here again, I am adopting a different aspect of this imprinting, referring instead to a *relationship-based conscience* or more briefly a *relational conscience*.

One important difference between a conscience based on rules and one based on relationships is evident from the following example. In mid-August 2022, Bassam al-Sheikh Hussein attacked a bank in Beirut, Lebanon, and took six hostages. He needed money to pay the medical costs of his gravely ill father. Since the collapse of the banking system, the Lebanese had scarcely been able to access their accounts. It was clear to all that Bassam was demanding only what was due to him. Far from condemning him for this action, the public celebrated him as a hero. How can that be explained in terms of our model? In a rules-based society, robbery is regarded as a violation of the law. But in a mainly relational culture such as prevails in Lebanon, cleverness, vigilance or cunning in breaking the law can evoke such admiration that the perpetrator can even be cheered as a hero. Moreover, the evaluation becomes even more complicated through the fact that Bassam al-Sheikh Hussein wanted to get only what really was his due.

By highlighting the influence of the number of nurturing adults on the development of the conscience, Spiro has provided an interesting model for a typology of the personality and change in worldview. However, Spiro's model explains only part of the matter. An African infant growing up in a nuclear family in an urban environment in Africa will develop and possess a relational conscience despite the small number of adults rearing him. This can be explained by the presence of other factors influencing the development of the conscience, in particular the *type of upbringing*. If the adults teach the norms in terms of explanations and arguments (rules), the conscience of the child is more likely to become rules-based. If they emphasize the relational aspects of the norms, the child's conscience will probably become relational. So, for example you might hear "If you do that, Papa will beat you." Or conversely, someone might ask, "What will people say?"

If a child is given only a few norms, its conscience will become relational or will not develop as it should. This is what appears to have happened to the post-war generation in Western Europe, which rejected the traditional norms of Western society. As a consequence of an anti-authoritarian upbringing, its children developed either a relational conscience, or an under-developed conscience with inadequate functioning, neither relational nor rules-based. Instances of a poorly developed conscience are apparent when we see youth kill one of their comrades with no uncomfortable feelings, a phenomenon which we encounter today more and more frequently in our big cities around the world.

Let's look at cycling in our cities. In the 1960s and 1970s, the overwhelming majority of cyclists observed the Highway Code. Today only a fraction of them stops at a red light. Instead, they look each way to see if a car is approaching, or if a policeman or a traffic camera is there, and then proceed without waiting for the light to change. What has happened here? The rules-based conscience has largely given way to the relational or underdeveloped forms, which act in disregard of the rules (cf. section 5.3.5).

Concerning change in the conscience orientation, it should be noted that at conversion the deep structures of the personality are not automatically altered, except through the sovereign work of the Holy Spirit. The only human way to effect change in the conscience is to influence it specifically. The deeper layers of the personality, which have been imprinted in early childhood, permit fewer changes than the layers acquired in later life. Relational elements can be added through corresponding education or lifestyle – for example, through a close relationship with the God of the Bible. Rules-based elements are activated through introducing rules into daily life, such as the Ten Commandments, other rules, a strict lifestyle or a tight agenda. I will return to this topic in more detail in section 3.6.

If you would like to get to know your conscience orientation, you can test yourself as follows. Imagine that you are driving at night and the traffic light in front of you is red. How would you behave? If you stop, your conscience is in all probability focused on rules. If, on the other hand, you look in both directions to see if a car is coming or a policeman or traffic camera is about, and then (if not) go through the red light, your conscience is probably relational.

Of course, Spiro's observations remain a model (or an ideal type) and do not describe all of reality. Each of us is a blend of relational and rules orientations. A more precise way to understand a personality profile is by means of six basic pairs of values with which the conscience orientation is imbued. This typology will be set forth in section 5.1.1 and in the Appendices 2 and 3.

3.3.3.4 The Psychoanalytic Model of the Conscience

I will now describe three models of the conscience which will enable us to refine our understanding of its orientations. The first one considers the conscience from the perspective of psychoanalysis. It locates the conscience in Freudian terminology within the *ego* (in today's psychological terminology the self) and distinguishes two different spheres: the ego ideal on the relational axis and the superego on the rules axis (see Table 8).

On one hand, a child identifies with its parents: typically, a boy would desire to be like his father and a girl like her mother. The parents become their ideal, their ego ideal. If a child cannot fulfil its parents' expectations, it will feel shame. On the other hand, a child will submit to the rules of its parents and integrate them into its conscience, the *superego*. And if it contravenes the rules, it will feel guilty. In this way, the ego ideal and the superego create representations of the parents in the conscience of the child. In psychoanalytic terms, if a child has a tendency to behave in such a way as to dishonour its parents or contravene their rules, it will sense a tension between the ego and the ego ideal, evoking shame, or a tension between the ego and the superego, manifested as a feeling of guilt. The psychoanalytic model is presented in Table 8.

Table 8: The Psychoanalytic Model of the Conscience

Ego	Relational Axis	Rules Axis
Motivation	Identification	Submission, obedience
Compartment of conscience	Ego ideal	Superego
Feedback regarding a goal or norm	Failure	Transgression
Produced feeling	Shame	Guilt

One might ask which educational method of motivating a person is stronger: identification with a role model or subordination to the latter's rules. The apostle Paul operated according to both: on one hand, he commanded us to imitate himself, but also God and Christ (1 Cor 11:1; Eph 5:1), thus arguing in view of identification on the relational axis. On the other hand, his aim was to lead non-Jews to "obedience to the faith" (Rom 1:5; 15:18). Here he is reasoning according to obedience to what the law prescribes, an argument on the rules axis. By contrast, Islam, the name of which means literally "submission," points us only to the rules axis, or submission to the Islamic law, the *sharia*.

Interestingly, the psychoanalytic model of the conscience, developed indeed by the Jewish psychoanalyst Sigmund Freud, is not far removed from the biblical concept of sin. The Hebrew word *hata'* relates to the picture of the arrow which "misses the target," an image taken over by the Greek word *hamartia*. If the arrow falls short or just misses its target, this means from the perspective of our model a shaming failure. However, if the arrow overshoots the target, that is equivalent to stepping over the boundaries or transgression, evoking feelings of guilt. This second way of looking at this relates, on the one hand, to the Hebrew word *pēscha'*, and, on the other hand, to the Greek word *paraptoma*, both meaning "to step over" (the edges of the path). All this broadens the dimensions of failure and transgression and throws light on different facets of sin according to the Bible. It expresses itself both in inadequate behaviour regarding the rules, and also in lack of relationship to the creator.

3.3.3.5 The Cognitive Model of the Conscience

The second model introduces us to the practice of the child psychiatrist Michael Lewis in New York, allowing us to understand other aspects of the conscience orientations.[45] He experimented with small children, getting them to play

---

45. Michael Lewis, *Shame: The Exposed Self* (New York: Macmillan, 1992).

games (which require following the rules). These games were deliberately somewhat too difficult for the children. When they predictably failed, Lewis observed two reactions. One group of children let their heads drop and ceased all activity for a moment. The children may have said to themselves, "I really cannot play any game." The other group became very active, trying to find a solution to the problem. The self-evaluation in this case may have been: "No problem; I will be able to play other games." Lewis interprets the reaction of the first group as awareness of complete failure in the game, expressed in his view as a sense of shame (lowering of the head, inhibition). The second group, according to Lewis, feels they have only partly failed, expressed as a response of guilt (intensive search for a solution). Lewis concludes from this experiment that shame and guilt are not primary emotions like fear, joy, rage, sadness and disgust, but *composite feelings*, the result of cognitive assessment of one's own behaviour with regard to the rules of the game (*"self-conscious" emotions*). Table 9 suggests that shame and guilt are the result of an assessment (B) of situational norms, game rules or life goals (A) with a total or partial attribution (C).

Table 9: The Cognitive Model of the Conscience

A. Norms, rules and goals		
B. Assessment: failure		
C. Attribution:		
Total	→ Shame	"self-conscious"
Partial	→ Guilt	emotions

To understand what I mean by "self-conscious" emotions, note that in general a child becomes aware of itself around the age of eighteen months. Before this age, if you put a red dot on its nose in front of the mirror, the child points its finger towards the mirror. After eighteen months it points to its own nose. By then it has developed an awareness of itself, a self-consciousness. Thus, shame and guilt are quite specific feelings reflecting a cognitive process, a "moral" assessment of norms, rules or goals. Clearly, an infant can sense these two feelings only after self-awareness has developed. It appears, according to Lewis's observations, that the reaction of shame is more comprehensive and inhibiting than the guilt reaction, which is more likely to have a stimulating effect.

3.3.3.6 The Soteriological Model of the Conscience

The model of the conscience orientation also lends itself to developing a typology of the concepts of salvation, forgiveness and sin – in other words, soteriological notions. Since shame and guilt are, among other things, an expression of sin, any model of the conscience is also a soteriological one. This means it has links to the five soteriological concepts.

According to the Bible, the condition of sin has to do with disgrace, with salvation relating to honour. The prophet Isaiah says, "But Israel is saved by the Lord with everlasting salvation; you shall not be put to shame [*bosh*] or disgraced [*kalam*] to all eternity" (Isa 45:17). By the same token, the psalmist writes, "All worshippers of images are put to shame" (Ps 97:7). The apostle Paul states, "All have sinned and fall short of the glory of God" (Rom 3:23). And: "The Scripture says, No one who believes in him [Jesus Christ] will be put to shame" (Rom 10:11, citing Isa 28:16).

On the other hand, provision for atoning for a violation of a law is made by the guilty person bringing the priest a sin offering (Hebr. *hata'at*) or a guilt offering (Hebr. *'asham*, Deut 5:14–6:7). The prophet Isaiah refers to the servant of God in the same way:

> But he was wounded for our transgressions [*pēsha'*], crushed for our iniquities [*'awon*]; upon him was the punishment [*musar*] that made us whole [*shalom*], and by his bruises we are healed . . . Yet it was the will of the Lord to crush him with pain. When you make his life an offering for sin [*'asham*] . . . through him the will of the Lord shall prosper. (Isa 53:5, 10)

In turn, the Lord's prayer puts great emphasis on the necessity of forgiveness in the life of a disciple of Jesus: "Forgive us our debts [*opheilēma*], as we also have forgiven our debtors" (Matt 6:12 NRSV). Whereas in most classic English translations *opheilēma* (lit. "that which is owed") is translated by "debts" (KJV, NKJV, NIV, NRSV, NJB), newer English translations (e.g. NLT) and various translations in other languages also use neutral terms such as omission or offence, which bring in the relational aspect.

Figure 4 shows the positive and negative values of the soteriological model of the conscience. On the left are the biblical terms (sin, forgiveness and salvation), in the middle the rules axis (justice and guilt) and on the right the relational axis (harmony, honour and shame). As I describe these concepts in detail, I will begin at the bottom and will trace the functions of the conscience to the top.

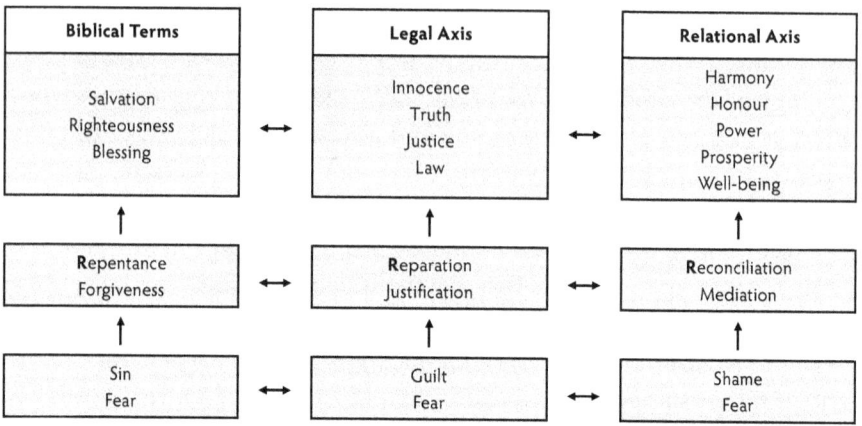

Figure 4: The Soteriological Model of the Conscience

Sin, that feeling or condition that is aroused by violating a norm, can surface as guilt or shame. Both are accompanied by fear – either fear of punishment in the case of rules-based persons, or fear of losing affection or esteem in the case of relational persons. A rules-based person will want to make amends for the transgression of the rule, the individual guilt, which normally happens through the payment of a fine, an offering or even a term in prison. The biblical and theological term for this is *justification*. Luther viewed this in terms of God placing him before a law court on account of his guilt. Hence, he looked for a God who would be merciful towards him, acquitting him and restoring his innocence – in other words, justifying him. Luther's doctrine of justification is recognisably rules-based. On the other hand, as a person, Luther was certainly relational. When it comes to forgiveness, a relational person will respond differently from a rules-based person. Under the influence of shame, the person will be unable to face the situation and especially not the person she has offended, but will require a third person to mediate a reconciliation. In my opinion, forgiveness must be carefully weighed so as to touch deeper layers of persons, cultures and religions. The Bible offers us a balanced model of forgiveness involving the three Rs: *repentance, reparation and reconciliation*.

In terms of positive values, a rules-based person strives for freedom from guilt, a sound government legal system, obedience to the law, and truth. By contrast, a relational person will strive to restore harmony, honour, social status, power, prosperity and well-being. These values express themselves in life in the form of objectives and priorities. For rules-based persons and societies, human rights are important, whereas for relational persons and cultures, what matters most is harmony, collective honour and dignity. Here it is important to add a nuance in relation to the positive relational values. In addition to those mentioned, we have to include pride as a positive value, but also arrogance as toxic feeling. A relational person can be proud of her family, social or ethnic group. However, this positive feeling can easily turn into vanity.

The different dimensions of the model can be illustrated by a classic case: the story of the cartoons of Muhammad in 2004. The Danes and the French insisted on the right to freedom of opinion, as a rules-based conscience would expect, whereas Muslims in some countries reacted with violence, attacking embassies and committing murder, responses driven by the collective disgrace suffered. We can also consider three American presidents. George W. Bush led two wars in the Near East to establish human rights and democracy. This objective is clearly rules-centred. Then came Barack Obama, benefiting especially from the youth vote. Before important decisions with geopolitical outcomes, he largely consulted other statesmen. We can conclude from this that he is recognisably relational. He was followed by Donald Trump with his slogans "America first" and "Make America great again" (MAGA). Trump's strongly developed relational axis is conspicuous, but unfortunately his rules axis is underdeveloped. He respects neither the laws of the United States nor the rules of international diplomacy.

This typology noticeably represents Weberian ideal types. In reality, every person harbours a diverse blend of both conscience orientations. It can be very helpful for us to know our own profile, so that we can better comprehend how and why we behave as we do, and also improve our understanding of our neighbours, friends, colleagues and students. Section 5.1.1 will present a personality typology with six pairs of values (cf. appendix 3). It enables a deeper and more nuanced analysis of a person's worldview.

3.3.4 Time Orientation

The model of the conscience orientation caused us to recognize two different ways of handling time. The actions of rules-based persons are governed by time in a particular way. They keep a diary and plan how long a piece of work should take, and they value punctuality. By contrast, relational persons are not so bothered about time. Their focus is on people, relationships and things they have experienced together.[46] The well-known passage in Ecclesiastes 3:1–8 ("a time for everything") is typical of how relational cultures handle events.

---

46. Cf. Sherwood G. Lingenfelter and Marvin K. Mayers, *Ministering Cross-Culturally: An Incarnation Model for Personal Relationships* (Grand Rapids: Baker, 1986, 2003, 2016), 37–50, https://books.google.com.

However, this fourth model of worldview, again a cognitive model, suggests the introduction of an additional aspect of time, with particular significance in daily life and in current theological discourse. This is the focus on the past or the future.

Many people, such as the Hebrews, look back to their ancestral traditions. Like rowers in a boat, they are looking backwards. They think that the future lies behind them (Hebrew 'ahor "back, backwards," Ps 143:5; Isa 46:10; Jer 29:11).[47] John Mbiti observed something similar in Swahili: the term *zamani* incorporates several stages of the past, and the term *sasa* an aspect of the present. On the other hand, in several Bantu languages Mbiti discovered no linguistic terms referring to the future. In his doctoral thesis, he goes so far as to say that Africans have no notion of the future.[48] Several authors have rightly criticized this extreme approach.[49] For myself, I would say that it is not about the inability to conceive of the future but a fundamental difference in focus, towards either the past or the future. Sherwood Lingenfelter and Marvin Mayers call the future orientation a "crisis orientation" in which crises are seen in advance, and the past orientation, which conceives the problems of the future as lying behind them and therefore of no concern, "non-crisis orientation."[50] It is extremely difficult for people or a culture with a focus on the past to anticipate problems which will occur in the future, such as a shortage of drugs for a chemist, or to plan for future objectives, as is the normal practice in Western societies in school and project management. Table 10 describes the different orientations with regard to time.

Table 10: Time Orientations

Conscience Orientation	Punctuality orientation	Event orientation
Predominant Focus	Future orientation	Past orientation

So how did the people of the Old Testament move the focus from the past on to the future? According to Gerhard von Rad, it was after the continuous announcement of the day of Yahweh through the prophets that the Israelites

---

47. Wolff, *Anthropology of the Old Testament*, 83–92.

48. John S. Mbiti, *New Testament Eschatology in an African Background* (London: SPCK, 1969), 24ff; John S. Mbiti, *African Religions and Philosophy* (London: Heinemann, 1969b), 15–29.

49. E.g. Byang H. Kato, *Theological Pitfalls in Africa* (Nairobi: Evangel, 1975); Leonard Nyirongo, *The Gods of Africa or the God of the Bible? The Snares of African Traditional Religion in Biblical Perspective* (Potchefstroom: University of Potchefstroom, 1997), 89–98.

50. Lingenfelter and Mayers, *Ministering Cross-Culturally*, 65–77.

began to look to the future and their concept of time became linear.[51] The focus on the future, especially on the "end time," became an important feature of the New Testament concept of time. Its writers considered themselves as in the in-between, the *eschatological interim*, between the first appearing of Christ and his return, and they fixed their eyes on the eschatological future. This highly nuanced eschatological perception of time in the New Testament is an especially remarkable phenomenon in the ancient Near East. Even today many find it hard to understand. This is probably why it is neglected by many contemporary movements. Thus, the theme chosen by the ecumenical movement for its 1973 mission congress in Bangkok was "Salvation Today." Subsequently, the World Council of Churches went so far as to support revolutionary movements in southern Africa in order to expedite "salvation" for those peoples – salvation in a one-sided this-worldly and temporal sense.

3.3.4.1 The Health and Wealth Gospel

The health and wealth gospel is another movement with a theology which neglects the dimension of the eschatological interim. Predicated on the cultural concept of salvation, which is closely related to the Old Testament concept of shalom, this theology associates genuine Christian faith with assurance of health and success in life. If I give something to God, he will return it to me a hundredfold. According to this view, a Christian with real faith can be neither ill nor poor.

From a theological perspective, this movement ignores the New Testament perception of salvation, according to which Jesus Christ made salvation possible through his sacrificial offering. Salvation is a gift and cannot be manipulated. However, we have not yet attained the perfect condition of the New Jerusalem (Rev 21–22). Certainly, the kingdom of God has come near with the first advent of Jesus (Mark 1:15), but it will not come to full fruition until the return of Christ and the new creation. The biblical position is one of *inaugurated eschatology*, that of the health and wealth theology a *realized eschatology*.

From an anthropological perspective and especially with regard to the worldview of the health and wealth gospel, the following elements emerge by way of summary: in relation to the layers model of the order of creation, the health and wealth gospel results from an anthropocentric and holistic worldview. In terms of the five basic soteriological concepts, it identifies the cultural concept of salvation with that of the Old Testament while ignoring the

---

51. Gerhard von Rad, *Old Testament Theology, vol. 2: The Theology of Israel's Prophetic Traditions* (Edinburgh: Oliver and Boyd, 1965; Westminster: John Knox Press, 2001), 99–127.

New Testament nuance, particularly the eschatological dimension. As for the conscience orientation, at the root of the health and wealth gospel is a relational worldview which seeks harmony, honour and power in the eyes of others, but wellness and wealth for the self. As we will see in the next section, prosperity can also be regarded as a sign that a lot of mana is involved.

This explains why a significant percentage of the world's population lean towards the health and wealth gospel and fills churches of pastors who adopt this theology. This factor has enabled the massive growth of churches such as the Universal Church of the Kingdom of God and Salt of the Earth in Brazil, El Shaddai in the Philippines, the Church of the Lord (Aladura), the Celestial Church of Christ and the Redeemed Christian Church of God in Nigeria, and the Kimbanguist Church in the Democratic Republic of the Congo. For the Africa Chapter of the Lausanne Theology Working Group, this raises the question whether, "much popular Christianity is a syncretized super-structure on an underlying worldview that has not been radically transformed by the biblical gospel."[52]

3.3.5 Mana

The fifth model which can assist in the practical outworking of a worldview is the concept of mana.[53] It stems from the Austronesian (oceanic) group of languages and was incorporated into cultural anthropology in 1891 through the missionary Robert Codrington.[54] In the animist worldview, mana serves to explain the principle of cause and effect, especially extraordinary causes with extraordinary effects (in Western understanding, mana is partly reckoned to have a supernatural cause). If a hunter's arrow always hits the target, it possesses a lot of mana. If a man or woman is successful in life, owns a big house and has many children, that person has a lot of mana. In such a case, mana becomes a symbol for happiness and affluence. Mana can also manifest itself in terms of authority, charisma, good fortune, miracles, prestige, social status, power or vitality. This indicates that mana is related to the relational conscience in its striving for prestige, honour, power and wealth. In folk Islam, the concept of *baraka* is somewhat similar, but it has a wider meaning in terms

---

52. Lausanne Theology Working Group. "Statement on the Prosperity Gospel," *Evangelical Review of Theology* 34, 2 (2010): 99–102, 101.

53. Cf. Käser, *Animism*, 66–87.

54. Robert H. Codrington, *The Melanesians: Studies in Their Anthropology and Folklore* (New York: Clarendon Press, 1891), 118.

of the "power of blessing." The millennial generation has become particularly interested in this – a generation which I would describe as relational – has become particularly interested in this power in order to indicate that someone has special talent or good fortune (cf. section 5.3.5).

There is positive mana, e.g. in prayers for blessing, and negative mana, as in imprecations and curses. These are *forms of speech with great effect*. They are based on the concept of "words of power" exemplified in the Hebrew term *dabar*. This concept relates approximately to what the linguistic speech act theory calls "performative speech," equating speech to the corresponding action (e.g. "I swear").[55] This phenomenon forms the basis of the cursing psalms.

Mana can be attributed not only to forms of speech but also to objects, occurrences and beings: those with no mana are regarded as profane, and those with a lot of mana as holy or taboo. *Holy* describes the positive aspect, that which is required, whereas *taboo* describes that which is forbidden.

3.3.5.1 Acquiring Mana

How does one acquire mana? One possibility is to touch the person or object which possesses it. In Buddhist temples, you can observe believers rubbing their hands or forehead on statues of the Buddha. The desire to touch the garment of Jesus surely has to do with attributing mana to him (Mark 6:56). One can also take up mana into one's own body. According to animist perception, one can acquire the capabilities of a brave hunter or an intelligent chief by eating his heart or brain respectively. This assumption lies at the root of *cannibalism*. A third way to get mana is through rituals containing spells, prayers and offerings. With the aid of these rituals, one can charge various objects with mana: an *amulet* serves to protect from misfortune. It can consist of pages from holy writings, a mirror or a pearl. In Islam, it is the hand of Fatima and the numbers three or five. A *talisman* is used to bring good fortune: for example, pomegranates in the story of Leah and Rachel, the wives of Jacob (Gen 30:14–16). A *fetish* (from Portuguese *feitiço*) is another object which can be charged with mana through a ritual. It has a variety of functions. Fetishes form the basis of what is commonly called magic. A fetish can be contained in a vase or a horn, or represented by a statuette or a mask. In animist medicine, a fetish can also be a "medicinal item." Indeed, in many languages of animist cultures, the same word is used for both fetishes and medicines.[56] Finally,

---

55. For speech act theory "saying is doing," cf. John L. Austin, *How to Do Things with Words* (London: Oxford University Press, 1955); Wiher, *Sharing the Good News*.

56. Cf. Käser, *Animism*, 72–76.

mana can be acquired through sexual intercourse with a virgin. Some men seek intercourse with an intact young girl in order to be cured of AIDS disease. Tantric Tibetan Buddhism has a similar notion: men believe that intercourse with a virgin will enable them to accumulate cosmic energy (positive karma), prepare themselves for the encounter with the invisible world, and attain or improve the social status of a lama.

3.3.5.2 Mana and the Folk Religions

In societies with an animist and folk religious background, the use of the concept of mana to help interpret anything unusual can also have outcomes in terms of how current religious phenomena are understood.

Examples of *procedures* where mana is involved include worship services, rituals, prayers, blessings, recitations, baptism and the communion service. The new airport in Colombo (Sri Lanka) was cleansed for three days through the recitation of sutras. The prayer mills of Tibetan Buddhism claim to multiply the efficacy of the recitations. The animist notion of mana can create confusion concerning sterility in hospital operating rooms. According to this notion, sterility is transferable: a sterile object endowed with mana transfers its quality to unsterile ones. The Western notion is opposite: the unclean object contaminates the clean object. Interestingly, we find both instances in the Bible. In Leviticus 5:2 we read that if someone touches something unclean, he becomes unclean. On the other hand, cleansing water, a pure object, can remove this impurity (Num 19:11–12, 18–19; 31:23).

Objects endowed with mana are instruments for holy acts, especially holy books such as the Koran, the Hindu Bhagavad-Gita, the Buddhist Tripitaka and the Bible. Christians with an animist background tend to deal with abdominal problems by drinking anointing oil or holy water, or they apply the holy object (endowed with mana) to the medical problem. A personal experience illustrates this. An evangelical family had adopted a formerly possessed girl but the demon kept on returning, and they had to continually drive it away through prayer. On one occasion it so happened that the demon returned while the adoptive parents were away. What did their children do? They filled containers with water, dipped their Bibles in it to enrich them with mana, and sprayed the demon with this "holy water," forcing it eventually to depart. The parents returned to find the house sopping wet and the exhausted children sound asleep. Holy water is used in a number of religions: water from the Ganges in Hinduism, water from the interior of Orthodox cave churches, and holy water in Catholic, Anglican and African initiated churches.

There are also *locations* endowed with mana, such as places of sacrifice, cemeteries, caves, waterfalls, volcanoes, temples and mountains. The Ka'ba in Mecca and the Dome of the Rock and the Al-Aqsa-Mosque in Jerusalem are places with a lot of *baraka*. This is also why the mausoleums of Timbuktu have become places of pilgrimage. For the Christians, the Church of the Holy Sepulchre is such a place, where people go on pilgrimage to touch Jesus' grave. Buddhists and Hindus build temples on mountain tops, which are regarded as places containing mana. By the same reasoning, the American Indians and the Australian Aborigines consider certain mountains holy and so do not climb them. Crowds of Western tourists, however, are quite shameless in ascending them. Spiritual warfare is important for Christians of animist or charismatic background, for which certain places such as mountaintops are of spiritual significance.

In folk Islam, fasting is a *period* full of *baraka*, especially the Night of Destiny (*laylat-ul-qadr*). On this night, the twenty-seventh of the month of Ramadan, it is claimed that Muhammad rode on horseback from Mecca to Jerusalem, from where he ascended to heaven (Sura 17:1–2; 53:13–18). On this night, the believer can make wishes and count on them to be fulfilled. This is because at this time the angels are on their way to earth. According to the beliefs of folk Islam, "The Night of Destiny is of more value than a thousand others."

Certain *persons* are also endowed with mana, such as shamans, mediums, healers, imams, priests, pastors and significant deceased personalities. The latter include, for example, Buddha, Muhammad, Gandhi and Jesus. Animists in Guinea who have seen the Jesus film wonder where Jesus could have acquired his great power. After thinking about it, they concluded that his great power derived from the fetishes in his bag, whereas it had not occurred to any of the Christians of secular background who had produced the film that this detail might have any significance. Christians with an animist background have a clear tendency to entrust prayer in general, and particularly prayer for an ill or possessed person, to a member of the clergy rather than a lay Christian, to an ordained rather than a non-ordained minister, and to a personality from outside more than to a local pastor. It is assumed that special people of these types have greater mana.

3.3.5.3 Mana and the Bible

Does the concept of mana have anything to do with the Bible? Indeed, in the Bible unexpected and supernatural effects are ascribed to divine activity. In Isaiah 29:14 we read, "So I will again do amazing things with this people, shocking and amazing" (cf. Matt 11:25; 1 Cor 1:25–28). The Bible grants us no latitude for interpreting such events from the animist perspective of mana. Clearly, the people groups living in Palestine at the time of Jesus thought and acted on the basis of a holistic perspective permeated by the concept of mana: "Wherever he [Jesus] went into cities or villages or farms, they laid the sick in the market places, and begged him that they might touch even the fringe of his cloak" (Mark 6:56; cf. 5:25–34 for the woman with haemorrhages). One can conclude from this explanation that there were animists among the inhabitants (in the Decapolis, Sidon and Tyre). One can assume that such beliefs also existed within the Jewish folk religion, creating a mixture of Judaism and Animism. This is probably the case with the former sorcerer Simon's wish to pay for the power of the Holy Spirit, which was imparted by the imposition of Peter's and John's hands (Acts 8:9–25). I have already mentioned the Hebrew concept of the "word (in action)" (Hebrew *dabar*) present in the cursing psalms and in the introduction of John's gospel: "All things were made through him [the word] . . . the word became flesh . . . and we have seen his glory" (John 1:3, 14). John's gospel as a whole is an interpretation of these declarations.

Nevertheless, some passages remain difficult to explain. How are we to understand what happened to the corpse which came back to life after being thrown into the grave of Elijah and coming into contact with his bones? (2 Kgs 13:21). Or the idea that pure objects can convey their quality to impure ones? (Num 19:11–12). In interpreting the Bible, the concept of mana would seem very far-fetched to Christians of secular background, whereas for Christians of animist background it underlies many biblical interpretations and everyday behaviour patterns.

Following this discussion of the five models of worldview, we will now consider identity, the second concept describing the deep structures of the personality.

3.4 Identity

As already noted, the concept of identity is closely linked with that of worldview. Besides the perception by others, self-awareness exercises a strong influence on identity. A change of worldview leads to a crisis of identity and a search for a new one. Hence it becomes acute in our rapidly changing globalized world and during the conversion process.

Identity is also an interdisciplinary human phenomenon. Almost all branches of the humanities have concerned themselves with this concept. One can find one's identity in roles, activities, locations, rites, or customs, in one's history, one's language and one's ethnicity. Here I am limiting my discussion to the biblical, psychological and philosophical approaches.

3.4.1 Biblical-Theological Approach to Identity

In the biblical view, the foundation of our identity is God: from the perspective of creation, we are creatures of God, made in his image (Gen 1:26f). In relation to redemption, all who have accepted Christ and believe in him are children of God (John 1:12). In the course of our discipleship, we are changed more and more into the image of Christ (2 Cor 3:18). And "all who are led by the Spirit of God are children of God . . . You have received a spirit of adoption, through whom we cry: Abba, Father!" (Rom 8:14–15). Finally, with regard to missions, we are sent out by Jesus just as he, the Son, was sent by the Father (John 17:18; 20:21). In the Greek term *apostolos* "apostle," literally meaning "the sent one," we perceive the missional identity of the disciples. The apostle Paul begins most of his letters with the formula "Paul, apostle of Jesus Christ."[57] Forming and preserving an identity "in Christ" is a vital objective of discipleship: being children of the Father and messengers of Christ. The Bible commands us, "Keep your heart [your identity] with all vigilance, for from it flow the springs of life" (Prov 4:23).

3.4.2 Psychological Approach to Identity

Psychologists consider that identity develops out of the dialogical tension between the self and the other, between self-awareness and awareness of the other. At first the infant is aware only of itself. Then it sees a face and a voice, which it identifies with its mother. Later, within a nuclear family, it can distinguish the face of its father. Gradually the circle extends to brothers and sisters, uncles and aunts, neighbours and friends, members of the church fellowship, society, and eventually to the supreme being, God. During this process, the development of identity is closely linked with the formation of worldview, arising by means of the conscience out of the same dialogical tension between the self and the other. In other words, the association of worldview with identity is secured through a conscience which, because of its particular orientation, gives priority to certain values. In this psychological model of

---

57. Romans 1:1; 1 Corinthians 1:1; 2 Corinthians 1:1; Galatians 1:1; Ephesians 1:1; Colossians 1:1; 1 Timothy 1:1; 2 Timothy 1:1; Titus 1:1.

identity, we are thus operating within a triangle consisting of conscience orientation, worldview and identity.

Looked at from another angle, identity emerges through a process during which past experiences, values and thought systems acquired through socialization are integrated into a unified, organized and coherent personality structure. This involves first the values, thought systems and behaviour patterns conveyed by the parents, then those of society, school and church (Figure 5).

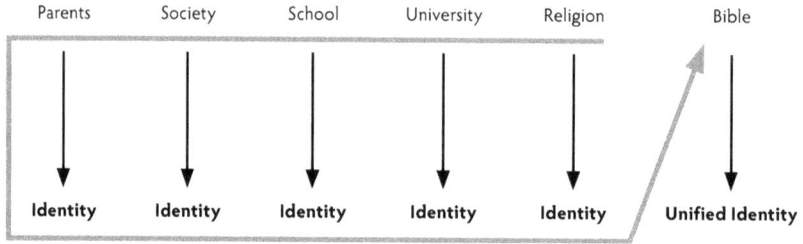

Figure 5: Formation of a Unified Identity

During maturation and the conversion process, two or more non-integrated cultural systems are present alongside each other. As long as this continues, several worldviews compete with each other to determine the person's identity. This struggle consumes a large part or even all of a person's psychic energy, resulting in a small impact in personal life and society. In social psychology, this is called *cognitive dissonance*, or an inner tension between a person's thought systems, convictions, emotions or attitudes that arises when several of them contradict each other or when behaviour goes against their ideas or beliefs. This adds special importance to integration in the processes of personal maturing and change. Such integration can be achieved through a critical evaluation of aspects of personality in the light of Scripture. Undertaking such an evaluation has as its objective "taking every thought captive to obey Christ" (2 Cor 10:5). Figure 5 reflects this process of biblical evaluation of worldviews which have come from the varied contexts of socialization, with the development of a unified identity on the basis of the biblical worldview.[58]

If physical and spiritual memories and worldview are influencing our emotional and physiological reactions, as well as our decisions, it is only

---

58. This critical evaluation is similar to the process which Hiebert calls "critical contextualization." Paul G. Hiebert, "Critical Contextualization," *Missiology* 12 (1984): 287–96. Reprints: *Anthropological Insights for Missionaries* (Grand Rapids: Baker, 1985), 171–92; *International Bulletin of Missionary Research* 11.3 (1987): 104–12.

through memory that a coherent identity can be preserved. It is therefore important to connect our personal and cultural memories with Scripture. Since forgiveness (granted or requested) is often involved, this constitutes inner healing. The challenge of this process of integration consists in knowing which kind of identity will gain the upper hand, the cultural identity or the identity "in Christ."

3.4.3 Philosophical Approach to Identity

In his book *Oneself as Another* (1992), the philosopher Paul Ricœur (1913–2005) touches on the issue of the relationship between the influence of genetic inheritance (nature) and that of the environment (culture) on identity.[59] Genetic inheritance influences character, which Ricœur defines as "the totality of enduring dispositions by which a person can be recognized." Character is the unalterable pole of identity. Ricœur calls it "selfhood" (*mêmeté*). By contrast, the environment exposes the person to a great variety of biographical and cultural situations. By the term "ipseity" (*ipséité*), Ricœur means the phenomenon by which persons possess the capacity to remain themselves despite the multitude of circumstances around them. According to this definition, identity is a matter of personal choice. This element of continuity is harder to grasp than character. Hence, Ricœur introduced the new concept, *narrative identity*: persons tell their story and remain true to themselves by promising to do so and abiding by it. This incorporates an element of loyalty into character. On one hand, we have continuity of character ("selfhood," *mêmeté*); on the other hand, there is constancy in friendship through keeping one's word (narrative identity, *ipséité*). In this way, Ricœur brings together the concepts of orality and identity: our identity becomes a matter of "telling our story," just as the identity of God is related in the Bible. It is interesting that the narrative approach of Paul Ricœur expressed in philosophical terms reappears in the narrative approach of Kwame Bediako in theological terms.

3.4.4 Kwame Bediako and the Search for Identity in Theology

In his survey *Theology and Identity* (1992) on the relationship of theologians in the church's patristic period and the present day to their cultural environment, the evangelical theologian Kwame Bediako (1945–2008) from Ghana appears to combine the two psychological models of identity – the dialogical tension

---

59. Paul Ricœur, *Oneself as Another* (Chicago: University of Chicago Press, 1992).

between the self and the other, on one hand, and the integration of thought systems and past experiences into memory on the other hand.[60]

Among the church fathers, Justin Martyr (100–165) and Clement of Alexandria (150–215) looked for continuity between Greek philosophical tradition and the Christian faith. By contrast, Tatian (died c. 170) and Tertullian (c. 150–220) were emphatic advocates of discontinuity. Among contemporary African theologians, Bolaji Idowu (1913–1995), Vincent Mulago (born 1924) and John Mbiti (1931–2019) defend continuity, whereas Byang Kato (1936–1975) is alone in advocating a radical discontinuity.

Bediako, together with Mbiti and Idowu, appears to recognize a continuity in the so-called "monotheism of the African traditional religions." According to this way of thinking, Africans have already acknowledged the creator God. For Bediako, the new identity in Christ is bound up with the reality of Christian living, and therefore with the socio-cultural context in which it is manifest. As to how this new identity in Christ, the universal mediator, is envisaged, the question for Bediako is this: "How should Christ and African Christianity be represented in the context of African traditional religions?" Bediako holds that in Jesus the African is confronted with an "adopted past." In him the African Christian can identify beyond the clan ancestors with Abraham and David, with Luther and Calvin. Although Bediako corroborates aspects of continuity between the African traditional religions and the Christian faith, he also perceives significant discontinuities. For him, the Scriptures are a catalyst in the integration process between African and adopted culture: "We recognize the Scriptures as the narrative explaining who we are, and therefore as our story."[61] Bediako makes clear that the biblical story has become *our* story through Christ, our narrative identity.

3.5 Otherness

Having reflected on identity (in other words, the self), which is the second concept describing the deep structures of the personality, I want to briefly look at the other from the perspective of self. Recall that the notions of conscience orientation, worldview and identity are all three involved in a dialogical field of tension between the self and the other.

---

60. Kwame Bediako, *Theology and Identity: The Impact of Culture upon Christian Thought in the Second Century and in Modern Africa* (Oxford: Regnum Books, 1992).

61. Kwame Bediako, "Scripture as the Hermeneutic of Culture and Tradition," *Journal of African Christian Thought*, 4.1 (2001): 2–11.

Different personalities, different communication and leadership styles and different priorities in life can cause tensions and later, if they are not resolved, lead to conflicts. In this way, the other becomes a challenge. Personalities can be structured or chaotic, rules-based or relational. Communication styles can be direct or indirect, needing a mediator or not. One can imagine a style of leadership either hierarchical or flat, democratic or autocratic. Concerning priorities in life, the accent can be placed on efficiency or harmony, power and prosperity. We will return to this issue in chapter 5 (section 5.7).

Otherness also presents a challenge because of the multitude of its different perceptions. Those who incline towards a mystical approach argue that culture has no significance. Others worry that one might no longer be at home in one's own household. Utopians believe that there are no differences between people and that we are all the same. Moreover, some hold the view that identity can more or less be reduced to culture: "I am a British Christian, an African Christian, an Asian Christian, an American Christian." Cultural determinism, for its part, asserts that one is the product of one's culture and that culture can be neither criticized nor changed. Finally, there are those who stereotype identity: "the Africans are . . .," "the Europeans are . . ." The consequence in our churches is often a lack of intercultural pastoral care which takes account of cultural differences – an individualistic, communal, charismatic or ethnocentric religiosity.

Missiologist Theo Sundermeier (born 1935), in *Understanding the Other* (1996), proposes a step-by-step model towards better understanding of the other (see Table 11).[62]

Table 11: Steps in Approaching the Other

Level of . . .	Subjectivity	Objectivity	Action
Phenomena	Experience of otherness	Descriptive analysis	Awareness from a distance
Signs	Sympathy	Contextual analysis	Participatory observation
Symbols	Empathy	Comparative interpretation	(Partial) identification
Relevance	Respect	Contextualization	Coexistence

---

62. Theo Sundermeier, *Den Fremden verstehen: Eine praktische Hermeneutik* (Göttingen: Vandenhoeck und Ruprecht, 1996).

When we are confronted with a person, or when we are getting to know a society with a different culture, we begin our approach on the level of phenomena. We describe them, perhaps only in our thoughts, while keeping our awareness at a certain distance. Then we develop more of a feeling for this new environment and move into the role of a participant observer. The third stage is a comparative exploration of this new environment in an attitude of empathy and partial identification. Finally, we reach the phase of relevance, that of respect for the other culture, comprising attempts to contextualize and efforts to coexist. Sundermeier refers to this as "convivence." This model provides a "gentle" access to what is other and alien.

Following this brief discussion of worldview, identity and otherness, we arrive at the problem of changes in worldview and identity.

3.6 Transformation of Worldview and Identity

Bringing about change in a person's inner being and the formation of a new identity in Christ is the goal of everyone working in God's kingdom. But how is that to be achieved? It is the Holy Spirit who effects deep change within a person and bestows a new identity. This is about genuine transformation, as witnessed in the story of the apostles and the tales of revivals in church history.

In times of revival, God's most urgent desire, bringing people back to himself, also becomes that of his followers. Significant missionary movements and the great denominations have originated from revivals: the Moravian revival in the eighteenth century, the great Anglo-Saxon revivals of the eighteenth and nineteenth centuries and the Chinese, Korean, Indian and East African revivals in the twentieth century. In Korea, morning prayer meetings and systematic Bible study kept the revival going for almost a hundred years, until it came to a halt due to growing materialism in the now affluent South Korean society. But beyond the regions where revival occurred, one often meets Christians whose daily lives are no different from those of the rest of the population. If we want to understand nominal Christianity (the behaviour of people who have experienced a change of religion without inner transformation, or people who maintain Christian behaviours but have lost faith), we must first understand the deep structures of person, culture and religion, including how we can change them.

I will now investigate how worldview and identity can be changed with the help of an anthropological approach, while remaining aware that the Holy Spirit is sovereign and can transform people with or without human cooperation.

3.6.1 Transformation in Practice

The imprinting of the deep layers of the personality that happened in early childhood is less amenable to change than later imprinting. The former relates to the emotional and evaluative layers, whereas the latter concerns the cognitive layers. Transformation of worldview in cognitive models takes place via a cognitive approach: the five soteriological concepts and the layers model of the order of creation are taught through stories, and the time agenda is altered. This is similar to the process of chronological Bible teaching, which can change the cognitive aspects of worldview and identity (cf. appendix 5).

However, the models of worldview relating to the emotional and evaluative levels require a different approach. With regard to the conscience orientation, the relational axis can be strengthened through a relational upbringing or a relational way of life, such as through intense relationships with friends or a close relationship with the biblical God. Rules-based elements are made effective through the introduction of rules in daily life, e.g. the Ten Commandments or a strictly regulated lifestyle and a tight agenda. It becomes apparent that the notion of mana is closely linked with a relational conscience if one separates into a hierarchy the parts of life filled with mana and those without. We recognize that any transformation of worldview and identity requires a combination of cognitive, emotional and evaluative approaches to effect change, whether in ourselves or in others.

3.6.2 Transformation of the Core of Personality and of the Cultural Skin Layers

With regard to a person's relationship to culture and its interaction with the process of conversion, there are two diametrically opposed positions: the first draws on the older Authorized Version translation of 2 Corinthians 5:17: "If any man be in Christ, he is a new creature: old things are passed away; behold, all things are become new." According to this interpretation, after conversion everything in a person becomes new. This interpretation leads some Christians to believe that after one's conversion, cultural elements are no longer of any importance. Another verse seems to confirm this interpretation: "There is neither Jew nor Greek, there is neither bond nor free, there is neither male nor female: for ye are all one in Christ Jesus" (Gal 3:28 KJV). However, it is also apparent that following conversion cultural, social and sexual differences are still present in some way. Those who interpret the Bible in such a way as to eliminate these differences among believers ignore the ongoing presence of "cultural skin layers" (cf. appendix 1).

The second position is represented by more recent translations which are better renditions of the Greek text: "Anyone who is joined to Christ is a new being; the old is gone, the new has come [*gegonen kaina*]" (NIV). This means that the core or the centre of the person has been newly created. It is like being given a new name (Isa 43:1; 62:2). As for the cultural layers, the process of sanctification of this new creation has only just begun, meaning that the transformation of worldview and identity is yet to happen. This second position regards conversion as a transformation process in which persons progress in their personality through the guidance of others and their own efforts. This is very different from any kind of determinism and is based on Ephesians 4:22–24:

> You were taught to put away your former way of life, your old self, corrupt and deluded by its lusts, and to be renewed in the spirit of your minds, and to clothe yourselves with the new self, created according to the likeness of God in true righteousness and holiness. (Eph 4:22–24)

The transformation is described in figurative language: put off the old self and put on the new. This second position offers a more realistic view. In evangelism and the process of conversion, our aim is not only change at the heart of the human personality through the new creation, but also transformation of one's "cultural layers" through conscious sanctification. As the letter to the Hebrews says, "Without holiness no one will see the Lord" (Heb 12:14).

I will now discuss the change of worldview and identity during the conversion process, change which includes a transformation of the centre of the personality and of the "cultural layers."

3.6.3 Conversion Alters One's Worldview and Identity

Let us look at what happens when conversion changes one's worldview and identity. From the biblical-theological perspective, the core of the person is re-created anew by the Holy Spirit. According to the Bible, the person receives a new "name" (Isa 43:1; 62:2), signifying a new identity (Gen 17:5; Rev 2:17).

From an anthropological perspective, one's worldview changes following conversion when the person undergoes a change in social context, that is, joins a new community with its different subculture. For example, if the person comes from an animist background with a holistic worldview, the content of the preaching and teaching could move her towards a two-tiered worldview.

The worldview could also change in terms of conscience orientation, if the person moves from a relational community to a rules-based one, or vice versa. If, for example, the society is relational and the fellowship of believers is rules-based, and if in addition it is influenced by a rules-based kind of preaching and instruction, the conscience of the newly converted person will gradually change and become more rules-centred.

The worldview will also change if the five soteriological concepts are taught systematically. If in a context the supreme being is regarded as the source of one's fate and perceived as potentially both good and evil, then the teaching of the biblical concepts of God and of evil will show that God is good in every respect, and that everything he has created and everything that he grants in life are also good. Evil comes from his adversary, Satan. If prosperity is understood as a gift from God and not the result of one's own merits, the person will no longer try to influence his good fortune in life (cf. sections 2.3.4.1 and 3.2.3.1).

3.6.4 Conversion Does Not Alter Worldview and Identity

The opposite case is also possible – one in which worldview and identity remain unaffected by conversion. From the biblical-theological perspective, there is no change of worldview and identity if no new creation occurs. This is the situation, for example, if a person makes a decision for Christ through social pressure, economic factors (so-called "rice Christians"), or to win the favour of a potential marriage partner.

From the anthropological perspective, worldview does not change if society is no different from the fellowship of believers. For example, believers in an Islamic society can maintain an Islamic worldview, which is similar to the Hebrew worldview regarding the structuring of creation, although different concerning most of the soteriological concepts. Also, the worldview does not need to change if the five soteriological concepts in society are the same as in the fellowship of believers. This is the case in a Christian community with a syncretistic form of belief. As for the conscience orientation, a person from a relational society can come and enter a similarly oriented fellowship of believers.

If concepts of worldview between society and the fellowship of believers are widely different, then it is necessary to impart biblical concepts systematically, for those concepts will not change without conscious intervention. Regrettably, this does not happen in most churches, because systematic and chronological Bible teaching is seldom regarded as a foundational element in the conversion and discipleship process, and because in most churches Bible study is not all that popular. We must always bear in mind that our worldview influences our everyday behaviour patterns and our identity. In the above-mentioned case, believers will behave just like other members of society and exhibit no difference from the rest of the population. When this happens, their witnessing impact on society will thus be almost non-existent.

3.6.5 Pre-Christian and "Christian" Worldview Side by Side

So far, we have seen that worldview and identity may or may not be changed through conversion. A third possibility is that the pre-Christian worldview persists despite the emergence of a "Christian" one. For example, this is the case when the two worldviews determine different areas of life: the "Christian" worldview may regulate behaviour on Sunday, at church and in family life, while the pre-Christian worldview influences public life and the workplace. This situation is encouraged by the fact that a relational personality or culture operates according to an *and-and logic*, in which contradictory worldviews regulating the same spheres of life or different ones can co-exist without disturbing the person concerned. In such a case, the Christian worldview has practically no effect on working life or on society. In contrast, rules-based persons with an *either-or logic* are reluctant to tolerate contradictions in their lives or at least have great problems in imagining a Christian life like that. They would call it *syncretism*.

If two worldviews are present together in a person, we have what Paul Hiebert calls *split-level Christianity*.[63] Here, both worldviews compete for expression in the person's identity. This is illustrated in the question: "Am I a Christian European or a European Christian? A Christian African or an African Christian? A Christian Asian or an Asian Christian? A Christian American or an American Christian?" In other words, does our cultural identity take priority over our identity in Christ or vice versa? The predominance of a cultural identity and the lack of a unified identity in Christ were regrettably apparent in the conflict in Rwanda, which led to a tragic fratricide among Christians, in the violence perpetrated against the indigenous populations in North America and Australia, or in the massacre of the Jews by the Nazis.

In most cases the cultural identity predominates, because after conversion no work has been done on the worldview, meaning that there has been no evaluation of the culture in the light of Scripture. Here we pick up on the model of forming a unified identity in Christ through an evaluation of the worldviews

---

63. Hiebert et al., *Understanding Folk Religion*, 15–30, 73–92.

acquired through socialization. These worldviews are then expressed in cultural identities in the different sectors (see Figure 5 in section 3.4.2). Such a "split-level Christianity" with a predominance of a cultural identity (or multiple cultural identities) can only be addressed through in-depth Bible studies during the discipleship process. These must include comparative studies of the worldviews acquired during socialization and the biblical worldview. This means practically that the ordering of creation, the soteriological concepts, and the orientations of the conscience and of time must be compared between the person's culture and the Bible. The overriding importance of systematic and chronological Bible study during the discipleship process, both before and after conversion, must once more be emphasized (see appendix 5). This enables not only a change in worldview but also the integration of different cultural systems and the creation of a new identity in Christ. In other words, this means that all the "cultural skin layers" of the personality must undergo a transformation during the discipleship process (see appendix 1).

3.7 Summary

In our approach to the deep structures, we have considered personality, culture, religion and identity as functions of worldview. This assumption brings with it an enormous simplification in terms of analysing personality and culture, normally involving several academic disciplines (history, philosophy, psychology, sociology, cultural anthropology and religious studies). This is why my own in-depth interdisciplinary analysis of culture proceeded on the level of worldview. Because of its fuzzy nature, I have used five models to make it practical. These provide us with an interdisciplinary approach on several levels, progressing in depth from the cognitive to the emotional and evaluative levels (see Table 12).

Table 12: Operational Level of Worldview Models

Model	Level		
	cognitive	emotional	evaluative
Layers model of creation	+		
Five soteriological concepts	+		
Time orientation	+	+	
Mana		+	+
Conscience orientation		+	+

The emotional and evaluative levels lie deeper than the cognitive one. Hence, I have avoided a purely cognitive analysis such as is often used in philosophy and theology. Three models of worldview are located on the cognitive level: the layers model of the order of creation, the five soteriological concepts and time orientation. These should be conveyed through teaching, preaching or stories during chronological Bible teaching. The two models of worldview which operate on the emotional and evaluative level are the conscience orientation and mana. These require different approaches.

In the next two chapters, I will apply these models: in chapter 4 to Scripture, theology and church practice, and in chapter 5 to persons, cultures and religions in the various contexts of our globe.

For Further Reading

Käser, Lothar. *Foreign Cultures: A Cognitive Approach*. Nuremberg: VTR, 2014.

———. "Concepts of the World in Different Societies." Pages 56–64 in *Animism: A Cognitive Approach*. By Lothar Käser. Nuremberg: VTR, 2014.

Lingenfelter, Sherwood G., and Marvin K. Mayers. *Ministering Cross-Culturally: An Incarnation Model for Personal Relationships*. Grand Rapids: Baker, 1986/2003.

Mbiti, John S. *African Religions and Philosophy*. London: Heinemann, 1969.

Wiher, Hannes. *Shame and Guilt: A Key to Cross-Cultural Ministry*. Bonn: Culture and Science Publications, 2003.

4

In-Depth Analysis of Scripture, Theology and Church Life

I shall now apply the models presented in chapter 3 to Scripture, theology and church life. I will have to be very selective, giving priority to the models which enable in-depth analysis. There will thus be an intentional bias in my analysis.

4.1 Scripture

My journey through the Bible will be chronological, choosing some of the stories and situations and putting forward for discussion some models derived from them.[1]

4.1.1 The Creation

The first account of creation (Gen 1) portrays the biblical God creating human beings as the final element, the crown of creation, and God's representatives.

---

1. For an in-depth discussion, I refer the reader to other authors who have given an overview of the subject: David A. deSilva, *Honor, Patronage, Kinship and Purity: Unlocking New Testament Culture* (Downers Grove: InterVarsity Press, 2000); Jayson Georges and Mark D. Baker, *Ministering in Honor-Shame Cultures: Biblical Foundations and Practical Essentials* (Downers Grove: InterVarsity Press 2016); Christopher Flanders and Werner Mischke, ed., *Honor, Shame, and the Gospel: Reframing Our Message and Ministry* (Pasadena: William Carey Library, 2020); Jackson Wu and Ryan Jensen, *Seeking God's Face: Practical Reflections on Honor and Shame in Scripture* (Pasadena: William Carey Library, 2022); Müller, *Conscience – The Moral Law Within*. Others have tackled a special aspect: Bruce J. Malina and Richard L. Rohrbaugh, *Social-Science Commentary on the Synoptic Gospels* (Minneapolis: Fortress, 1992); Jerome H. Neyrey, ed., *The Social World of Luke-Acts: Models for Interpretation* (Peabody: Hendrickson, 1991); Jerome H. Neyrey, ed., *Honor and Shame in the Gospel of Matthew* (Louisville, KY: John Knox, Hendrickson, 1998); David A. deSilva, *Despising Shame: Honor Discourse and Community Maintenance in the Epistle to the Hebrews* (Atlanta: Scholars Press, 1995); Jackson Wu, *Reading Romans with Eastern Eyes: Honor and Shame in Paul's Message and Mission* (Downers Grove: InterVarsity Press, 2019).

He grants them a place of honour, telling them they are to rule just as God himself as creator rules over the creation. Being created according to the image of God implies that human beings have a conscience and a will (Gen 1:26–28). Already in the first chapter of the Bible, we are given precise teaching about the biblical worldview: the doctrines of God and man, with both their similarities and the great difference between the creator and his creation.

The second account of creation (Gen 2) introduces some nuances. God creates humankind as the first element of creation, which also signifies a place of honour. He orders them to care for creation in the same way as God does, and to name the animals. In an intimate scene between partners, God breathes life into the man (*'ish*) and creates for him a female counterpart (*'ishah*) (Gen 2:7, 15, 19, 22–23). We can conclude from this that human beings were created to have an intimate relationship with God. The Bible employs several images for this relationship: God and his people (Lev 26:11–12; Jer 24:7; Ezek 34:30; 36:28; 37:27; Rev 21:2–3); the father and his son (2 Sam 7:8, 14) or daughter (Ezek 23); husband and wife (Ezek 16; Hos; Rev 17–18; 19:6–8; 21:9). Hence, human beings are relational beings created by a relational God. Having been created in the image of the triune God, they exist as unity in diversity (Gen 1:27; 2:22–24). In terms of the five soteriological concepts, we find in Genesis 1–2 the introduction to the concepts of God and man.

The two accounts of creation end with this statement: "The man and his wife were both naked, and were not ashamed" (Gen 2:25). One might say they were in a sense like children, who are also not aware of shame when naked. The child psychiatrist Michael Lewis, for example, adopts this interpretation.[2] In his view, they feel no shame because at this stage of their development in life, they are not yet aware of their own self. However, from a theological perspective, this interpretation is questionable with regard to Genesis, since Adam and Eve were functioning as adults. In addition, this biblical statement relates to a period in salvation history before our time, that of paradise before the fall. By contrast, we are in the period after the fall.

So how should we interpret this statement in the Bible? It would appear that the man and the woman have no reason to have a bad conscience. Their nudity is not an issue; being in paradise before the fall, they are in harmony with God. Moreover, their conscience not yet being influenced by a code of law, they would feel shame if they had a bad conscience. This mention of the absence of shame is a first indication that Hebrew culture is predominantly relational in its orientation.

---

2. Lewis, *Shame: The Exposed Self*.

4.1.2 The Fall

To enable the conscience to develop and function properly, God, like any competent educator, issues a norm: "Of the tree of the knowledge of good and evil you shall not eat" (Gen 2:17). This norm could at first sight seem petty, stingy and difficult to reconcile with a generous and merciful creator God. However, it receives a deep pedagogical sense when we take into account the absolute necessity of a norm for the development of the conscience. Through the choice involved, the evil one exploits the weakness of the human heart. Adam and Eve do not follow God's instructions. Violating the norm triggers within a relational conscience the awareness of the self and a feeling of shame. This results in several typical patterns of shame behaviour: fear, concealment, covering the body and blaming another (Gen 3:7–13). The attempt to conceal the disgrace with fig leaves fails. So, God takes pity on them and covers the disgrace with animal skins, an action linked to the shedding of blood (Gen 3:21). The removal of shame through divine intervention, meaning forgiveness, must have made an unforgettable impression on Adam and Eve, which they surely shared with their two sons.

The lack of any indication of guilt feelings after violating God's norm is a problem for some commentators. They speak of an "ontological guilt," although there is no mention of it. Proceeding from what will become evident in my examination of issues of Bible translation and interpretation, most commentators appear to operate on the basis of a rules-based conscience (cf. section 4.3.1). Clearly, they expect guilt to follow from infringing a norm. But there is no mention of guilt in the biblical text. Why is that the case? The most obvious explanation is that the conscience has not yet come under the influence of rules. Later on in Exodus, we shall see that God's introduction of a set of laws leads to the Israelites having to pay for every sin. This repeated influence eventually leads to the development of a rules orientation. In this way, the conscience adds a functioning legal axis to its relational axis. At this stage in God's revelation and in salvation history, there is still no code of law for the first human pair to follow in order for a feeling of guilt to develop after the transgression.

Speaking to the serpent, God also announces in this chapter how he will restore harmony in the relationship between himself and humankind through a mediator, "the son of the woman": "I will put enmity between you and the woman, and between your offspring and hers; he will strike your head, and you will strike his heel" (Gen 3:15). The "son of the woman" will destroy evil, but he will suffer. Thus, God points beyond the concept of evil and sin, towards the prospect of redemption. So, salvation comes via a mediator, and through the shedding of blood (Gen 3:21; cf. Deut 17:14; Heb 9:22).

With regard to the five soteriological concepts, we have in Genesis 3 the introduction of the concepts of evil, sin and salvation. Thus, the first three chapters of the Bible set out the essence of the five soteriological concepts. This is why a new missiological approach to Bible translation and to the conversion or discipleship process recommends beginning with chronological Bible teaching at the start of the Bible, with Genesis 1, in order to base the process on the five soteriological concepts (cf. appendix 5).[3]

4.1.3 The Relational Conscience in Genesis

Following the account of the fall, we find in Genesis a clear account of how a relational conscience functions. As mentioned in the previous section, it is very probable that Adam and Eve told their sons Cain and Abel about their failed attempt to cover the source of their shame with fig leaves, and also about their astonishment over the disappearance of their sense of shame after they received the animal skins from God (Gen 3:21). The feeling of shame was suddenly gone. But despite this, Cain does not consider that he should approach God with a blood sacrifice for the forgiveness of sins. Since his non-sacrificial offering was not accepted, he lowers his head as an expression of his shame and becomes enraged (Gen 4:5–7a). In psychological terms, he succumbs to a *shame-rage cycle* and then commits a criminal act. Here is a simple way to understand this phenomenon better. After being humiliated once or several times, relational persons can react in two ways: they either "implode," becoming depressed, or they "explode," becoming aggressive and liable to commit a crime. These mechanisms help to explain why most people suffering from depression and most of those who end up in prison are relational. In the West, girls seem to be socialized for the "imploding" form, whereas boys tend rather towards aggressive reactions. The phenomenon of the shame-rage cycle could also explain the violence of football fans after their team has lost a match, of Muslims after the publication of caricatures of Muhammad, and of Vladimir Putin after the eastward expansion of the European Union (EU) and of the North Atlantic Treaty Organization (NATO).

The blessing, the covenant with God, the new name and the promises bring Abraham honour (Gen 12:1–3; 15:4–6, 18; 17:5–7). A new name represents

---

3. Cf. John R. Cross, *All that the Prophets Have Spoken* (Olds, Canada: GoodSeed, 1999), https://www.goodseed.com.

a new identity: "father of a great nation" (*'abraham*). By contrast, infertility is a disgrace (Gen 15:2; 16:1–2). God shows Abraham that he desires to be an exclusive and ever-present covenant partner: "I am God Almighty [*'el shadday*]; walk before me, and be entirely to me [*tamim*]" (Gen 17:1 translation by Hans Bürki). Hagar experiences him as the "God who sees" (*'el roi*). Following the disgrace of infertility, harmony between Abraham and Sarah is restored after the birth of Isaac (Gen 21:2; cf. also Hannah in 1 Sam 2, and Elizabeth in Luke 1:25).

Jacob receives honour through Isaac's blessing, but Esau loses face and gets himself into a shame-rage cycle (Gen 27:27–30, 39–41). After deceiving his brother, Jacob flees (Gen 27:42). He then believes he is out of range of God's oversight. But in Bethel he realizes that God is an ever-present partner (Gen 28:16–17). God's revelation in Bethel is an important lesson for relational persons who need to know that the attachment figure is never absent. Only so is the relational conscience fully operational. It is in this sense that we should understand the "eye of God" on the screen of icons (iconostasis) in Orthodox churches: it signifies the presence of the "God who sees." Jacob has to learn that God is the "God who sees," just like Hagar and any other relational person (Gen 16:13; cf. Prov 21:2). Jacob's success brings him honour (Gen 30:25–43). And his encounter with God in Peniel honours him, but is the cause of a humiliating disability: he will have a limp for the rest of his life (Gen 32:30–32). One might ask oneself; is a typical situation for the servants of God – to be simultaneously honoured and humiliated?

Through the dreams that he tells his family, Joseph causes his brothers and his father to lose face and plunges the brothers into a shame-rage cycle: they commit a crime against him (Gen 37). At first, he is humiliated, but later honoured. The biographies of relational patriarchs who were humiliated and then restored to a status of honour indicate a biblical pattern of divine pedagogy and human behaviour.

4.1.3.1 The Pattern of Honour-Shame-Honour

Several biblical characters exemplify this pattern of honour-shame-honour. They start from a position of honour, humiliate themselves or are humiliated by God, and then are restored to a high position in society: Abraham, Job, Jacob, Joseph, Moses, David, Daniel, Nehemiah, Esther, Mordecai, Paul. Jesus himself is a prime example of this (Phil 2:5–11), and he challenges us to follow his example (Matt 23:12; Luke 14:11; 18:14; 1 Cor 11:1). In the same way, God challenges us to trust him, in quietness and humility (Exod 14:14; Ps 46:11; Isa 7:9; 30:15; Mic 6:8).

There are opposite examples of those who seek a high position and are then humbled. We could describe this as a pattern of shame-honour-shame. Typical examples are Satan (Isa 14; Ezek 28); his threesome – Satan, the Antichrist and the false prophet (Rev 13); and the "whore" of Babylon (Gen 11; Rev 17–18).

4.1.3.2 The Merciful Face of God

In Genesis, we encounter a second concept important for the relational conscience: the "face" of God, indeed a completely relational concept. God, full of grace, is always prepared to turn (*panah*) his face (*panim*) towards sinful persons, to favour, forgive and guide them. Thus, he says to Abraham: "Walk before my face!" (Gen 17:1 literal translation). The shining of his face is transferred to the faces of those who believe in him: "Those who look to him are radiant" (Ps 34:5). This explains why the face of Moses was shining after his stay of forty days on Mount Sinai in the presence of Yahweh (Exod 34:29–35). It is also the prayer that God gave to Aaron and which becomes our prayer that God will let our faces become radiant as he lets his face shine upon us: "The LORD make his face to shine upon you" (Num 6:24–26; cf. 2 Cor 3:7–18). Thus, through the gift of the "Aaronic blessing" God enters into the covenant relationship with the Israelites and subsequently also with those who believe in Jesus, giving us both the text of the prayer and also the command to pray. In the same way, communication theory indicates that when people meet each other their glances always focus on the centre of the face, the area around the eyes and nose, unless the gaze has to be lowered because of social prescriptions. Thus, the notion of the "face of God" is an expression of the relationship between the creator and his creatures. On this basis, God's exhortation to seek his face becomes understandable in its very depth: "Come, my heart says, seek his face! Your face, LORD, do I seek (Ps 27:8).

4.1.3.3 Purity and Holiness

Purity and holiness are likewise an expression of the relational conscience, and can be traced throughout the whole Bible. Moreover, a survey of religions leads us to understand that in all cultures purity plays a central role. In all religions purity is essential for approaching the deities. Access to a deity, as cultural anthropology has found in all cultures, requires impure persons to purify themselves before they approach the holy being. The Bible emphasizes this process in the Holiness Code (Lev 11–15; 17–25): "You shall be holy, for I, the LORD your God, am holy" (Lev 19:2). This idea underlies the name given in the book of Isaiah to the God of the Bible, "the Holy One of Israel" (Isa 12:6; 30:12; 41:14; etc.).

The Holiness Code contains various regulations concerning external purity, e.g. food, women's monthly period and leprosy. Psalm 51 offers further insight into this regard, pointing out that what really counts is inner purity: "Create in me a pure heart, O God" (Ps 51:10). As in the rite of sacrifice this is acquired through the shedding of blood: "Cleanse me with hyssop, and I will be clean" (Ps 51:7). During the sacrificial rite, the hyssop branch is dipped in blood and then the blood is sprinkled on the altar to effect forgiveness.

impure → pure → holy

After the coming of Jesus, the regulations for external purity no longer apply. Jesus mixed with sinners: prostitutes, tax collectors, collaborators with the colonial power and non-Jews. According to the Jewish teaching, these were all unclean. But Jesus said, "It is not what goes into the mouth that defiles a person, but it is what comes out of the mouth that defiles . . . For out of the heart come evil intentions, murder, adultery, fornication, theft, false witness" (Matt 15:11, 19; cf. Mark 7:14–23). This teaching of Jesus is confirmed by the repeated vision of Peter while praying on a roof in Joppa:

> He saw the heaven opened and something like a large sheet coming down, being lowered to the ground by its four corners. In it were all kinds of four-footed creatures and reptiles and birds of the air. Then he heard a voice saying, "Get up, Peter; kill and eat." But Peter said, "By no means, Lord; for I have never eaten anything that is profane or unclean." The voice said to him again, a second time, "What God has made clean, you must not call profane." (Acts 10:11–15)

This experience embedded itself in Peter's memory, since he repeats this central statement of the Holiness Code for the churches in Asia Minor: "You shall be holy, for I am holy" (1 Pet 1:16).

Purity and holiness are of great importance in Scripture and in religions generally. They have a particular connection with the relational conscience. So one should not be surprised that they carry special emphasis in relational religions, for which maintaining harmony is also of central importance (cf. section 4.4.2).[4] Purity remains a great challenge for contemporary relational generations, especially in relation to certain contents of the internet such as

---

4. I include among the relational religions animism, Hinduism, Shintoism, Chinese and Tibetan Buddhism, Daoism and Confucianism.

pornography (cf. section 4.3.5). Hence, our prayer remains: "Father in heaven, may your name be held holy" (Matt 6:9 NJB).

4.1.4 The Formation of a New Worldview in Exodus

So far, we have seen in the book of Genesis how a relational conscience functions. In Exodus and Leviticus, we see God take a new step by giving the law. And when Moses breaks the tablets on which the Ten Commandments are written (Exod 33), God provides them a second time (Exod 34). We realize that God's action here is fully intentional. From now on, life will not only be determined by relational norms but by very precise divinely given regulations.

4.1.4.1 Activation of the Legal Axis

It is possible to imagine that people could manage their lives satisfactorily on the relational axis alone. But God has other plans: he provides the law (Exod 20–Lev 27). These regulations are benchmarks for the relational conscience with its lack of an internalized code of rules within the human psyche. They order all aspects of everyday life: religious, social, individual. Any infringement of the rules has to be paid for by a sacrifice (Lev 1–7). This activates the rules axis of the conscience.[5]

Subsequently, one can observe in the Old Testament how life becomes progressively rules-based for those people who become involved with the law on a daily basis: priests, Levites and scribes. By contrast, the ordinary folk continue to act for the greater part of everyday life on the relational axis, apart from the purely religious aspects.

The prophets are quick to warn of the danger of lack of balance in a purely rules-based life (1 Sam 15:22; Pss 40:7–10; 51:17–18; Isa 1:11). The increasing rules-based approach of the scribes can be deduced from the Greek translation of the Old Testament, the Septuagint, from the third century BC. Here a number of relational Hebrew terms are changed into rules-based ones: instruction (Hebr. *torah*) becomes law (Greek *nomos*); the word for covenant (*berit*), expressing a mutual relationship, is translated by a Greek word indicating a final legal decree, a testament (*diathēkē*). This is despite the presence in Greek of a corresponding term containing the idea of a mutual relationship (*synthēkē*).

---

5. For a discussion of some important features of the law, see section 4.1.4.5.

Among the scribes and Pharisees of the New Testament, we also find a strong rules-based approach. When Jesus addresses them in Matthew 23, he criticizes the lack of balance in how their conscience is oriented:

> Woe to you, scribes and Pharisees, hypocrites! For you tithe mint, dill, and cumin, and have neglected the weightier matters of the law: justice and mercy and faith. It is these you ought to have practised without neglecting the others. (Matt 23:23)

The Pharisees go to the extent of paying a tenth, according to the law, for the herbs used in cooking, but neglect the relational side of life with God: justice (Hebr. *tsēdēq*), compassion (Hebr. *hēsēd*) and faith (Hebr. *'ēmunah*). Based on the Hebrew meaning, *tsēdēq* (righteousness) relates to behaviour in line with the covenant with God and the fellowship of believers; *hēsēd* (compassion) describes one's attitude when a partner violates the covenant, also translated as loyalty, love or grace; and *'ēmunah* (faith) speaks of trust in the path God has prepared. In Hebrew culture, all three are relational terms, although righteousness also includes a rules-based aspect, namely keeping God's commands. When a Pharisee asks Jesus which is the most important law among the 613 regulations of the Pharisaic code, he does not say that it is the 327th (which would have been a rules-based answer), but quotes the Old Testament:

> "You shall love the Lord your God with all your heart, and with all your soul, and with all your mind." This is the greatest and first commandment. And the second is like it: "Love your neighbour as yourself." (Matt 22:37–39; cf. Deut 6:5; Lev 19:18)

The answers Jesus gives are altogether relational, and as such are a counterweight to the excessive concern of the Pharisees regarding the 613 rules. In addition, he warns the disciples that the righteousness of the Pharisees, being limited to those rules, is not sufficient to ensure entry into God's kingdom (Matt 5:20). This makes clear that God wants us to have a balanced conscience orientation, directing us to act in love for God and our neighbour, and at the same time to observe God's commands.

4.1.4.2 A Balanced Covenant Formula

From this formula we deduce a covenant principle within the kingdom of God. In the Old Testament, God frequently says: "Love me" (stressing the relational aspect of the covenant) "and keep my commands" (representing the legal aspect).[6] Instead of speaking of commands, the Hebrew language can also use the term "words" (e.g. Deut 29:8; Ps 119:11). In this sense, the Bible speaks also of the "ten words" (Exod 34:28; Deut 10:4). In some occurrences, the formula also appears in slightly different versions: "to love the LORD, and to walk in all his ways" (Josh 22:5) or to "keep the commands of the LORD, by walking in his ways and by fearing him" (Deut 8:6; cf. 10:12; 11:22; 26:17; 28:9; Eccl 12:13).

In the New Testament, Jesus uses the same formula, with variations: "They who have my commands and keep them are those who love me" or "If you love me, you will keep my commands" or "If you do not keep my commands, you do not love me."[7] I believe that this formula reveals very clearly God's desire that we should function on both axes: relational and rules-based.

4.1.4.3 A Balanced Forgiveness

In the same way, I believe God wants us to demonstrate a balanced culture of forgiveness in our lives, determined by the three concepts of *repentance*, *reconciliation* and *reparation* (the three Rs of forgiveness). For rules-based societies, reparation is of central importance. Reparation for offences is prescribed by law: fines and years-long imprisonment. By contrast, in relational societies reconciliation procedures through mediators are made available. In the Bible, both processes can be observed, supplemented by a third component: repentance involving a change of thinking and behaviour (Hebr. *shub* "turn around"; Gr. *metanoia* "change in thinking"). All three components of forgiveness are contained in the story of Zacchaeus and his resolve: "Lord, half of my possessions I will give to the poor, and if I have defrauded anyone of anything, I will pay back four times as much" (Luke 19:8). The first part shows the relational aspect, entailing the restoration of harmony in society, and the second fulfils the Mosaic law, restoring four times what has been stolen (Exod 22:1). The whole process is proof of the sincere and honest change of mind of Zacchaeus.

4.1.4.4 The Fear of the Lord

Many may be surprised to discover that these two aspects of the covenant are contained in the expression "the fear of the Lord." On the relational side, it can evoke submission or abasement before God as creator and redeemer (Matt 5:3;

---

6. Deuteronomy 6:5–6; 7:9; 11:1, 13; 30:16; Joshua 22:5; 23:6, 8; 1 Kings 9:4; Nehemiah 1:5; Psalm 119:63; Ezekiel 36:26–27; Daniel 9:4.

7. John 14:15, 21, 23–24; 15:10; 1 John 3:23–24; 2 John 6.

Rom 3:23; Eph 5:21). On the legal axis, it can signify obedience to his will and his commands (Deut 10:12–13; 13:4; Rom 1:5; 15:18). Both orientations spring from the fear of the Lord as the beginning of knowledge (Prov 1:7). Where this expression occurs in the covenant formula, fear in terms of reverential awe is used instead of love: "Love (fear) God and keep his commands" (e.g. Deut 10:12–13; 13:4; Eccl 12:13).

4.1.4.5 The Formation of a New Worldview

The introduction of numerous regulations in Exodus and Leviticus activates not only the legal axis of the conscience but also other elements involved in forming a new worldview. This can be observed through several models.

The fundamental motivation consists in launching in the people of God the transformation of the animist worldview into a worldview which we describe as biblical. What I call Hebrew worldview describes the layers aspect of the biblical worldview. As we have seen, the Hebrew worldview, in contrast to the holistic (animist) worldview, separates the creator from the universe he created, but without separating the invisible world from the visible, as the two-tiered worldview does. This intentional divine approach is revealed in the way the giving of the law begins:

> I am the LORD your God, who brought you out of the land of Egypt, out of the house of slavery; you shall have no other gods before me. You shall not make for yourself an idol, whether in the form of anything that is in heaven above, or that is on the earth beneath, or that is in the water under the earth. You shall not bow down to them or worship them. (Exod 20:2–5)

Only the creator is to be worshipped, not deities "made by human hands" (Ps 115:4). They correspond to the "spirit doubles" of statues and masks and objects in nature (trees, waterfalls, mountain peaks) to which animist cultures attribute extraordinary effects, which is interpreted as mana. This capacity confers honour, affluence and well-being, which all relational persons strive for. Among other things this is also an indication that animist cultures are relational. The Bible clearly accepts that idols have power, emanating from the demons behind them, which Christopher Wright describes as the "two paradoxes" (cf. sections 1.3.2 and 2.3.5).[8]

Commands five to ten (Exod 20:12–17) concern the foundational prerequisites a society requires if it is to function properly: honour parents,

---

8. Wright, *The Mission of God*, 136–47.

do not murder or commit adultery, do not steal, lie or covet. Their objective is to raise the ethical standard of the people of God. Paying back stolen property fourfold aims to deter theft and serve as a protective measure (Exod 22:1). These commands can certainly be termed *anthropological constants*, because they are found in many societies throughout our planet (cf. the Buddhist "ten commands"). If they are not observed, a society cannot function as it should.

One particularly important section of the Law relates to the introduction of the blood sacrifices and gift offerings (Lev 1–7), together with explanations concerning which is required for each kind of sin. In animist cultures, the diviner, after consulting with the invisible world, decides what kind of offering should be made. So on one hand, God's instructions can be seen as being in continuity with the animist cultural context. On the other hand, however, God introduces a discontinuity, for he decides what kind of offering is appropriate, not the diviner. The laws of blood sacrifice and gift offerings reach their climax in the instructions for the Day of Atonement (*yom kippur*, Lev 16). On this day, the High Priest offers sacrifices for the people's sins and for his own. This also has its parallels in animist cultures, where the diviner also has to make his own offering. The basis for the blood sacrifice is that the blood deals with the sin: "For the life of the flesh is in the blood; and I [God] have given it to you for making atonement [*kipper*] for your lives on the altar; for, as life, it is the blood that makes atonement [*kippur*]" (Lev 17:11). It is God who gives life, portrayed in how the blood pulsates. And it is God who accomplishes forgiveness, indicated through the blood that is poured out. Blood sacrifice is a further element in continuity with animist cultures.

We find another significant passage in the purity laws (Lev 10–15). In relational and animist societies, the concept of purity is of the greatest importance. A first-century Jew was not allowed to eat with a non-Jew, just as today a Hindu may not eat with someone who is not a Hindu or not a member of his caste. According to this reasoning, only the pure may approach a deity. So it must be made clear what is pure or impure, and how cleansing can be achieved. Certain foods, certain diseases, certain garments, and the menstrual period make one impure. On these issues, God also provides regulations, again in line with animist cultures.

Over against the profane sphere, comprising the pure and impure spheres, stands the holy sphere. Following the concept of purity, God addresses that of holiness, which lies at the centre of the Levitical code (Lev 17–25). Here we find the formula, "You shall be holy, for I, the LORD your God, am holy" (Lev 19:2). The Hebrew word *qadosh* "holy" signifies a cutting and a separation: the creator is distinct from the universe he has created. Hence, his people must be cut off from the surrounding (animist) world. His people are called to identify themselves with God and cross over from the world they are living into the world of God and his kingdom. As the apostle Paul says: "He has rescued us from the power of darkness and transferred us into the kingdom of his beloved son" (Col 1:13). The apostle John describes the tension that is created in this way: "in the world, but not of the world" (John 17:11, 16). And because this aspect is so important to the apostle Peter, he uses the Leviticus formula in his exhortations: "You shall be holy, for I am holy" (1 Pet 1:16).

In short, in Exodus and Leviticus God creates a new worldview out of the relational notions of the spirit double, mana, purity and holiness, concepts which are all very widespread in the animist environment (cf. section 5.4.1).[9] This is achieved through the introduction of regulations that promote a higher ethical standard, differing from that of the animist life-setting. In so doing God is acting within the framework of intercultural communication, which in general prescribes elements of continuity which are interspersed in small degrees with aspects of discontinuity.[10] This divine process is, of course, continued in the rest of the Old Testament and into the New. We can name this new worldview "biblical" (cf. sections 3.6 and 4.1.9).

4.1.5 Jesus Christ, the Answer to Human Need

What does the Bible say about Jesus Christ? We have seen that in Genesis 3:15 he is presented as "the son of the woman," the required mediator, and as the one whose heel the serpent (Satan) will strike, who must suffer, but who will also crush the serpent's head.

4.1.5.1 The Person of Jesus

The introduction of Jesus Christ as "son of David, son of Abraham" at the beginning of Matthew's gospel (Matt 1:1) corresponds absolutely to Jewish expectations: he is the expected mediator and saviour and the blood sacrifice needed for forgiveness (cf. appendix 5). By contrast, the declaration by the angel to Mary that Jesus is the "Son of the Highest" (Luke 1:32) is blasphemous for the Jews. Also within Islam, the reaction is to deny the blasphemy: Allah did not procreate (Sura 9:30–31; 4:171; 5:75). However, the assertion is confirmed during the baptism (Matt 3:17) and the transfiguration of Jesus (Matt 17:5), by

---

9. Cf. Mary Douglas, *Purity and Danger* (London: Routledge & Kegan Paul, 1966); Mary Douglas, *Leviticus as Literature* (Oxford: Oxford University Press, 1999).

10. Cf. Wiher, *Sharing the Good News*.

the demon-possessed man in the region of the Gerasenes (Mark 5:7) and by Jesus himself (John 10:36). Jesus is on the same wavelength when he says that he and the Father are one (John 5:18–23; 10:30). So there is a discontinuity in terms of communication to Jews. On the other hand, Jesus conceals his identity by his choice of the title "Son of Man" used for the prophet Ezekiel (e.g. Matt 8:20; cf. Ezek 2:1, 3, 6, 8; 3:1, 3–4 etc.). With this title, Jesus' communication is in continuity with the ideas of the Jews. By choosing this expression, he indicates also that he can complete his saving work only as "truly God and truly man," a formula adopted by the Council of Chalcedon (451).

4.1.5.2 Jesus' Work on the Cross

From the perspective of the legal axis, Jesus Christ is the ransom, the payment of our guilt (Mark 10:45). In so doing Jesus places himself within the tradition of Old Testament redemption. Moreover, the writers of the New Testament consider his death the blood sacrifice necessary for the forgiveness of sins, although in reality very little blood is shed in the process of flogging and crucifixion. In Romans 3, the apostle Paul links the cross with the lid of the ark or the horns of the altar (*hilastērion* "means of atonement"). The priest has to sprinkle it with the blood of the sacrifice, using a branch of hyssop: "whom [Christ Jesus] God put forward as a sacrifice of atonement [*hilastērion*] by his blood, effective through faith, to show his righteousness" (Rom 3:25). The letter to the Romans also confirms that we are justified before God through the sacrifice of Jesus Christ (Rom 3:21–22; 5:1).

In terms of the relational axis, Jesus Christ has borne our shame on the cross (Heb 12:2). He is the mediator of our reconciliation with God (2 Cor 5:17–20; 1 Tim 2:5). But be careful: the cross of Christ is a disgrace and foolishness (1 Cor 1:18–28). This is a second reason why in the work of missions it is necessary to start at the beginning of the Bible: this is where we learn why Jesus Christ had to be exposed to such disgrace on the cross. He had to become the mediator between God and humankind, the blood sacrifice for the forgiveness of sins (cf. appendix 5).

4.1.5.3 Jesus' Receptor-Oriented Communication

In his relationships, Jesus Christ behaves in accordance with *receptor-oriented communication*, a concept described by Charles Kraft.[11] When confronted with the predominantly rules-based Pharisee Nicodemus, Jesus chooses very direct communication: "No one can see the kingdom of God without being born

---

11. Kraft, *Christianity in Culture*, 169-92.

from above" (John 3:3). By contrast, with the Samaritan woman, he chooses an indirect approach (John 4). At Jacob's well, he begins the conversation with a topic familiar to her, water: "Give me a drink!" (v. 7). He pursues it to a point where tension arises, leading to a change in the situation as she asks, "Sir, give me this [living] water, so that I may never be thirsty or have to keep coming here to draw water!" (v. 15). Then Jesus guides the dialogue to a different topic: "Call your husband" (v. 16). This leads her to perceive that he is a prophet (v. 19). Subsequently, the woman realizes that following the commands of the Samaritans is not a valid approach, "for salvation is from the Jews" (v. 22). And it is not about the place of worship, for "God is spirit, and those who worship him must worship him in spirit and truth" (v. 24). Finally, after a whole series of topics, questions and answers, the Samaritan woman understands that Jesus is talking about the messianic age whereupon Jesus gives the crucial answer: "I am he [the Messiah], the one who is speaking to you" (v. 26).

We can see from this comparison that the approaches to Nicodemus and the Samaritan woman correspond to the two kinds of conscience orientation. With Nicodemus Jesus is very direct, for as a Pharisee he knows all about the law and is very rules-based. But with the Samaritan woman his approach is indirect, for she is an ordinary person with a relational conscience.

4.1.6 Four Case Studies

On our journey through the Bible, I have so far limited myself to the main avenues of the biblical record. But we can now apply my models to an in-depth analysis of particular Bible passages.[12] I will analyze the stories of Balaam (Num 22–24), the regulations for levirate marriage (Deut 25:5–19), the story of King Saul and the woman in Endor (1 Sam 28), and the parable of the two sons (Matt 21:28–32).

4.1.6.1 King Balak of Moab and the Diviner Balaam (Num 22–24)

Afraid of Israel's military force, Balak, king of Moab, sends messengers to Balaam, a diviner from Mesopotamia with an international reputation, asking him to curse Israel on the way from Egypt to the promised land. Interestingly, Balaam consults Yahweh before deciding whether to accept the request (22:8). God says, "You shall not go with them; you shall not curse the people, for they are blessed" (22:12). So Balaam refuses to go with the messengers. However,

---

12. Cf. Hannes Wiher, *Shame and Guilt: A Key to Cross-Cultural Ministry* (Bonn: Culture and Science Publications, 2003), 216–81.

Balak gives it a second try. Again, Balaam asks God. In a very relational way, God gives in, while limiting the risk of a curse: "Go with them; but do only what I tell you to do" (22:20). Nevertheless, God is angry about the shameless second request (22:22). This is probably why the angel of the Lord obstructs Balaam's path several times during the journey. His donkey seems at first sight a proverbially stubborn one. Ironically, the diviner, who is supposed to have access to the invisible world (24:3, 16), does not see the angel of the Lord, except at the very end. Only the donkey sees him. King Balak receives Balaam with a feast (22:40). He pays him well, just as contemporary diviners are well paid. It is both surprising and intriguing that Balaam prepares seven altars and offers on each one a bull and a ram to God, not to his own deities (23:4). Probably, God compels him to do so. Then, at four different sites, Balaam utters oracles given to him by God. In these oracles, each time after seven offerings, he does not curse but blesses Israel. King Balak is not happy about it and says to Balaam, "What have you done to me? I brought you to curse my enemies, but now you have done nothing but bless them" (23:11; cf. 24:10). Instead of speaking only through Israelite prophets, as we usually assume, God also uses an animist diviner to pursue his purposes with his people.

4.1.6.2 The Regulations for Levirate Marriage (Deut 25:5–19)

In a relational culture, the sanctions for disgraceful behaviour consist of actions and events which evoke feelings of shame. The levirate marriage custom requires a widow to marry her dead husband's brother (Deut 25:5–19; cf. de Vaux 1964). The refusal by the husband's brother to follow the levirate marriage rules of the levirate evokes a response from the widow:

> Then his brother's wife shall go up to him in the presence of the elders, pull his sandal off his foot, spit in his face, and declare, "This is what is done to the man who does not build up his brother's house." Throughout Israel his family shall be known as "the house of him whose sandal was pulled off." (Deut 25:9–10; cf. Gen 38: the story of Judah and Tamar)

In Israel the taking off of one's own sandal signified the legalization of an act (cf. Ruth 4:7–8). Taking off the other person's sandal indicated that the person was disobeying the law. Spitting in another's face caused one to suffer seven days of impurity (Lev 15:8; Num 12:14). A woman spitting in a man's face is shaming in itself. Hence, this passage describes a matter of disgrace with lasting effect. The most shaming punishment is public stoning and banishment from the community (Deut 22:13–21; 23:1–7). The punishments shame not only the offender but the whole family. As such, they act as a deterrent in a relational society.

4.1.6.3 King Saul and the Woman in Endor (1 Sam 28)

The Philistines muster their troops to go to war against Israel. The prophet Samuel has died. King Saul has removed all necromancers and diviners (the mediums) from the country. When Saul sees the army of the Philistines, he is afraid. So he enquires of God, but the latter does not answer him, "neither through dreams, nor the casting of lots, nor through the prophets" (v. 6). Then Saul orders his servants to take him to a woman "who commands a spirit of the dead" (*baʿalat ʾob*). Saul disguises himself, goes to her at night and asks her to call Samuel up from the realm of the dead (*sheʾol*). When Samuel appears, Saul asks the woman what she sees. She says: "I see a god [*ʾelohim*] coming up out of the ground" (v. 13).

The first question to consider here is why this spirit being is referred to as *ʾelohim*. In the 2,570 occurrences of the term *ʾelohim* in the Old Testament, the great majority concern the creator God, the God of Israel. But in some instances, the same word is used of other deities (Exod 18:11; 20:3; Ps 97:7). Psalm 96 turns it into a play on words: "For all the gods of the peoples [*ʾelohei haʿamim*] are idols [*ʾelil*]; but the Lord made the heavens" (Ps 96:5). To avoid this problem, the Septuagint, the Greek translation of the Old Testament, translates *ʾelohim* in certain passages with *angeloi*, "angels" (Ps 8:6; 97:7; 138:1).

The second question of interest is whether the spirit being was really Samuel or a demon. This raises the broader question of how to understand the relationship between animism, a human cultural and religious system, and the demonic world (cf. sections 2.3.2 and 5.4.1). Let us assume that an animist wishes to make contact with his deceased father. Following the prescribed rituals, his father appears to him and he hears his voice. But is it really his father's face and his father's voice? Back to the question of the spirit being. Interestingly, about half of commentators on this passage hold that it was the prophet Samuel, and the other half that it was not. In other words, there is no answer. And if there is no answer, this is not the main point of the story. Rather, the main point is the announcement of judgement of a disobedient and syncretistic king: the death of King Saul and his sons and the defeat of Israel the next day (v. 19).

Third, I want to make a remark concerning the woman in Endor "who commands a spirit of the dead" (*baʿalat ʾob*). Usually, Bible translators and commentators refer to her as the "witch" of Endor. However, in animist cultures, witches cause harm to other members of society. People fear and avoid them. From the biblical text, we have no clue that this was the case. It would therefore be more precise and appropriate to refer to this woman as a diviner, in anthropological terms a medium, a mediator between the visible and the invisible world in animism of type 2 (cf. section 5.4.1.2).

In summary, we can say that it is impossible for an animist calling up his father to know whether he is really seeing and hearing his father or a demon seeking to manipulate and destroy him. That is why Scripture forbids contacting the spirits of the dead (Deut 18:10–12; Isa 8:19).

4.1.6.4 The Parable of the Two Sons (Matt 21:28–32)
Jesus relates a parable about a father and his two sons (Matt 21:28–32). The father asks them to help in the vineyard. The first says yes, but doesn't go. The second says, "I won't!" Later he regrets and goes after all. It is clear that neither son wants to go and work. The behaviour of the first reveals a relational conscience. He wants to maintain harmony and not snub his father. He says yes. The behaviour of the second son reveals a rules-based conscience. He tells the truth without concern for damaging the relationship with his father or disrespecting him. He communicates directly: "I don't want to work!" But then he goes. Jesus then asks which son has done the will of his father. In the relational environment of the eastern Mediterranean, the response of the first son is seen as normal behaviour. Nevertheless, all the listeners agree that the second son fulfilled the will of his father. So does this mean that being rules-based is better? Not necessarily so, based on a background analysis of the Bible as a whole. Jesus is here correcting the cultural values of the Mediterranean region: what matters in the kingdom of God is not outward consent but the actual deed. At the last judgement, the Son of Man will reward all of us according to our deeds (Matt 16:27). So, with regard to certain issues, the gospel is intended to have a transforming influence on the local culture.

4.1.7 Analysis of Cultures in Scripture

My rapid journey through the worldviews in the Bible concludes with a brief analysis of the worldviews of some of the peoples, cultures and religions, and a reflection on multiculturalism in Scripture and on the so-called biblical or "Christian" worldview. This will include looking at aspects of Hebrew culture in the Old Testament, together with features of Greek and Roman culture in the New Testament. Although the Old Testament cultures can all be described as Hebrew, they span a period of over a thousand years, so they will obviously exhibit considerable differences. Although I do not recommend going beyond individual analyses to make generalizations, the latter can with caution assist in interpretation or translation of the Bible in terms of overall biblical context. What follows is an attempt to approach certain cultures in a fairly general way, expressing the results of my reflections with all necessary reservations. In general, we can agree that the ancient Near East cultures where God revealed himself at the time of both the Old and New Testaments can be characterized as animist and hence as predominantly relational.

4.1.7.1 Analysis of Hebrew Culture

We have seen that in Genesis God began to communicate in a relational context. In a second step, in Exodus and Leviticus, he introduced a set of rules intended to reshape the conscience of those layers of the population which had an affinity for the sacrificial rites and the law.

When one considers the Hebrew language, one is impressed by the limited number of grammatical rules and the breadth of meaning of its words, which are frequently very broadly defined. The term *hēsēd* is one example. Depending on the context, it can be rendered by numerous English words: loyalty, devotion, grace, mercy, compassion, love, etc. Such observations indicate the importance of the relational axis. We can also see that God, Jesus and the prophets pursued a holistic communicative approach comprising the total spectrum of styles of communication: being, doing and speaking, verbal and non-verbal, direct and indirect. All in all, we find in the Hebrew language a holistic way of thinking, characteristic of a relational conscience.

Moreover, God's introduction of the law activates the legal axis, so that we can speak of a balanced conscience, both relational and rules-based. However, in my view, the balance tilts somewhat in favour of the relational axis. This is apparent when we consider what has been said in the preceding paragraph and also Jesus' remarks about the Pharisees. This reasoning takes us already into the New Testament, but still within the Jewish context. Judging by how Jesus criticizes the Pharisees in their attachment to the law, they appear to be extremely rules-based (Matt 22:34–40; 23). By contrast, the Samaritan woman with her origin among the ordinary people is much more relational (John 4). She comes to draw water in the midday heat so as to avoid the gaze of others. Finally, the apostles Peter, John and Paul, simple but also very educated Jews, appear very balanced in their writings, hence both relational and rules-based. I will return to this point when discussing the influence of Greek (Hellenistic) culture on the disciples in the next section.

4.1.7.2 Analysis of Greek Culture

Greek culture, the foundation of Hellenist culture, was animist with a relational and holistic worldview. It underpinned philosophical systems representing, according to Luc Ferry, secularization of a religion, in this case Greek animism.[13] In Greece we must distinguish between philosophies with a two-tiered perspective and those with a secular one, but both of them having fragmented worldviews which are a feature of a rules-based conscience.

The Greek language has more grammatical rules than Hebrew, and its grammatical structure is very elaborate and precise. Greek philosophical thought was very analytical, but among the general population the tendency was more probably holistic. So what we have here is at root a relational conscience based on Greek animism, but with a more significant legal axis than in Hebrew culture – facts which are clearly visible in Greek language and philosophy.

Hellenistic culture was already having an influence on Israel in the centuries before the coming of Jesus Christ. At the time of Jesus, it predominated in certain regions of Palestine, such as Galilee, the Decapolis and Perea. This means that in analyzing New Testament culture, one must take account of the connection between the worldviews of Hebrew, Greek and Roman culture, although for teaching purposes, and in line with the Weberian logic of ideal types, I am discussing them separately. Herman Ridderbos similarly points out that in interpreting the anthropological language of the New Testament we must bear in mind the link between Hebrew and Greek perceptions.[14] In addition, Andrew Walls presents the idea that a large part of the letters of the apostle Paul can be interpreted as promoting principles for a Hellenistic way of being Christian – in other words, developing a new style of Christian living and a new identity.[15]

4.1.7.3 Analysis of Roman Culture

We find the same relational aspects of animism with the Romans, evident for example in the *mystery religions*.[16] The grammatical structure of the Latin

---

13. Luc Ferry and Lucien Jerphagnon, *La tentation du christianisme* (Paris: Grasset, 2009), 100.

14. Ridderbos, *Paul: An Outline of His Theology*, 114-21, 288-93.

15. Andrew F. Walls, "Converts or Proselytes? The Crisis over Conversion in the Early Church," *International Bulletin of Missionary Research* 28.1 (2004): 2-6.

16. Mystery cults are forms of religion which originated in the Greco-Roman world and experienced their widest spread in the early centuries after Christ. They embraced the notions of individual salvation, death and resurrection. Entry was through initiation.

language is even more developed than in Greek. In addition, Roman law had a significant influence throughout the Roman Empire, apparent even in the Europe of today. We regard the Roman legal system as a powerfully effective rules-based force, leaving its legacy in the cultures which arose in the wake of the Roman Empire. These aspects of Roman culture combined with Hellenist culture around the Mediterranean, including with Hebrew culture in Palestine at the time of Jesus.

4.1.7.4 Comparative Analysis

If we may generalize with due caution, we can say that Hebrew culture is more relational than Greek culture, which in turn is more relational than Roman culture. Of course, all three also have rules-based elements of ascending importance. This general cultural background must be taken into account when we are interpreting and translating the Bible.

4.1.7.5 Relational Aspects in the Bible

In the covenant relationship between YHWH and the people of Israel, the love, mercy, grace and faithfulness of God (Hebr. *hēsēd*) underlies everything (e.g. Pss 100:5; 106:1; 118:1, 29; 136:1). The refrain "his goodness [*hēsēd*] endures forever" in Psalm 118:2–4 and through the whole of Psalm 136 underscores this fact. The natural response by the people of Israel to this affirmation is love for their God (e.g. Josh 22:5; 23:6, 8; 1 Kgs 9:4; Neh 1:5; Ezek 36:26–27; Dan 9:4). Jesus and later his disciple John integrate the command to love God in the instructions to their disciples (e.g. John 15:10; 1 John 3:23–24). When the Pharisees ask him which is the greatest command, a rules-based question, Jesus gives a relational answer: "You shall love the Lord your God with all your heart, and will all your soul, and with all your mind. This is the greatest and first command. And a second is like it: you shall love your neighbour as yourself" (Matt 22:37–39). In the Sermon on the Mount, Jesus condenses the Old Testament requirements in terms of the Golden Rule, a relational summary of the content of the law: "In everything do to others as you would have them do to you; for this is the law and the prophets" (Matt 7:12). The apostle Paul exhorts the Christians in the new, multicultural churches to accept one another (Rom 15:7), indeed to love one another warmly (Rom 12:10), and to forgive one another just as God in Christ has forgiven us (Eph 4:32). This also includes providing for one another (1 Tim 5:8). In so doing we are back in a covenant relationship, in which God's behaviour is to be reflected in ours.

4.1.7.6 Rules-Based Aspects in the Bible

As the section on the formation of a new worldview in the books of Exodus and Leviticus shows (cf. 4.1.4), sacrifices in general and the guilt offering in particular indicate that God's intention was to bring more balance into the orientation of the Israelite conscience through the payment of a penalty (Lev 1–7). Also, the frequently occurring demand to demonstrate love (or fear) of God by keeping his commands indicates the same intention (e.g. Deut 6:5–6; 7:9; 11:1, 13; 30:16; John 14:15, 21, 23–24; 15:10). Psalm 119 is a song in praise of the importance of God's commands. Jesus points to the importance of the law as the foundation of the life of a disciple: "Do not think that I have come to abolish the law or the prophets . . . until heaven and earth pass away, not one letter, not one stroke of a letter, will pass from the law" (Matt 5:17–18). Jesus urges his disciples to give clear and unambiguous answers: "Let your word be 'Yes, Yes' or 'No, No'" (Matt 5:37). The apostle Paul in turn commands the churches in Asia Minor to "make the most of the time" during their lives (Eph 5:16) and to maintain order in the worship service (1 Cor 14:40). All of us, each individual, must appear before the judgement seat of Christ (2 Cor 5:10).

4.1.8 Scripture and Multiculturalism

Now that we have looked at the different worldviews and cultures in Scripture, the time has come to reflect on the experience of living with culturally different others as depicted in the Bible.

In relation to multiculturalism, Scripture combines unity and diversity; the triune God is *unity in diversity*. Moreover, he is the sovereign over the whole universe, but acts at the same time in particular situations. When he tells Abram to leave his country and to be a blessing for all nations, he introduces an action which concerns one person but has a universal perspective (Gen 12:1–3). With the election of the people of Israel and their calling to be a blessing for all the nations, the universal God commits himself to a particular people (Exod 19:5–6). In the same way, his intervention through Jesus Christ has the salvation of all humankind in view (John 3:16). This tension between God's universality and particularity is perhaps best visible in Deuteronomy 10:14–15: "Although heaven and the heaven of heavens belong to the Lord your God, the earth with all that is in it, yet the Lord set his heart in love on your ancestors alone and chose you, their descendants after them, out of all the peoples."[17]

---

17. Cf. Howard Peskett and Vinoth Ramachandra, *The Message of Mission* (Downers Grove: InterVarsity Press 2003), 109–12.

On this theological basis, one can conclude that the personal and cultural variety in humankind is no accident, but the result of God's plan (Gen 1:28; 10–11). This variety is both a burden (Gen 10–11) and at the same time an enrichment (Rev 5:9). However, the problematic nature of this variety is often in the foreground. After Pentecost unity is once more possible (Eph 2). The Bible does not favour any particular culture. The gospel can take root in any and every culture.

The fact that God created all human beings according to his image (Gen 1:26–27) provides us with a foundation for intercultural communication. It means that all of us have the same basic needs, which Abraham Maslow arranged in the form of a pyramid. For Maslow, the bottom layer consists of the fundamental physiological needs for survival; above that level come our needs for security, belongingness, esteem and love, and at the top the need for self-realization and transcendence.[18] Maslow's theory has been frequently criticized, developed further and complexified.[19] However, in our view, his assessment of basic needs presents a simple overview of human constants. Every person has a longing for deep, satisfying relationships, respect, significance and a sense of meaning. These basic needs are then enacted very differently by individuals. Beyond all cultural differences, we can achieve communicative access to others by building on these human constants, because we are all created in God's image.

> The Bible does not favour any particular culture. The gospel can take root in any and every culture.

The church, through conveying the gospel across all cultures, is "on a mission." We are called to be aware of our own imprinting and pattern of interpretation, and of those of our conversation partners. We should desire to maintain an attitude of respect towards adherents of other cultures. We do not say, "The way we do it is the best and only right way." Such arrogance has negatively impacted much missionary work. Rather, our attitude should express an openness towards and an interest in other cultures: "This is how we do it. What about you?"

---

18. Abraham H. Maslow, *Motivation and Personality* (New York: Harper & Row, 1970).

19. E.g. Clayton Alderfer's ERG theory (existence, relatedness and growth) and Manfred Max-Neef's fundamental human needs. The latest development in the research on intrinsic motivation and personality is the self-determination theory. See e.g. Edward L. Deci and Richard Ryan, *Intrinsic Motivation and Self-Determination in Human Behavior* (New York: Plenum, 1985); Richard Ryan and Edward L. Deci, *Self-Determination Theory: Basic Psychological Needs in Motivation, Development, and Wellness* (New York: Guilford Publishing, 2017).

4.1.9 The Biblical or "Christian" Worldview

Following this analysis of the different cultures in the Bible and their worldviews, I now consider what exactly a biblical or "Christian" worldview is, so as to assess how my reflections on Scripture compare with other approaches. Many publications, particularly by Reformed authors, emphasize the importance of forming a biblical or "Christian" worldview after conversion.[20] I am in complete agreement with these writers. Which workers in the reign of God would not want their converts to form a biblical worldview? (cf. section 2.6). However, the question remains: how does one define a biblical or "Christian" worldview?

The problem with defining it is that there are several worldviews in the Bible: in the Old Testament, with its time span of over a thousand years, one can detect various forms of expressing a worldview. In the New Testament, the Greek vocabulary used by mainly Jewish writers conveys notions of the Greek two-tiered perspective. The biblical writers incorporated these notions in varying degrees into their worldview. It becomes clear that the problem of the plurality of biblical worldviews cannot be solved. One provisional solution consists in looking for a common denominator among the different perspectives in general basic themes, such as the five soteriological concepts: the triune, monotheistic and personal biblical God, reference point of all reality and foundation of both the unity and diversity of the universe and of his personal character; salvation history in terms of creation, fall, redemption and fulfilment; the sovereignty of God; the reality and activity of the forces of evil, and the fallen nature of man. Beyond this approach, I suggest defining a biblical worldview in terms of a special configuration of three of the five models already proposed: the layers model of the order of creation (the Hebrew worldview), the five soteriological concepts (God, man, evil, sin, salvation), and time orientation. The fourth model, conscience orientation, is not typical of a biblical worldview and is therefore not workable here. Mana is in itself an animist concept and must therefore be excluded.

Other writers prefer to speak of a "Christian" worldview. A "Christian" worldview can be defined as "the worldview held by Christians." But a word of caution is needed here! Converts who have grown up within a Hindu worldview retain their Hindu worldview at the start of their life with Christ and behave accordingly in their daily lives. Similarly, converts with an animist background still behave after conversion according to their animist worldview. This is the case in most parts of Africa. Converts with a Muslim background still live in accordance with their Islamic worldview, particularly at the beginning of their

---

20. E.g. Ryken, *What Is the Christian Worldview?*

life with Christ. And converts with a secular background behave at first in accordance with their secular worldview. Such Christians will believe neither in the existence of the devil, nor in hell, nor in miracles or demons. Most authors who write about the "Christian" worldview take no account of these intercultural aspects in their deliberations, nor of the fact that the elements of one's worldview are formed during childhood and can be changed only step by step with a good deal of educational effort. In general, significant change in worldview usually develops only after several years of the life of faith, and sometimes not until the next generation, with children who have been raised by practising Christian parents.

Others in turn define the "Christian" worldview in philosophical terms derived from the Western cultural sphere.[21] But Christians from the global South brought up in a relational, non-Christian society enter into the Christian life with a different background and different worldviews. On this basis, they interpret the Bible differently and are unable to conform to Western definitions of a "Christian" worldview.

Bearing all these things in mind, what should be our objective after conversion? The only possible approach is to work towards changing one's worldview through intensive Bible study, as chronologically as possible, and by stages integrate the different cultural systems into a biblical worldview and an identity "in Christ." This is a lifelong process, which we call sanctification (2 Cor 7:1; Heb 12:14).

An understanding of the Old Testament foundation of the "Christian" worldview makes clear that a Hindu or animist worldview cannot replace the biblical equivalent as an underpinning of the Christian faith. Only the biblical record can create a worldview with the capacity to so change personalities and cultures that they have a lasting influence on private and public life. Nevertheless, all cultures and religions have enough in common with the biblical worldview to prepare their adherents for the gospel. In this regard, it is important to understand that the worldview of every culture and every religion contains elements corresponding to the biblical worldview, as well as those which run counter to it. These correspond to the divine respectively human or demonic imprint of cultures according to the tri-polar perspective. Thus, one must always analyze commonalities and differences thoroughly. Kwame Bediako goes so far as to regard the animist worldview as very fruitful

---

21. E.g. Ryken, *What Is the Christian Worldview?*

soil for the gospel.²² His position is backed up by the very rapid spread of the Christian faith among previously animist peoples, especially in North and South America, Africa and Europe, and also among mountain people in Asia.

4.2 Theology

After this journey through the worldviews in Scripture, I come to the analysis of theological study. Due to space limitations, I will again proceed very selectively. Conscience orientation is the model which touches the deepest layers of worldview, and so I will depend on it extensively in my consideration of the various notions. I will first provide a survey of theological study during church history, and then I examine theological and soteriological concepts. Finally, I will take a critical look at the field of ethics.

4.2.1 Brief History of Theological Study

In this section, I give a brief historical survey of theological study from the perspective of conscience orientation. It should be borne in mind, however, that my generalizations are reductionist simplifications. The aim is to provide general guidance as a foundation for subsequent individual in-depth analysis.

We have seen that the apostles, most of them of Jewish origin, appeared to have a balanced conscience orientation, both relational and rules-based. This would therefore also be true of the early church, since it consisted mainly of Jews. With the massive inflow of Greeks and Romans (with their animist and relational background), the conscience of the early church became mainly relational. The theology of the church fathers was formulated on the foundation of largely relational Greek philosophical ideas. Interestingly, to this day the theology and practice of the Orthodox Church have remained essentially relational. For example, the concept of *theosis* ("deification"), expressing the striving to "become like God," is of central importance for Orthodox theology. By contrast, for the Roman Catholic Church, it represents the mortal sin committed by Adam and Eve which led to the fall (Gen 3:5). In the same vein, Anselm of Canterbury (1033–1109) developed a relational approach to the concept of forgiveness, in terms of the *satisfaction theory of atonement*. According to this theory, after humankind's fall, God himself

---

22. Kwame Bediako, *Jesus in Africa: The Christian Gospel in African History and Experience* (Minneapolis: Fortress, 2000).

satisfied his honour by sending his Son. I will discuss this in more detail below (cf. section 3.2.3.3).

Subsequently, the Catholic Church, by introducing indulgences[23] in the high medieval period, became more and more rules-based: a payment had to be made for every sin, as at the time of the introduction of the Mosaic law. Along the same lines, some five hundred years after Anselm and the introduction of indulgences, Martin Luther brought in his primarily rules-based doctrine of justification. However, Luther's personality reveals itself to be relational in several respects. Similarly, John Calvin, a trained lawyer, engaged with Catholic theology according to rules-based categories. Nevertheless, he developed significant trains of thought concerning Jesus Christ as the mediator between us and God.[24] In the wake of the reformers, the theology of Protestant and evangelical churches became essentially rules-based. The great missionary movements of the nineteenth century, triggered by the Anglo-Saxon revival, emphasized obedience to the Great Commission of Jesus in Matthew 28, a rules-based motivation. Western missionaries brought a rules-based message to the relational peoples of the global South and East: to pronounce a preformulated conversion prayer, to learn the catechism by heart, to assist the worship service, not to drink, not to smoke, not to steal, not to commit adultery, not to be a polygamist. Questions of allegiance, worldview and culture were not in view. Misunderstandings, superficiality and a dominance of cultural identity are the abiding result.

4.2.2 Conscience and Theology

If one follows the logic of the Weberian ideal types of conscience orientation, one can postulate two kinds of theology: a mainly rules-based theology such as was mainly developed by the Catholic and Protestant Churches, and a relational theology as represented by the Orthodox Church.

A *rules-based theology* typically looks as follows:

- As *dogmatic theology*, a rules-based theology is very much occupied with questions of doctrine.
- As *systematic theology*, it develops a logical system of thought.

---

23. Indulgence (Latin: *indulgentia*, from *indulgeo* "permit") is a way to reduce the amount of punishment for sins for oneself or another person. Indulgences were already introduced by the early church, but became increasingly popular in the eleventh century.

24. John Calvin, *Institutes of the Christian Religion* (Grand Rapids: Eerdmans, 1541, 2009).

- Theology is understood in terms of studying the word of God and proclaiming the gospel verbally (*kerygma*); it develops a *theology of the word*.
- Western rules-based theologians have developed a *kataphatic theology* (from Greek *kataphasis* "positive affirmation"), which uses precise terms to describe God by listing his attributes and to formulate doctrinal statements.
- A rules-based theology focuses on the cognitive aspect, promotes analytic thinking and is directed towards defining of and distinguishing between theological concepts; one result of this is the production of theological *dictionaries*.
- With regard to the encounter with non-Christians, it develops a theology of *apologetics*, involving verbal *truth encounter*;
- Acquisition of knowledge is scientific, based on maintaining distance between subject and object.

A *relational theology* looks very different. It has been characteristic of Orthodox theology. In the second half of the twentieth century, it also has become a feature of theologians in the global South, and of some theological projects in the various theological trends in the global North.

- A relational theology expresses itself chiefly as *narrative theology*. It analyzes the stories of the Bible and tells them in a missionary approach. It is no accident that Western theology has (re)discovered narrative theology at a time when its population has become more relational (cf. section 4.3.5).
- The relational theologians of the Orthodox Church have developed an *apophatic theology*, a way of reflecting about God and certain doctrines which avoids precise descriptions and prefers to remain silent about some things.
- A relational approach often focuses on the emotional and non-verbal dimension, and can also manifest as *spiritual warfare or power encounter* with "the unseen forces."
- A relational theology attributes greater value to *holistic thinking* as opposed to analytic thinking.
- Acquisition of knowledge is relational; it proceeds from proximity to and even intimacy between subject and object, according to the Hebrew term *yada'* "know, recognize (in a sexual encounter)."

These two expressions of theology are shown in Table 13 as alternative approaches.

Table 13: Conscience and Theology

Rules-based Theology	Relational Theology
Dogmatic theology	Narrative theology (stories)
Systematic theology	
Theology of the word	
Kataphatic theology	Apophatic theology
Apologetics (truth encounter)	Spiritual warfare (power encounter)
Analytic thinking (distinguishing theological concepts)	Holistic thinking
Scientific acquisition of knowledge through distance between subject and object	Relational acquisition of knowledge through proximity of subject and object

4.2.3 Conscience and Soteriology

Following the preceding historical survey of theological study and reflections on alternative theological approaches, this section discusses some selected soteriological notions from the perspective of the two conscience orientations and the five soteriological concepts.[25] This will again have to be selective. I will then present four approaches to forgiveness during church history: Christ as victor, the satisfaction theory, the vicarious atoning sacrifice of Jesus on the cross and the doctrine of justification. Finally, I discuss more recent developments in the doctrine of justification.

4.2.3.1 Some Soteriological Terms

The Bible understands sin as "missing the target" (*hata'*), a meaning taken up by the Greek term *hamartia*, and as "deviating" from the path marked out by God (*'awon*). Both are primarily relational approaches, but can, of course, also be interpreted as rules-based. The rules-based aspect of sin is highlighted particularly through the Hebrew word *pēschaʻ* and the Greek word *paraptoma*, both meaning "stepping over the edge of the path." In most societies, the definition of sin (error, fault) is in relation to the community. In contrast, the Bible's definition of sin relates to God and his commands, as he himself is the goal of our life and ordains our journey. These precepts became part of the norms of the Israelite community, reflected in the understanding of

---

25. Soteriology comprises reflection on sin, forgiveness and salvation.

righteousness (*tsēdēq, tsedaqa*) as behaviour in harmony with God's covenant and with the Israelite community. Hence, the Bible provides not only a social definition of sin along with most societies, but also one directed towards God – in other words, a theological definition of sin.

The notion of grace or mercy can be understood on the basis of the Hebrew concept of *hēsēd* as the normal behaviour within the covenant when its norms are violated by the partner. In this regard, the righteousness of God (*dikaiosynē theou*) – the standard behaviour according to his covenant with the people of Israel – demanded the sending of his Son Jesus Christ in an attitude of love, solidarity and faithfulness towards humankind (Rom 1:16–17). In this case, the righteousness of God becomes identical with his grace (*hēsēd*). Jesus Christ exemplifies the concept of grace in both conscience orientations by two parables: the parable of the lost son (Luke 15:11–32) brings out the relational aspect, the parable of the magnanimous king and the unmerciful servant (Matt 18:21–35) the legal aspect.

In the Old Testament, the notion of faith is based on the Hebrew root *'aman* "be firm," familiar to us in the expression "amen" or "so be it." The terms derived from it indicate the attitude of trust captured in the Greek term *pistis* "faith, trust." The Catholic Church has developed the various aspects of the notion in its systematic theology. The Latin word *assensus* "assent" conveys belief in the doctrines. Clearly, this aspect of faith is rules-based. Further, we have the word *fiducia*, faith or trust in God's love and mercy, a relational aspect. An additional relational aspect of faith is expressed through *fidelitas* "loyalty, faithfulness." This aspect of the meaning indicates that believers should live their lives in loyalty to God. The final Latin term *visio* describes a holistic understanding of the life of faith nourished by God. Proceeding from a holistic understanding of life, this term likewise indicates a relational aspect of faith.

Finally, there is the concept of salvation, summed up in the Hebrew word *shalom*, indicating harmony and integrity of life, clearly a holistic and relational concept. This Old Testament approach to salvation has re-emerged in the so-called health and wealth theology, in a reductionist way, as the concept of prosperity. It holds the view that salvation is already a reality in all its material and spiritual dimensions. As such it represents a *realized eschatology*. It ignores the circumstances of the eschatological interim, the period between the first and second coming of Jesus Christ. The biblical view is that salvation is "already" realized in the spiritual dimension, but "not yet" completely in the material world. The Bible therefore presents us with a "Christ-centred *shalom*" in terms of the dawn of the kingdom of God through the coming of Jesus Christ, a so-called *inaugurated eschatology*. From another perspective, salvation includes being on the side of the mightier God, a relational aspect, or believing in the true and just God, which conveys a rules-based faith.

Following these reflections on some of the soteriological concepts from the perspective of conscience orientation, I will now examine four approaches to the concept of redemption in church history, which taken together could be described as a "kaleidoscopic model" of forgiveness: the model of Christ as victor, the satisfaction theory, the substitutionary atoning sacrifice of Jesus on the cross and the doctrine of justification.

4.2.3.2 Christ as Victor, a Relational Approach

The patristic model of *Christus Victor* highlights Jesus Christ as the supreme God, mightier than all other deities. It expresses a relational approach typical of the animist context of the Mediterranean world. The titles "Lord" and "Saviour" applied by Paul to Jesus are an exact reflection of this relational approach, and they place Jesus Christ in opposition to the Roman emperor. This approach finds expression in the words of Colossians 2:15: "He [God] disarmed the rulers and authorities and made a public example of them, triumphing over them." Jesus Christ triumphs over all powers.

4.2.3.3 The Satisfaction Theory, a Relational Approach

Anselm of Canterbury (1033–1109) was not content with the patristic model of *Christus Victor*, and during dialogue with Spanish Muslim philosophers formulated the theory of satisfaction. He presented it in his work *Cur Deus homo?* (Why God Had to Become Man, 1098). According to Anselm, it is the task of humankind to honour God. If they fail to submit to God, they put him to shame. Their moral failure is so great that they cannot resolve the problematic situation by themselves. The solution depends on God, who must either provide satisfaction himself or punish humanity. God decided to provide that satisfaction himself by sending Jesus Christ. This offering is of supreme value because of the sublime life of Christ, as it is indeed God who is giving his life, and doing this for the whole of humankind. Anselm's concern is for the honour of God and the salvation of us all. It is a relational approach for collective salvation.[26]

---

26. Interestingly, the Catholic Church still maintains today satisfaction as the final stage in the process of forgiveness: 1) repentance (*contritio cordis*), 2) confession (*confessio*), 3) absolution by the priest (*absolutio*), 4) satisfaction in the sense of penance (*satisfactio*).

4.2.3.4 The Vicarious Atoning Sacrifice, a Rules-Based Approach

For Martin Luther (1483–1546), four and a half centuries later, it is a matter of individual salvation: "How can I gain the favour of a merciful God?" Not content with the doctrine of satisfaction, and mentally in turmoil through an inner experience of God, he discovered afresh the vicarious atoning sacrifice of Jesus on the cross: "He [Jesus] himself bore our sins in his body on the cross" (1 Pet 2:24; cf. Heb 9:28). Peter is here quoting Isaiah 53:5: "But he was wounded for our transgressions, crushed for our iniquities; upon him was the punishment that made us whole, and by his bruises we are healed." Jesus became a curse for us: "Christ redeemed us from the curse of the law by becoming a curse for us" (Gal 3:13). The emphasis is on reparation through punishment, a rules-based concept.

4.2.3.5 Justification, a Rules-Based Approach

In relation to his engagement with the vicarious atoning sacrifice of Jesus on the cross, Luther was also wrestling with the concept of the "righteousness of God" (*dikaiosynē theou*). Since he was reading the New Testament in Greek, he did not rely on the wording of the Vulgate, the Latin translation of Jerome in the fourth century. The latter translated the Greek word *dikaioō* "justify" by the Latin word *iustificare*, shifting the meaning to "make righteous." By contrast, Luther interpreted "the righteousness of God" as the gift of freedom from guilt in a lawsuit before God (an objective genitive[27]). The expression thus contains the notion of "declaring righteous," a righteousness which is an external and passive gift. Luther and the other Reformers distinguished the declaration of righteousness, "justification" as an external gift, from inner transformation, which they called "sanctification." By contrast, the Catholic Church, following Augustine, interpreted *iustificare* as a constant inner transformation, particularly after the Council of Trent (1545–1547). These are therefore contradictory positions.

So as not to limit ourselves to the official Reformation teaching, we should mention the Anabaptists, who, while adhering to the doctrine of justification, place themselves between the two official positions, on account of their conscience orientation. Their doctrine and practice, being very much affected by persecution, contain a very strong communal element. In addition,

---

27. In the objective genitive, righteousness becomes the object, making it an "external" gift from God. In the subjective genitive, righteousness remains bound to the subject; righteousness as a feature of God's character becomes an "inner" gift to the believer.

their emphasis on a theology of non-violence represents a significantly relational approach.

4.2.3.6 More Recent Developments in the Doctrine of Justification

Much later, in the first half of the twentieth century, the German theologian Adolf Schlatter (1852–1938) began to perceive in the expression "righteousness of God" (*dikaiosynē theou*) a subjective genitive, indicating righteousness as an attribute of God in terms of saving power. In the second half of the twentieth century, his two colleagues, Ernst Käsemann (1906–1998) and Peter Stuhlmacher (born 1932), suggest a balance between the two genitives (Käsemann 1964; Stuhlmacher 1989): the subjective genitive which perceives *righteousness as power* in the sense of "making righteous," and the objective genitive which understands righteousness as the *gift of freedom from guilt*, leading to its translation as "declaring righteous." In so doing, the genitive in the expression "righteousness of God" becomes an "author's genitive," conveying power and gift. It is apparent that the two genitives represent the two conscience orientations: the rules-based perspective of the reformers ("declaring righteous") and the relational perspective of the Catholic Church ("making righteous"). Thus, the theological debates reveal two conscience orientations (two worldviews). It is not surprising that debates have been heated and are not quite satisfactorily resolved. Not until the twentieth century were the two genitives brought into balance, enabling a rapprochement of the two theological positions with a degree of reconciliation at the time of the five hundredth anniversary of the Reformation in 2017.

4.2.3.7 The Current Situation

At the start of the twenty-first century, we can observe a somewhat more pragmatic attitude with regard to these discussions, which have been going on for five hundred years. This shift has naturally been influenced by aspects of late modernity and globalization, both of them advocating a relational approach and a downgrading of doctrinal views, as we will see in chapter 5 (sections 5.3.3 and 4.3.4). Common among those who share this pragmatic relational orientation is the response, "So what?" within the meaning of an ethically coherent faith. The next section will look at this issue in more detail.

4.2.4 Conscience and Ethics

Following the above discussion of the influence worldview exercises on theological and soteriological positions, I will now analyze ethics as a function of conscience orientation. We will ask what rules-based, relational and balanced ethics look like.

4.2.4.1 Rules-Based Ethics

A rules-based ethic is one which people in the West understand and are familiar with: a set of rules as the foundation of our behaviour. This conception begins with the law imparted by God in Exodus and Leviticus, and continues with the prospect of promoting an ethically correct life, determined by rules. The essence of this code is clearly found in the Ten Commands (Exod 20:1–17). This places us within the logic of the second part of the balanced covenant formula: "Keep my commands" (e.g. John 14:15).

4.2.4.2 Relational Ethics

The best-known relational ethic derives from Jesus' answer to the question from the Pharisee who wants to know which the most important law is. Jesus answers that the most important law is to love God, and your neighbour as yourself:

> You shall love the Lord your God with all your heart, and with all your soul, and with all your mind. This is the greatest and first commandment. And a second is like it: you shall love your neighbour as yourself (Matt 22:37–39).[28]

The first element of this *great command to love* corresponds to the first half of the balanced covenant formula: "Love God." It is relational and theocentric. One could draw up a *theocentric relational ethic* of this kind with the aid of various aspects of the relational conscience:

- *Live to the honour of God* (Matt 5:3–11; 1 Cor 10:31; Eph 1:6, 12, 14). A theocentric ethic of this sort is spelled out in the exhortations of the apostle Paul to the Colossians and the Corinthians: "Whatever your task, put yourselves into it, as done for the Lord and not for your masters" (Col 3:23); "You say: I am allowed to do anything – but not everything is good for you. You say: I am allowed to do anything – but not everything is beneficial" (1 Cor 10:23 NLT; cf. 6:12).
- *God sees all*. The God of the Bible is omnipresent; that is one of his main messages to the relational persons in Genesis and beyond (Gen 17:1; 28:10–22; Exod 3:14; Ps 139; Eccl 12:14; Heb 4:12).

---

28. Other biblical passages indicating a relational approach to ethics: John 13; 1 John 4:7–11, 19; 1 Corinthians 13:1–7.

But in the second half of the command to love, God broadens his ethical charge to us: "You shall love your neighbour as yourself" (Matt 22:39). Such a broader theocentric relational ethic directed to us could be expressed as follows:

- *Live to the honour of God and of the community.* We find a practical application in "providing honourable things [*kala* "good things"], not only in the sight of the Lord, but also in the sight of men" (2 Cor 8:21 NKJV).
- *Live in harmony with your neighbour.* The *Golden Rule* is the typical example of this approach: "In everything do to others as you would have them do to you" (Matt 7:12).

It is also possible to construct a theocentric relational ethic with the help of God's divine qualities in terms of challenges to his covenant partners. I will limit this summary to the attributes of righteousness, grace, faithfulness, wisdom and humility (Hos 2:21; Mic 6:8; Eph 5:9):

1. *Righteousness* (*tsēdēq, tsedaqa*): it sums up normal behaviour under the covenant, observing the obligations towards God and the community. Hence, in the Bible the term includes a relational *and* a rules-based dimension (Matt 6:33; 5:20; 23:23; Rom 1:17; 3:21–26; 5:1).
2. *Love and grace* (*hēsēd*): the Hebrew term describes normal covenant behaviour when the partner breaks the agreement (Pss 25:10; 40:10–11; 136; Prov 16:6; John 1:14, 17).
3. *Faithfulness, faith, truth* (*'ēmunah, 'ēmēt*): the Hebrew root *'mn* indicates the constancy and steadfastness of God; a relationship can only endure on the basis of faithfulness and truth (Ps 89; Hab 2:4; Isa 7:9; 28:16; John 1:14, 17).
4. *Wisdom* (*hokhma*) and *knowledge* (*da'at*): what links these two terms is the application of knowledge to practical living through wise behaviour (Prov 1:7; 11:2; 15:33; 1 Cor 1:18–2:16).
5. *Humility*: this acknowledges the superior status of the creator over us, his creatures (Prov 11:2; Matt 23:12; John 13; Phil 2:5–11; 1 Pet 5:5).

It is also possible to construct a *Christ-centred relational ethic*. The apostle Paul does this in his first letter to the Corinthians:

- "All belongs to you, and you belong to Christ" (1 Cor 3:22–23).
- "Your bodies are members of Christ" (1 Cor 6:15).
- "Follow Christ's example, imitate Christ" (1 Cor 4:16; 11:1).

In the Beatitudes, Jesus in turn develops a relational ethic based on the concepts of blessing ("Blessed are...") and honour ("Honoured are..."). Most translations retain the wording "Blessed are..." corresponding to the Greek term *makarios*. The prevailing conscience orientation of the populations around the Mediterranean reminds us that for those people, Jesus' Beatitudes represent a restoration of the honour of the "poor" and a blessing for them.

> Blessed are the poor in spirit, for theirs is the kingdom of heaven.
> Blessed are those who mourn, for they will be comforted.
> Blessed are the meek, for they will inherit the earth.
> Blessed are those who hunger and thirst for righteousness, for they will be filled.
> Blessed are the merciful, for they will receive mercy.
> Blessed are the pure in heart, for they will see God.
> Blessed are the peacemakers, for they will be called children of God.
> Blessed are those who are persecuted for righteousness' sake, for theirs is the kingdom of heaven.
> Blessed are you when people revile you and persecute you and utter all kinds of evil against you falsely on my account.
> (Matt 5:3–11)

One finds this "reversal of values" of the Beatitudes again in the foot washing of Jesus around the Passover meal (John 13). It is significant that Jesus places this symbolic action in the context of the disciples' question about who was the greatest (Luke 22:24). In general, in the societal rank order around the Mediterranean the "smallest" has to do the foot washing: the servant of the house, or the host himself, if he wants to honour the guest with a special gesture. Here it would have been the duty of John, the youngest disciple. It is typical that it is exactly and exclusively him who relates this episode. He will never forget the shame he felt during Jesus' action. In the context of the exhortations to humility in the Gospels and the Epistles, one could speak of a "reversal of values" and a "praise of weakness" (Matt 23:12; Luke 14:11; 18:14; 1 Cor 1:27; 9:22; 11:23–33; 2 Cor 4:7; 12:10). This ethical guideline runs exactly in the opposite direction relative to the values of Mediterranean societies.

In short, it is apparent that Jesus and the apostle Paul placed special value on a theocentric relational ethic.

4.2.4.3 Balanced Theocentric Covenant Ethics

The balanced covenant formula "Love God and keep his commands" combines a relational theocentric ethics with a rules-based ethics. We find this balanced covenant ethic in many places.[29] Proverbs 21:3 presents a somewhat hidden variant: "To do righteousness and justice is more acceptable to the Lord than sacrifice." Righteousness (*tsedaqa*) and justice (*mishpat*) represent here the relational and rules-based dimension. However, the balanced covenant ethic is expressed very clearly at the end of Ecclesiastes, beginning with the fear of God:

> The end of the matter; all has been heard. Fear God, and keep his commands; for that is the whole duty of everyone. For God will bring every deed into judgement, including every secret thing, whether good or evil. (Eccl 12:13–14)

Essentially, then, the Bible presents a theocentric, balanced covenant ethics.

4.3 Church Life

Having discussed how worldview influences theological, soteriological and ethical positions, I will now examine its influence on some aspects of church life (again selectively due to space limitations). I will consider interpretation and translation of the Bible, church leadership, counselling and the communication of the gospel.

4.3.1 Interpretation and Translation of the Bible

In this section, we will look first at the missiological concept of the cultural triangle, the basis for an investigation into interpretation and translation of the Bible "in the three horizons." Then we will consider transculturation ("translation") of the associated context, and finally problems of Bible translation and interpretation.

4.3.1.1 The Cultural Triangle
The linguist and anthropologist Eugene Nida (1914–2011) was the first to introduce the model of intercultural communication of the gospel via three

---

29. Deuteronomy 6:5–6; 7:9; 11:1, 13; 30:16; Joshua 22:5; 23:6, 8; 1 Kings 9:4; Nehemiah 1:5; Ezekiel 36:26–27; Daniel 9:4; John 14:15, 21, 23–24; 15:10; 1 John 3:23–24; 2 John 6.

languages and cultures, commonly referred to as the cultural triangle.[30] David Hesselgrave (1924–2018) subsequently developed this model further (cf. Figure 6).[31]

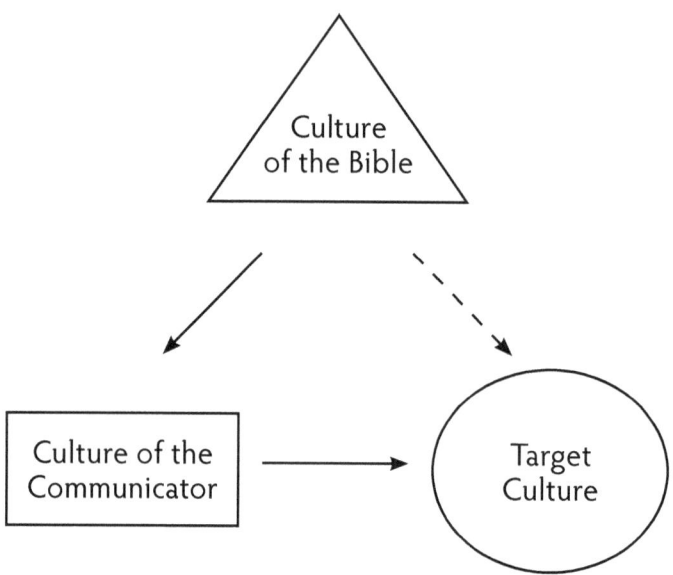

Figure 6: The Cultural Triangle

According to these authors, communication of the gospel involves three languages and three cultures, together with three worldviews. We read the Bible, the revelation of God into Hebrew and Greek/Roman culture, through the lens of (for example) English, African or Asian culture, or a cultural mix acquired during our socialization. Our interpretation of the biblical message is then decoded through the worldview of the receptor of this gospel message: members of the older or younger generation, intellectuals, workers or farmers, English, Africans or Asians.

The task of the communicator consists in trying to translate and interpret the message and intention of the Holy Spirit and the human authors of the biblical text and then conveying this message in a way that is relevant and

---

30. Eugene A. Nida, *Customs and Cultures: Anthropology for Christian Missions* (New York: Harper & Row, 1954).

31. David J. Hesselgrave, *Communicating Christ Cross-Culturally* (Grand Rapids: Zondervan, 1980), 107–13.

Mission."[40] The Micah Network, supported by theologians from the global South, adopts a holistic approach. This idea was taken up by the Cape Town Commitment of 2010, under the title "Bearing Witness to the Truth of Christ in a Pluralistic, Globalized World":

> As disciples of Christ, we are called to be people of truth. 1. We must *live* the truth. To live the truth is to be the face of Jesus, through whom the glory of the gospel is revealed to blinded minds. People will see truth in the faces of those who live their lives for Jesus, in faithfulness and love. 2. We must *proclaim* the truth. Spoken proclamation of the truth of the gospel remains paramount in our mission. This cannot be separated from living out the truth. Works and words must go together (IIA.1A).

In defining "witness," the Cape Town Commitment avoids the terms "evangelism" and "mission" because of possible misunderstandings. It begins with "*live* the truth" and continues with "*proclaim* the truth." Nine years previously, the Micah Network was still beginning its declaration with the aspect of proclamation. It seems that since then the holistic approach to mission and the importance of non-verbal communication have been acknowledged by the Lausanne Movement, which now is largely dominated by theologians from the global South with a generally holistic worldview.

Admittedly, probably not all Western Protestant theologians would share this perspective. Many prefer a narrow definition of evangelism which preserves its priority and distinguishes it from a broader view of mission. For example, David Hesselgrave, professor emeritus of mission studies at the Trinity Evangelical Divinity School in the USA, emphasizes that "the primary concern of our Lord has to do with meeting spiritual needs, not with meeting physical, material, or social needs." And he quotes Luke 19:10: "For the Son of Man came to seek out and to save the lost."[41]

In this journey through the interpretations of the terms evangelism and mission, we can observe a development from a two-tiered perspective to a holistic concept of mission. This development coincides with the shift of the centre of Christianity to the global South and the East, along with the simultaneous change of worldview in the West to an increasingly relational

---

40. Micah Global, "Declaration on Integral Mission," https://micahglobal.org/page/resources-external.

41. David J. Hesselgrave, *Paradigms in Conflict: 10 Key Questions in Christian Missions Today* (Grand Rapids: Kregel, 2005), 136.

conscience. Thus, the various developments are pointing in the same direction (cf. sections 5.3.3 and 5.3.5).[42]

4.3.2 Church Leadership

A good example of the influence of worldview on church life is the choice of the form of church leadership. In the New Testament, we cannot find normative texts relating to a definite form of church leadership. We are reliant instead on narrative texts that describe various models existing alongside each other in the early church. In what follows, I make no claim to offer a complete picture of the models of church leadership. I want instead to analyze certain models in relation to the worldview they are based on.

The *presbyterian model* derives the justification of its existence from how societies functioned in the ancient Near East, which honoured older people. The elders (Hebr. *zaqen*, Gr. *presbyteros*) are the leaders in society (Gen 50:7; Exod 3:16; Matt 16:21; 21:23; etc.). It is important to understand that this is not an indicator of age but an aspect of one's role. Therefore, in the societies around the Mediterranean where the first churches originated, the leaders were called elders. Luke notes that the apostle Paul appointed elders in the newly founded churches (Acts 14:23; 20:17). When Paul turns to the elders of the church at Ephesus, he gives them also other titles, in a synonymic perspective: "Keep watch over yourselves and over all the flock, of which the Holy Spirit has made you overseers, to shepherd the church of God that he obtained with the blood of his own Son" (Acts 20:28). Here Paul calls the elders "overseers" (Gr. *episkopos*) and links them with "shepherds" (Gr. *poimēn*). The title of pastor comes from the corresponding Latin word. We note that church leadership is regarded as team involvement with a variety of gifts. We also discover that the various terms are used synonymously. These two features indicate a relational approach. We have already seen that the societies around the Mediterranean were mainly relational, and are so today. By contrast, a collective functioning with a flat hierarchy, as observed below in the discussion of the congregational model, would be associated more with a rules-based approach.

The *episcopal model* understands leadership in terms of different levels, the leader of each being ordained or consecrated for that role. At the head of the hierarchy is the bishop, the "overseer" (*episkopos*), and on a lower level the

---

42. Cf. Hannes Wiher, *Holistic Mission: An Historical and Theological Study of Its Development, 1966-2011* (WEA World of Theology Series 25; Bonn: Culture and Science Publications, 2022).

deacon (*diakonos* "servant," cf. 1 Tim 3:1–13; Tit 1:5–9). Later the position of priest (*hieros*) was added to this hierarchy. This hierarchical structuring of church leadership follows the relational logic of the monarchy or "chiefdom," which prevailed in the animist and relational societies of the Mediterranean world. The Orthodox and Roman Catholic Churches, together with the Anglo-Catholic branch of the Anglican Church, place great value on the apostolic succession, considered of essential importance for the life of the church. Such a position has a time perspective towards the past, a feature which I have so far said little about (cf. sections 3.3.4 and 5.6.3).

Finally, there is the *congregationalist model*, which perceives the various Christian communities as autonomous and understands their leadership as democratically representative of the fellowship. As a result, the local church community chooses its leaders (cf. Acts 1; 6; 13:1–3) and the whole fellowship decides their destiny (cf. Acts 14:27; 15:2–3, 22). The congregationalist model correlates with the democratizing effect of the Lutheran concept of the priesthood of all believers. Those who favour this model regard the various terms for leaders as synonymous. The importance this model grants to the autonomy and democratic functioning of each fellowship is clearly a sign of a rules-based conscience, just as is the priesthood of all believers. Congregationalism naturally became widespread as Western societies became more rules-based (since the Reformation period).

In summary, the episcopal model reflects the relational framework of the feudal system. By contrast, the presbyterian model functions like a corporate body in the same way as a representative democracy, and the congregationalist model like a direct democracy. The first one reflects relational orientation, the last one rules orientation. With the exception of a short presence of the Presbyterian model in the early church, in church history we can observe a development from the episcopal model to the congregationalist model. It can be concluded that church leadership reflects the society of the period. Looking from another angle, we can perceive the development of a relational hierarchical structure into a more democratic form of leadership with a flat hierarchy, and hence more rules-based.

4.3.3 Counselling

Counselling is a further area of church life where the influence of worldview is very apparent. In discussing this sphere, I focus especially on those proposals which are trying to provide answers to questions of shame and guilt – those feelings which lie at the root of the two conscience orientations. One insightful resource is the approach of *strategic pastoral counselling* developed by Daniel Green and Mel Lawrenz. They argue that it is mainly psychoanalysts who deal with shame and guilt. Since psychoanalysis is a lengthy process and therefore difficult to access for most people, Green and Lawrenz propose a shortened scheme in five sessions, divided into three phases as summarized in Table 14.[43]

Table 14: Strategic Pastoral Counselling According to Green and Lawrenz

Phase 1	*Encounter and preparatory analysis* (session 1) Recognizing central problems and needs Pastoral diagnosis Defining a problem area acceptable to both sides
Phase 2	*Engagement* (sessions 2, 3, 4) Analysis of cognitive, emotional and behavioural aspects of the problem and ascertaining treatment options
Phase 3	*Disengagement and synthesis* (session 5) Assessment of progress and review of the remaining problems Referral (if required)

In the first session, the client and the counsellor make a survey of the problems and determine together which problem is to be tackled. In sessions two to four, they analyze the problem together and identify the client's resources and treatment options. In the final session an assessment of progress is made, together with a decision what to do next, possibly a referral to another therapist. In this shortened process, Green and Lawrenz pay special attention to resolving feelings of shame and guilt.

In their view, it is of the greatest importance to identify the perpetrator, the person who caused the feeling. For example, in sexual abuse the responsibility for the shame lies outside of the person suffering. By contrast, in a case of theft the perpetrator is both the locus and the cause of the feeling of shame or guilt. The process is similar regardless of on which side the responsibility lies, with the noteworthy exception that in cases where another person has caused the feeling and violated the boundaries of the self, as in cases of abuse, these boundaries must be restored (see Table 15).

---

43. Daniel Green and Mel Lawrenz, *Encountering Shame and Guilt: Resources for Strategic Pastoral Counselling* (Grand Rapids: Baker, 1994).

Table 15: Resolution of Feelings of Shame and Guilt

I am responsible	Someone else is responsible
Identification of responsibility Acceptance of responsibility Ownership of resulting emotions Confession of failure or wrong-doing Acceptance of forgiveness from God, the other person, and oneself Reconciliation and reparation	Reattribution of responsibility for the disconnection or wrongdoing Identification, ownership and resolution of all emotional reactions Restoration of the ego-boundaries Acceptance of love from another person Confrontation of the perpetrator (in person or symbolically) and confession of personal responsibility Acceptance of forgiveness from God, the other person, and oneself Reconciliation and reparation

With this model of strategic pastoral counselling, Green and Lawrenz have made an important contribution to overcoming shame and guilt. This is no longer simply the preserve of psychoanalysis, but is accessible to all involved in pastoral work.[44]

4.3.4 Communicating the Gospel

Having discussed interpretation and translation of the Bible, church leadership and counselling of believers in overcoming shame and guilt, I now turn to investigating the various aspects which need to be considered when we are communicating the gospel to others. I begin with some reflections on convergences and divergences of conscience orientation in intercultural communication of the gospel. I then, with the help of typologies of soteriology and personality, outline which forms of communication could be the most relevant with relational or more rules-based persons (cf. also sections 5.1.1 and 5.2.2). In actual practice, communicating the gospel will always consist of a blend of both conscience orientations. From another perspective, I examine

---

44. Cf. also David W. Augsburger, *Pastoral Counselling across Cultures* (Philadelphia: Westminster, 1986); David W. Augsburger, *Conflict Mediation across Cultures: Pathways and Patterns* (Louisville: John Knox, 1992); Edmund Ng, *Shame-informed Counselling and Psychotherapy: Eastern and Western Perspectives* (London: Routledge, 2020).

verbal and non-verbal communication, before concluding with a summary of the evangelism methods used by Jesus Christ.

4.3.4.1 Convergences and Divergences of Conscience Orientation

First, one must consider the problem of convergences and divergences between the conscience orientation of the communicator and of the conversation partner during intercultural communication of the gospel.

The content of the individual conscience depends on the cultural norms and values acquired in childhood during socialization. In an intercultural situation, one can expect both common and diverse content. In mission studies, we speak of convergences and divergences or continuities and discontinuities. Each participant is inclined to pass judgement on the other where he himself has a "good conscience." However, in this area the conscience of the other is "mute." Nevertheless, the conscience of each individual is close enough to God's benchmarks to serve as the first point of reference (Rom 2:1–16). Figure 8 portrays this situation schematically.

At the beginning of their encounter, the communicator (C) talks about biblical concepts with reference to the conscience of the conversation partner (P), especially that part of the conscience which is in agreement with biblical norms (upper two thirds of the grey area in Figure 8). It is advantageous to exclude the other areas at the beginning of evangelism and discipleship and to tackle them only in conjunction with teaching and counselling. These areas would probably alarm the conscience of the communicator, but not that of the conversation partner. Persisting with these areas would come up against lack of understanding on the part of the conversation partner, or would act as a challenge to accept the culture of the communicator. In such a case conversion would not rest on the conviction but on opportunism or blind obedience. The communicator would then have to stand guard, as it were, for an indeterminate period, making sure that this new and misunderstood culture was being complied with.[45]

In the next two sections, I describe evangelism from a rules-based or relational perspective. Then I briefly look at verbal and non-verbal communication. Finally, I will examine how Jesus Christ combines the two approaches in his evangelism.

---

45. Robert J. Priest, "Missionary Elenctics: Conscience and Culture," *Missiology* 22 (1994): 291–306.

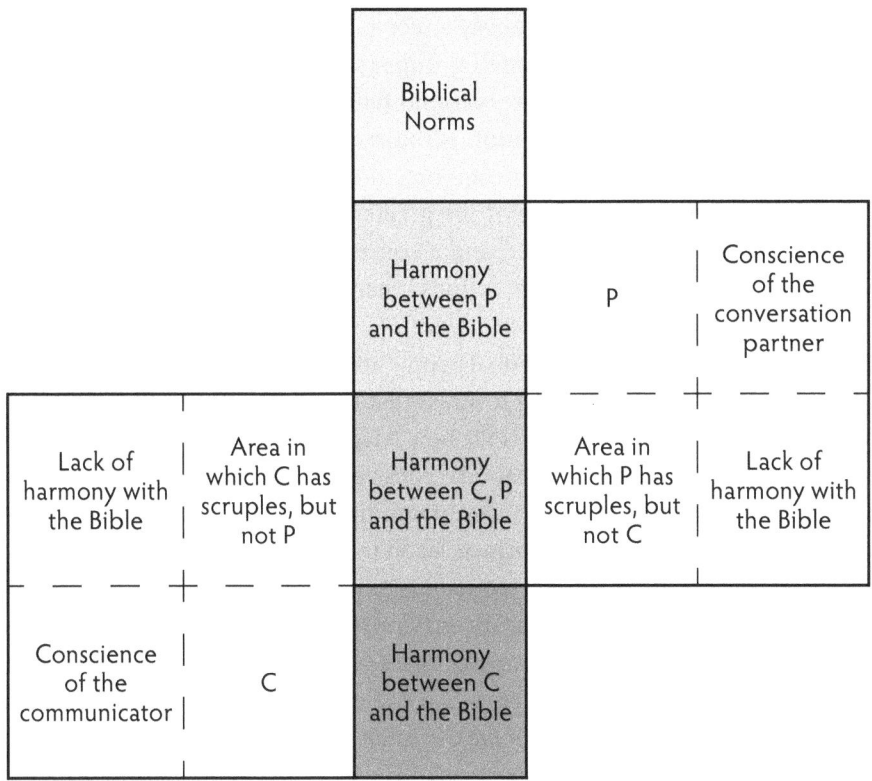

Figure 8: Convergences and Divergences of the Consciences

4.3.4.2 Rules-Based Evangelism

Rules-based communication of the gospel focuses on questions of *truth* and *right doctrine*. There are arguments in defence of the truth, such as are found in Paul's letters, and as understood and employed in apologetics. It is a *truth encounter*. The style of communication is normally verbal, and as such it is all about direct communication (John 3; Acts 2:38).

This communication points to the fact that God is true and just. Jesus Christ is the sacrifice through which we are justified (Rom 3:24–26). He is the ransom, the means of redemption, which pays the price of our guilt (Mark 10:45), and thus erases it through his grace (Matt 18:21–35; Luke 7:41–42; 16:1–5).

4.3.4.3 Relational Evangelism

In relational communication of the gospel, relationships have priority. The emphasis is on *persons* and not on truth. What is important is how we live – an authentic life of faith and a simple lifestyle. The communication occurs through dialogue, not on a one-way street as in preaching. Evangelism takes place among friends and in small groups (such as home cell groups). The style of communication revolves around telling biblical stories (a narrative approach). Verbal communication is indirect and pictorial, like that of the prophets and Jesus: parables, metaphors and riddles. In a relational context non-verbal communication is of the greatest importance: it consists of an attitude, a pattern of behaviour, and a communication expressing love and attention, e.g. through symbolic actions. There is also a place here for prayers for healing and release (*power encounter*).

In evangelism among relational people and cultures (animist cultures and Asian religions), it is important to stress that God is almighty, more powerful than other deities (Gen 17:1; Ps 96:4–5; 1 Kgs 18; Acts 13:11; 19:13–20). In addition, it is important for a relational conscience, where norms function only when the observant eyes of the attachment figure are present, that God is an ever-present partner, as he informed Jacob in Bethel (Gen 28).

With regard to Jesus Christ, one must emphasize that he is the almighty Lord (Phil 2:11), the victorious Christ (*Christus Victor*) of the church fathers who lived in an animist environment. Jesus is also the *mediator of reconciliation with God* (1 Tim 2:5; Luke 15:11–31), a subject treated by John Calvin in an important part of his *Institutes of the Christian Religion*. Jesus bore our disgrace on the cross (Heb 12:2). But the cross of Christ is an offence and foolishness (1 Cor 1:23). For Muhammad, it is unthinkable that Allah would allow such a great prophet to get into a situation of such great disgrace. And for Hindus and Buddhists, it is obvious that Jesus lacked positive *karma*, which is why he ended up on the cross. How could such a person bring us closer to *nirvana* if he himself lacked *karma*? Hindus and Buddhists find this ridiculous. Here the chronological Bible teaching becomes essential to explain the significance and necessity of the cross (cf. appendix 5). This places the conveying of the gospel within a process of both non-verbal and verbal communication.

4.3.4.4 Witness of Life and Witness of Truth

The witness of daily living represents the centripetal dimension of mission, because it attracts people. They would like to know why this or that person is different from other people. This is why the crowd followed John the Baptist and Jesus into the desert. Through the example of his life and his *non-verbal communication*, Jesus aroused not only people's curiosity but also a questioning attitude. In so doing he determined who in the crowd was really interested in the good news. To identify people with whom we can begin chronological Bible study together, we can put questions to those around us, or so-called

"Shema sentences."[46] Jesus advised his disciples to find people whom God has prepared, *people of peace* – people who receive the messenger and the message of the gospel favourably – and to stay with them longer in order to be more deeply effective (Luke 10:1–12; Matt 10:11).

Once questions had been evoked through non-verbal communication, Jesus continued with verbal communication of the gospel relating to the situation and context (*event speech*). The communicator of the good news must be able to answer questions and at the same time convey the gospel. How did Jesus do that? Jesus answered questions briefly or at length, being in good measure "salt of the earth." He used both direct and indirect communication. He involved himself in people's needs, feeding them or healing them – which we can summarize as quest for well-being – and he also answered the trick questions of the intellectuals (Pharisees) searching for truth. With the disciples on the road to Emmaus, he shared a perfect example of chronological Bible teaching to explain why the Messiah had to suffer, a key question for many people (Luke 24:44–46).[47]

How to stimulate questions?
- Through the example of our life
- Through Shema sentences, to find people of peace

How to answer the questions?
- Being salt in good measure
- Direct or indirect communication?
- Quest for well-being or truth
- Chronological Bible study

4.3.4.5 The Evangelism Model of Jesus Christ

To summarize, we can combine the different kinds of communicating the gospel, based on the particular conscience orientation, with the methods Jesus used in his evangelistic ministry. Of course, this schematic summary in Table 16 reflects a much more complex reality.

---

46. Shema sentences (from Hebrew *shema* "listen") are short sentences which can awaken curiosity.

47. Cf. Wiher, *Sharing the Good News*, ch. 5.

Table 16: The Evangelism Model of Jesus Christ

Ongoing non-verbal communication		
Jesus cultivates relationships and meets people's needs: *relational approach* ("relational encounter")	Being	Presence
Jesus involves himself in the struggles of people around him; he prays for the sick and frees the possessed: *antagonistic approach* ("power encounter")	Doing	Action
Verbal communication in favourable (kairos) moments		
Jesus explains his actions and answers questions evoked by his non-verbal communication (*event speech*). He engages in both dialogue and proclamation: *dialogical and kerygmatic approach* ("truth encounter")	Speaking	Words

Jesus spent his days among the parts of the population to whom he desired to proclaim the gospel. In this way, he came to know their needs and responded to those needs when they were brought to his attention. This was his *relational approach*. He also applied an *antagonistic approach*, consisting in the struggle against the forces of evil, as carried out in the healing of diseases and release from demons. Then he answered the questions of intellectuals and preached the gospel. This can be termed his *dialogical and kerygmatic approach*.[48]

4.4 Summary

In this chapter, I have analyzed the authors and the themes of Scripture to understand God's word better and produce an interpretive grid as a background for our reading of the biblical message which we want to pass on to the people around us. We have understood that God pursued a pedagogical approach with people, especially with the nation of Israel, in order to transform their originally animist worldview into a biblical one and raise their ethical level. Only in this way can they become a light and a blessing for the nations. God's intention for people is that they should function on both axes, relational and rules-based, and acquire a balanced conscience.

I then investigated the influence of the worldview of theologians on their theological work. I discovered that they prefer to deal with those aspects of a topic which agree with their worldview. They have a blind spot when it comes to elements which deviate from their conscience orientation; hence

---

48. Cf. Wiher, *Sharing the Good News*.

they unconsciously neglect these elements or deliberately blank them out of their theological writings.

Finally, I observed the effects of worldview on various aspects of church life, beginning with biblical interpretation and translation, then church leadership, the counselling of believers and the communication of the gospel. I have found that among the five models of worldview used when studying the deep structures of the Bible, theology and church life, the conscience orientation has proven to be the most fruitful model.

For Further Reading

Georges, Jayson, and Mark D. Baker. *Ministering in Honor-Shame Cultures: Biblical Foundations and Practical Essentials.* Downers Grove, IL: InterVarsity Press, 2016.

Richards, E. Randolph, and Brandon J. O'Brien. *Misreading Scripture with Western Eyes: Removing Cultural Blinders to Better Understand the Bible.* Downers Grove, IL: InterVarsity Press, 2012.

Wiher, Hannes. *Shame and Guilt: A Key for Cross-Cultural Ministry.* Bonn: Culture and Science Publications, 2003.

Wiher, Hannes. *Sharing the Good News: Evangelism in the Light of Scripture, Mission and Communication Science.* Nuremberg: VTR, 2024.

5

In-Depth Analysis of Personality, Culture and Religion

Having discussed the worldviews in Scripture, theology and church life in chapter 4, I now turn to persons, cultures and religions in the societies of our globe and apply the models presented in chapter 3 to analyze their worldviews. I then do the same with the worldviews underlying some other main features of world societies: the communication between the members of those societies, their models of leadership and their styles of managing conflicts. As in chapter 4, my approach remains very selective, giving priority to models that lend themselves to in-depth analysis.

5.1 Persons

The conscience orientation model enables one to compile a typology of personalities. In this section, I will present a typology that I have developed on this basis. I will then consider typical behaviour patterns of relational and rules-based persons and the origins of people's preference for functioning orally, audio-visually or in writing, and I will also relate this factor to conscience orientation. To conclude this section, I will offer some reflections on the bimodal functioning of the human brain, which provides a physical basis for the conscience orientation model, although, of course, conscience orientation itself derives from how children are socialized, not from brain functioning.

5.1.1 Typology of Personality

Classifications of personality types are useful if they help us understand people of different cultures and religions, without forcing them into stereotypes.

However, the danger always exists of falling into essentialism, or dividing people into categories without justifying those categories by careful and thorough individual analysis. In appendix 2, I have submitted some typologies which have been developed in the world of business and in mission, so that the reader can judge their relevance. In this section, I set forth my own personality typology, by reference to conscience orientation. It draws on the typologies presented in appendix 2, especially on the basic values model of Lingenfelter and Mayers.[1]

By adapting this model, the fifth one shown in appendix 2, combined with some elements of the other typologies, it is possible, with reference to conscience orientation, to define *two personality types on the basis of six pairs of basic values*. I will remove the pair of values of Lingenfelter and Mayers labelled crisis orientation and non-crisis orientation, which I have already established as located outside of conscience orientation, and rename them as past and future orientation with regard to how time is perceived. A future-orientated person anticipates crises, quite unlike a past orientated person (cf. section 3.3.4). However, as fundamental aspects of how the conscience functions, I add autonomy and heteronomy, labelling them *individualism* and *collectivism*; the former applies to rules-based persons, and the latter to relational persons. These opposing principles place the emphasis on the individual, and respectively on the community or the group. For the sake of clarity, I will remove questions of communication, leadership and decision-making from the typology of personalities and will discuss them in later sections (5.2 and 5.6). The two types of personality which I retain are summarized in Table 17 and described in more detail in appendix 3.

Table 17: The Personality as a Function of the Conscience

Rules-based Personality	**Relational Personality**
Individualism (individual identity)	Collectivism (group identity)
Punctuality orientation	Event orientation
Task orientation	People orientation
Achievement focus	Status focus
Analytic thinking	Holistic thinking
Courage to fail	Fear of losing face

---

1. Lingenfelter and Mayers, *Ministering Cross-Culturally*, 27–35.

In the context of the rules-based autonomy of the conscience, the personality is more likely to reveal itself as individualistic, time-oriented, keen on punctuality, task- and achievement-oriented, with a tendency towards the kind of analytical thought which underlies the development of science and technology, and not afraid to fail when taking up individual initiatives. By contrast, the relational personality is characterized by a preference for working on a team, has a group identity, is person-oriented, and strives for honour, prestige and status, with a tendency towards holistic thinking such as is typical of environmental protectionists. It fears the public prominence that comes with taking the initiative, because of the danger of losing face.[2]

I want to specify here that egoism and altruism cannot be attributed to one conscience orientation or the other. One could presume this on the basis of the relative autonomy of the rules-based conscience. However, narcissism can be an expression of a rules-based or a relational personality.

As models these two kinds of personality are simplifications of a complex reality. In sociological terminology, they are Weberian ideal types, representing a whole spectrum of personalities with a very mixed palette of values. The questionnaire in appendix 4 is intended to help readers to create their own personal profile in terms of basic values. Any person or culture should be able to place themselves within one or the other orientation with regard to certain values. As a result, this approach refines the simple, rough allocation of a person to one of the orientations. Values acquired in early childhood are rooted in deeper layers of the personality and are harder to alter than those internalized in adulthood. Nevertheless, the conscience orientation is subject to change throughout one's life. This means that one's personality profile can continue to develop until the end of life. The questionnaire should guide readers in getting to know their particular lens or "glasses" through which they perceive themselves and others, and in shaping more effectively how they convey the gospel through the cultural triangle.

Here is a personal example. I grew up in a relational family in a mountain village, where everybody knew everyone else. When about to embark on some activity, we always asked ourselves, "What will other people say?" Both my parents and all my siblings were relationally oriented. Hence, my socialization from early childhood enabled me to feel comfortable in a group context. It also meant that I was afraid of failing at any task and losing face. However, my time in Swiss schools taught me to be punctual and efficient in completing tasks

---

2. Cf. Lingenfelter and Mayers, *Ministering Cross-Culturally*, 30–34; Wiher, *Shame and Guilt*, 282–94, 428–34.

conscientiously and thinking analytically. I also learned to function and work effectively alone. Thus, school broadened my personality in regard to a number of rules-based abilities on top of my more deeply rooted relational layers. A Sri Lankan friend assessed my personality as 55 percent rules-based and 45 percent relational. Nevertheless, the more deeply rooted relational elements of my personality (group identity, status focus and fear of losing face) determine my basic orientation, despite the higher percentage of rules-based aspects. However, my rules-based elements have been further strengthened since the evaluation by my Sri Lankan friend and my return from Africa. The reason for this is the mainly rules-based work ethic of the majority of evangelical theological seminaries where I have taught.

5.1.2 Typical Behaviour Patterns of Rules-Based and Relational Persons

I include here a few examples of typical behaviour patterns.[3] For rules-based persons, it is normally acceptable:

- To officially confront others (and in so doing sometimes shame them);
- To refuse to let others avail themselves of one's resources;
- To expect borrowed items to be returned in immaculate condition;
- To express a negative opinion about others who bow to social pressure.

For rules-based persons, it is normally *not* acceptable:

- For someone to tell them what they should do;
- For social pressure to be used to make them conform to it;
- For their own property to be used without asking permission;
- For borrowed items not to be returned unless asked for.

For relational persons it is normally acceptable:

- To penalize people who take no responsibility for others in their group;
- To speak negatively about others who do not fit in;
- To take one's share when with others who do not voluntarily share with the community.

---

3. Cf. Heike Tiedeck, *Kulturen verstehen lernen: Wie interkulturelle Begegnungen gelingen können* (Nuremberg: VTR, 2018), 27–28.

For relational persons it is normally *not* acceptable:

- To fail to take responsibility for one another in the group;
- To fail to put those you are with under social pressure;
- To fail to share one's possessions;
- To do things which cause the group to lose respect;
- To finish the meal quickly and leave while others are still eating.

5.1.3 Preference for Functioning Orally, Audio-Visually or through Written Text

Following this brief look at some of the typical behaviour patterns of relational and rules-based persons, I will now consider in this section the fact that people have preferences for communicating and functioning either orally, audio-visually or through written text. I include this topic because of the special importance of reading and writing and literature in many societies and also in the traditional method of evangelism.

The traditional approach to conveying the message of the Bible has consisted in getting people interested in reading the Bible, and in teaching preliterate people to read and write. In the southern hemisphere, missionary societies set up extensive literacy programmes. It was a rules-based approach. Klaus Bockmühl (1931–1989) remarks that the oral dimension of faith has been marginalized since the Reformation.[4] The integration of relational peoples from the global South into world Christianity and the increased relational orientation of young Christians in the global North led to an awareness of many people groups' preference for oral functioning. In fact, this is the case for a majority of the world population (70 percent according to Lovejoy).[5]

> Preference for operating orally is a feature of most of the world's population.

In response, people began to reflect on how oral cultures function. This was foundational to the subsequent creation of the International Orality Network, a subgroup of the Lausanne Movement and the World Evangelical Alliance.[6] Its

---

4. Klaus Bockmühl, *Hören auf den Gott der redet* (Giessen: ABC-Team, 1990), 85–108.

5. Grant Lovejoy, ed., *Making Disciples of Oral Learners*, Lausanne Occasional Paper 54 (Lima, NY/Bangalore, Lausanne Committee on World Evangelization and International Orality Network, 2005).

6. Their website is https://orality.net. The publications of the network, including the *Orality Journal*, are available online, e.g. Lovejoy, *Making Disciples of Oral Learners*; Samuel E. Chiang and Grant Lovejoy, ed., *Beyond Literate Western Practices*, 3 vols. (Hong Kong: Capstone Enterprises, 2013, 2014, 2015).

first approach consisted in narrating biblical stories in a culturally appropriate way and with the necessary expert knowledge. N. T. Wright remarks in this regard:

> Stories are, actually, peculiarly good at modifying or subverting other stories and their worldviews. Where head-on attack would certainly fail, the parable hides the wisdom of the serpent behind the innocence of the dove, gaining entrance and favour which can then be used to change assumptions which the hearer would otherwise keep hidden away for safety.[7]

Besides telling biblical stories, the Orality Network developed theatre plays, dramatic sketches and pantomimes as well as films and artwork for presenting the biblical message. This led in a second step to the foundation of the Ethnodoxology Network.[8]

Beyond the preference for oral communication, the relational conscience also shows a preference for images, such as those offered by artwork and the internet. Studies in North American colleges have shown, for example, that the great majority of students are "audio-visual" learners, whereas their professors still prefer print media.[9] With regard to the communication of the gospel, Clyde Taber notes that after fifteen hundred years of preaching and five hundred years of print media the time has come to "portray" Jesus Christ in stories and images.[10] This transformation implies a change from a digital to an analogue communication mode with the consequence that the content of the message becomes fuzzier. Furthermore, the change leads from analytic to holistic thinking and from an individual, deductive and literary style to collective, inductive and audio-visual learning.[11]

The two networks for orality and ethnodoxology take account of the oral and audio-visual orientation of relational people and cultures. This is a completely new synthesis, taking up the model of conscience orientation and recognizing that different ways of functioning (oral, audio-visual, written)

---

7. N. T. Wright, *The New Testament and the People of God* (Minneapolis: Fortress, 1992), quoted in Lovejoy, *Making Disciples of Oral Learners*.

8. Cf. James R. Krabill, ed., *Worship and Mission for the Global Church: An Ethnodoxology Handbook* (Pasadena: William Carey Library, 2012).

9. Jay Moon, "I Love to Learn, But I Don't Like to Read: The Rise of Secondary Oral Learning," *Orality Journal* 2.2 (2013): 55–65.

10. Clyde Taber, "Contextualizing the Gospel in a Visual World," *Orality Journal* 2.1 (2013): 66.

11. Cf. Charles Madinger, "Coming to Terms with Orality: A Holistic Model," *Missiology* 38.2 (2010): 201–13.

relate to how the conscience operates and can coexist in one and the same person in the same way as one's value profile can contain values from both conscience orientations. This is, for example, the case with young people in the way they communicate via social media chat, which can be called "digital orality" (also secondary or modern orality).[12] Digital orality thus exists where literate people prefer audio-visual forms of communication but produce them in electronic media forms through lettered culture skills. Concerning this new phenomenon, Madinger remarks:

> From Baby Boomers onward, one trend is certain: the world is moving increasingly toward non-literate forms of communication for the diffusion of messages, even with (or perhaps especially with) the availability of today's advanced technologies.[13]

Any one of us, even if well educated, may prefer to follow the news on radio, TV or internet instead of reading a newspaper, or may listen to a book such as the Bible in an audio or audio-visual format instead of reading it. So what matters is to analyze how an individual, a subculture or a social group function in order to select the suitable approach – oral, audio-visual or written. The understanding of orality (and digital orality) as an aspect of the relational conscience enlarges the notion of orality to include different learning and leadership styles, as well as indirect forms of communication such as music, theatre and styles of worship, which are studied by ethnodoxology.[14]

5.1.4 The Bimodal Functioning of the Brain

In considering the development of conscience orientation in chapter 2, we noted that the anthropologist Melford E. Spiro devised a theory of the deep layers of the person based on childhood development, or how persons are socialized (cf. section 3.3.3). According to this theory, siblings with the same parents should develop an identical conscience orientation. In reality, there are different or even opposed orientations within the same nuclear family. What is the reason for this? Spiro developed his theory at a time when science believed

---

12. Samuel E. Chiang, "Editor's Note." *Orality Journal* 1.1 (2012): 8; idem, "Three Worlds Converged: Living in an Oral, Literate, and Digital Culture," in *Worship and Mission for the Global Church: An Ethnodoxology Handbook*, ed. James R. Krabill (Pasadena: William Carey Library, 2012), 179–83, https://orality.net/resources.

13. Madinger, "Coming to Terms with Orality," 211.

14. Cf. Hannes Wiher, "Worldview and Oral Preference Learners and Leaders," in *Beyond Literate Western Practices: Continuing Conversations in Orality and Theological Education*, ed. Samuel E. Chiang and Grant Lovejoy (Hong Kong: Capstone Enterprises, 2014), 109–25.

that the environment was the chief factor influencing personal development. Today, we know that genetic endowment and the environment have roughly equal influence on how a person functions.

What can we conclude from this about the physical basis of conscience orientation? Neuroscientists have discovered that the two halves of the brain do not function in the same way as the two kidneys or lungs do; rather each half of the brain has its own preferred function.[15] I have attempted to summarize the bimodal functioning of the brain in Table 18.

Table 18: Functions of the Two Hemispheres of the Brain

Left Hemisphere	Right Hemisphere
Analytic thinking	Holistic thinking
Abstract	Concrete
Partial perception	Complex perception
Separation	Integration
Verbal communication	Non-verbal communication
Digital communication	Analogue communication

The centres underlying analytic and abstract thought are located in the left hemisphere, together with the centres housing linguistic ability. The left hemisphere supports a partial perception of reality, whereas the right hemisphere tends towards holistic and concrete perception and thinking. In addition, spatial orientation and understanding of images and metaphor are located on the right side. This clearly means that in some way the left hemisphere supports rules orientation, whereas the right hemisphere could underlie relational orientation (cf. appendix 3).

The result of the competing influences of genetic endowment and the environment, of physical underpinnings and socialization, is that a relational upbringing can perhaps work against the dominance of the left hemisphere, or vice versa. However, the two conscience orientations do not coincide perfectly with the two brain functions. On the other hand, there is sufficient convergence between the two models for practical purposes.

---

15. Lingenfelter and Mayers, *Ministering Cross-Culturally*, 51–64; Rita Carter, *Mapping the Mind* (London: Weidenfeld & Nicolson, 1998; rev. ed.: Berkeley: University of California Press, 2010).

5.2 Communication

Drawing on this analysis of persons, we will next look at how people communicate with each other. If conscience orientation influences the personality, it must necessarily influence the style of communication. In this section, I will first consider the most important models of communication, then summarize the effects of conscience orientation on communication, and finally mention some examples of communication in the Bible and in intercultural situations.

5.2.1 Communication Models

In examining the communication models, we can observe a development from the linear to the circular, from the partial to the whole, and from the technical and rules-based to the relational. I begin with *psychoanalysis*, which postulates that communication develops essentially from unconscious intrapsychic processes. The conscience orientation model was created on this basis.

I then consider the *code model*.[16] This model originates from the cognitive framework of engineering science and structuralism, which analyzes processes and structures to discover the essential elements common to all communication events: the sender; the selection and encoding of the message; the medium; the selection and decoding of the message; and the receptor. The model therefore looks for those codes which are common to the communicator and the receptor. In so doing, it limits itself to words (signs, codes) – the cognitive aspects of communication. This mathematical and linear model has greatly stimulated mission studies. This is where we find the origin of the formal and dynamic equivalence approach which is widespread in Bible translation.

Next I consider the *speech acts theory*, which maintains that every communication is an act which alters relationships, and that speaking is doing.[17] It claims that every kind of speech has a performative function. I relate this concept to the Hebrew word *dabar* "word (in action)."

The next stage in the development of communication models is the inclusion of context through the *relevance theory*.[18] It includes the observation that the meaning of a communication is construed through cognitive activity

---

16. Warren Weaver and Claude E. Shannon, *The Mathematical Theory of Communication* (Urbana: University of Illinois, 1963).

17. John L. Austin, *How to Do Things with Words* (London: Oxford University Press, 1955).

18. Dan Sperber and Deirdre Wilson, *Relevance: Communication and Cognition* (Oxford: Blackwell, 1986).

common to the communicator and the conversation partner on the basis of contextual information. The relevance principle implies an optimal relationship between the effort involved in understanding the message and the gain in knowledge of the conversation partner.

Finally, the *systems theory* understands communication as a whole in terms of relationship.[19] It is the first model to include the emotional and evaluative aspects of communication. According to this theory, communication means defining a relationship, affirming one's own identity, negotiating one's own position, influencing the conversation partner, sharing feelings and values, and meaning in the broadest sense. Adopting systems theory means definitively giving up simple and linear models. One instead embraces circular and complex systems which do not discount instability, fluctuation, chaos, disorder, vagueness, openness, creativity, contradiction, ambiguity and the paradoxes of reality.

The application of systems theory to communication is at the origin of the slogan "*We cannot not communicate.*" The communicator, a key agent in the relationship, becomes an integral part of the communication. Systems theory which introduces the concept of the two levels of communication: the content and the relationship. Here we find the two conscience orientations. Since the relational aspect of communication includes the content (its informative aspect), the relational dimension of communication is *metacommunication*. Systems theory teaches us that the capacity for satisfying metacommunication is the condition for good communication. If metacommunication sends a message antithetical to the content of the communication, we call this state of affairs a *paradoxical communication*. The result is a pathological relationship.

> We cannot not communicate.

Thus, beginning with an analytic perspective limited to conveying information, restricted to essential elements common to all communication processes and leading to rules of communication, we have arrived at a relational theory of communication which is very fuzzy, full of paradoxes, and with a minimum of rules. With regard to this development from a rules-based concept of communication to a relational approach, it is interesting that during the same period of time, the second half of the twentieth century, one can perceive a similar development over time, from the rules-based pre-war generation to the relational X, Y and Z generations. The same phenomenon

---

19. Paul Watzlawick et al., *Pragmatics of Human Communication: A Study of Interactional Patterns, Pathologies, and Paradoxes* (New York: W. W. Norton & Co., 1967).

can be observed in the reflections on mission in the Lausanne Movement: there is a progression from a debate about the relationship between evangelism and social responsibility, a two-tiered concept of conveying the gospel, to a holistic concept of mission (cf. section 4.3.1.5).[20] I will return to this development later when discussing the generations and the transition from modernity to postmodernity (cf. section 5.3.3 and 5.3.5).

5.2.2 Communication as a Function of the Conscience

Like personality, communication can also be understood as a function of conscience orientation, whether it is rules-based or relational communication. These two ideal types of communication are also connected with direct and indirect communication, and with verbal and non-verbal communication. I have set out the effects of the two conscience orientations on communication in Table 19.

Table 19: Communication as a Function of the Conscience

Rules-Based Communication	Relational Communication
The essence of the message is communicated through precise utterances	The essence of the message is supported by a mutually recognized context
Minimal awareness of context	Strong awareness of context
Little non-verbal communication	Much non-verbal communication
Silence is suspect	Silence is acceptable
One must say "yes" or "no"	One seldom says "no"; a "yes" can mean "no"
One must say what is true, even when it hurts	One must maintain a harmonious relationship
Conflicts in relationships are normal	Conflicts in relationships are to be avoided
Conflict is brought into the open and discussed frankly	Conflict is hidden and not mentioned
One must know how to accept direct criticism constructively	Direct criticism ruptures the relationship; confrontation is to be avoided

---

20. Wiher, *Holistic Mission.*

Rules-Based Communication	Relational Communication
One must not lie	One must not lose face
Tendency to talk too much in an unfamiliar group and to listen little	Tendency to listen a lot in an unfamiliar group and say little
The focus is on solutions and actions	The focus is on relationship and trust
Linear reasoning	Cyclic reasoning
A mediator is viewed as a disturbing hindrance to (direct) communication	One needs a mediator for important communication and conflict resolution

To illustrate, here is how a friend described to me the way her brother communicates with her: "When I ask my brother how he is, he says 'Good.' And when I talk with him about sport, weather and politics, he gives me a detailed answer over half-an-hour long." My friend's brother is definitely a person who is receptive to indirect, relational communication.

5.2.3 Examples of Communication in the Bible

In general terms, the context of the ancient Near East can be described as animist, and its conscience orientation as relational. In this section, I offer some examples of how communicators in the Bible were attuned to communicating in this way.

In the Old Testament, God used mediators to communicate in an animist and relational context: the patriarchs, Moses and the prophets. The prophets used vivid imagery in their communication: lament (Amos 5:1–2), accusations (Amos 5:18; 6:1), proverbs (Amos 3:3–6), riddles (Amos 2:9; 3:12; 5:2, 7, 19, 24), symbolic names (Hos 1:3–9), symbolic actions (Hos 1:2–3; 3:1–2; Ezek 4; 12:1–20) and metaphors (Ezek 16). They employed indirect, non-verbal communication, appropriate in a relational environment.

In the New Testament, Jesus similarly communicated through images and parables. The context of the Mediterranean should also be viewed as animist and relational. But in addition, Jesus communicated according to the orientation of his conversation partner. With the Pharisee Nicodemus, he was very direct and rules-based (John 3). By contrast, with the relational Samaritan woman, Jesus proceeded in a very relational manner (John 4).[21]

---

21. Cf. Wiher, *Sharing the Good News*.

5.2.4 Examples of Intercultural Communication

I spent my final year of medical study with a colleague at a training hospital in Tanzania. We lived in the same house as the nursing staff and sang together in the gospel choir. We decided to invite a few friends to dinner on a Saturday evening. They gladly accepted. Several times we checked that the date and time suited them: Saturday at 6:00. On that Saturday, we very much enjoyed preparing quite a special meal. But no one turned up. At 8:00, we sat down to eat the now cold food on our own.

What had gone wrong in the communication between our friends and ourselves? We had not been able to receive the refined non-verbal signals of our friends. We Europeans are accustomed to conveying the main message verbally. But in Tanzania the main message is wrapped up with non-verbal signals, especially if it is delicate or painful. If we had been able to receive the message through their channels, we would have recognized their facial expressions, their gestures and their evasive answers.

During our mission work in Africa, we missionaries had periodical conferences with the church leadership. These often began hours later than planned. Before we could begin, all participants had to be present. Since they came by public transport, turning up late was the rule rather than the exception. Then there were hours-long discussions. Often we reached the point where all the Africans suddenly stood up. Astonished, the Europeans would ask whether we ought not first to come to a final decision. Equally astonished, the Africans would reply that a consensus had indeed been reached and so the conference was over.

What was the problem here in communication? This consensus was only accessible non-verbally. This was another example of how the Africans exchanged non-verbal signals which we Europeans could not perceive. We were waiting for a decision to be made in a formal way, whereas the Africans had registered their agreement and considered the conference to be at an end.

At other conferences, it sometimes happened that after various votes by both parties, the church president summarized a basic consensus verbally. It was then not unusual for a European to introduce an additional nuance, to which the Africans reacted with surprise. Why? In a relational society, the votes follow one another in ascending rank order. After a concluding and summarizing final vote by the highest-ranking person, no further opinion should be given.

There was a Bible translator living among the Deni Indians in the Brazilian rainforest. He brought them regular radio messages by plane and asked them to clear the runway so that the plane could safely land and take off. Most of the village inhabitants helped with the work. He wanted to pay them according to the amount of time and quality of their work. But since he didn't live in the village, he didn't know who had joined in the work and for how long. So he asked the village chief to repay each person according to their contribution. During the distribution, however, the more aggressive workers took more than their due. The others complained to the chief and also to the Bible translator.[22]

What was the problem? The Bible translator assumed that the Deni Indians were organized according to a hierarchy and that the chief had authority over the workers. But the latter were independent with regard to work. Communal working only happened when they were clearing the forest. Then each person specified how much land he could cultivate. For the Bible translator, the best way to proceed would have been to divide the runway into sections. Then each worker could have decided for himself how many sections he could work on, and wages could then have been allotted on an individual basis.[23]

5.3 Societies

Having considered how individuals have different ways of functioning and communicating, I will now do the same with reference to societies, that is, people in groups. Clearly, there are certain parallels in how individuals and societies function. The "Culture and Personality" School in San Diego in the USA focused particularly on this topic. It is at the core of the new scientific discipline of social psychology. Melford E. Spiro, whom we have already referred to in chapter 2, is a representative of this school. According to this school, the parallels between personality and culture indicate that the prevailing worldview represents the majority orientation of a population, but not that all members of a society subscribe to it. A society will always contain people with a divergent orientation.[24] To fully cover a particular culture, an analysis of its worldview must target individuals. Generalizations about social layers, e.g. generations, communities or religions, only provide general indications and must always be interpreted with reservations. This holds true all the more today, as in the course of history societies have increased in complexity and are now often fragmented.

It is therefore with caution that I now apply the typology of personalities to historical and contemporary societies. I begin with a typology of societies in terms

---

22. Sherwood G. Lingenfelter, *Transforming Culture: A Challenge for Christian Mission* (Grand Rapids: Baker, 1992), 59–68.

23. Tiedeck, *Kulturen verstehen lernen*, 36–37.

24. Cf. e.g. Melford E. Spiro, "Social Systems, Personality, and Functional Analysis," in *Studying Personality Cross-Culturally*, ed. Bert Kaplan (New York: Harper & Row, 1961), 93–128.

of their conscience orientation, and then I work through the major historical epochs: the Middle Ages, the Renaissance, the Reformation, baroque, romanticism, modernity, postmodernity (or late modernity), the phenomenon of globalization and the generations of the twentieth and twenty-first centuries in the West.

5.3.1 Typology of Societies According to their Conscience Orientation

Table 20, analogous to the typology of personalities discussed above, sets out a typology of societies by reference to their conscience orientation. We must again bear in mind that these are Weberian ideal types, representing abstractions of the extreme, between which there exists in reality a whole spectrum of mixtures of societies. Although the typology I will be developing is essentially determined by conscience orientation, I will also include the layers model of the order of creation and the soteriological concepts in the analysis of societies.

Table 20: Typology of Societies According to their Conscience Orientation

Rules-Based Society	**Relational Society**
Fragmented view of the world: separation between the material and the spirit world or no notion of a spirit world	Holistic worldview: unity of material and spirit world; harmony between the living and the living dead (ancestors)
Justice and law as main principles	Honour for elderly and ancestors
People want to live according to law	People want to live in harmony with others
"Bounded set"	"Centred set"
Egalitarian society	Hierarchical society
Achievement focus, efficiency of people and institutions	Status focus
Analytic thinking	Holistic thinking
Individual identity	Group identity
Salvation as correct behaviour towards God	Salvation as welfare, affluence and harmony
Sin as breaking the law	Sin as violation of harmony
Forgiveness as reparation for the infringement	Forgiveness as reconciliation and reintegration (through a mediator)
Punishment through payment	Punishment through humiliation

A *rules-based society* predicated on the layers model will typically possess a fragmented worldview, that is, a two-tiered or a secular worldview. Its principles will be justice and law. Its limits will be well defined; missiologically speaking, it will be a "bounded set."[25] In such societies, the response to certain situations will be simply: "Rules are rules; nothing can be done about it!" A person's rights will hold an important place. These are typically egalitarian and often democratic societies. Its members will be individualistic, their most important values being punctuality, efficiency and achievement, along with analytical thinking. They create the foundation for the development of science and technology. Their notion of salvation will be correct behaviour towards God. Sin will be regarded as breaking the law and forgiveness as reparation. Punishment is seen in terms of fines or deprivation of liberty.

Relational societies typically have a holistic worldview. Their principles are harmony in relationships and honour for the elderly and for ancestors. People will say, "We've always done it like that." Through this respect for tradition, there is a connection between conscience orientation and past perspective. Many such societies have a hierarchical structure. Persons in authority have great influence. Divergent behaviour is not welcomed: anything of that sort must be nipped in the bud. Relational societies are "centred sets" in which all members will pursue the same values. Such societies function on a relational basis, so rules are of little importance; in a sense, the rules are there to be broken. The members think holistically and promote ecological and social issues. Salvation is viewed in terms of welfare, affluence and harmony, but sin as violation of harmony, and forgiveness above all as social reconciliation. Punishment normally consists of humiliation – events evoking shame.

5.3.2 Historical Epochs

In this section, I will attempt to give a brief historical survey, which cannot avoid some degree of generalizations. I would not normally recommend this approach, preferring to apply the models of my analysis to individual persons. But drawing mainly on the results of the San Diego Culture and Personality School in the USA and on the later development of social psychology, I will look for parallels between personalities and societies. My aim is to discover a general orientation in the interpretation of the different historical epochs.

---

25. Cf. Paul G. Hiebert, *Anthropological Reflections on Missiological Issues* (Grand Rapids: Baker, 1994), 111–36.

I have already mentioned my analysis of the *ancient Near East* and *Mediterranean* world at the *beginning of the Christian calendar* as an animist and relational environment. As an example of the relational conscience of the ancient Near East and Mediterranean world, the victors in war deliberately humiliated the kings, commanders and soldiers of the opposing armies. Such events are also recorded in the Old Testament, e.g. placing one's foot on the necks of conquered kings (Josh 10:24), or cutting off the king's thumbs and big toes to mark him for the rest of his life with a shameful and visible disability (Judg 1:6–7). In the Roman Empire, the emperors led vanquished armies in a triumphal procession across the Forum in Rome to humiliate them. In the New Testament, a similar description is given to depict the victory of Jesus over demonic forces (Col 2:15; Luke 20:43 quoting Ps 110:1). Believers will join in this triumphal procession with Christ, the great victor (2 Cor 2:14).

When the animist Germanic peoples of Europe adopted Christianity, this did not significantly change their worldview, especially as during this process several elements of Germanic culture were integrated into *medieval Christianity*, as a number of historians have discovered.[26] Nevertheless, the christianizing of animist societies caused the worldview of certain medieval personalities to become two-tiered after the manner of Neoplatonism. This led to the integration of certain rules-based elements into social and church life, such as indulgences, because every sin had to be paid for. But for the most part, the societies of Europe up to the beginning of the modern period were mainly relational.

The *Renaissance* (fourteenth and fifteenth centuries) was characterized mainly by a relational conscience orientation. Their representatives made portraits and physical depictions and took initiatives aimed at discovering the human body and its functions.

The *Reformation* (sixteenth century) brought an important change: it was strongly influenced by a rules-based conscience orientation, which is very present in the Bible. The doctrine of justification influenced the conscience of certain people. According to Max Weber's thesis, a sense of duty, so greatly esteemed by Calvinism and later by Calvinist Puritanism, brought about the economic and scientific developments of Europe and North America.[27] However, this thesis has been criticized by many authors.

---

26. E.g. James C. Russell, *The Germanization of Early Medieval Christianity: A Sociohistorical Approach to Religious Transformation* (New York: Oxford University Press, 1994).

27. Max Weber, *The Protestant Ethic and the Spirit of Capitalism*, ed. Richard Svedberg (Los Angeles: Roxbury, 1905, 1996).

The *Baroque* (1575–1770) and *Romanticism* (1795–1835)[28] eras can be understood, in a certain sense, as counter-currents of modernity, which we will cover in the next section. They were characterized by a predominantly relational conscience orientation. Their leading figures of these eras liked to make portraits and representations of the body. Pleasure and personal well-being were valued in contrast to Calvinist and Puritan ethics which was built on duty. The emphasis on love, nature and the unconscious was clearly an antithesis to the reason and intellectualism promoted by the Enlightenment. It is here that pietism must be located, and with it the origins of evangelical piety.

5.3.3 Modernity and Postmodernity

The changes which took place in Europe during the Renaissance, the Reformation, the Enlightenment and industrialization, known as the *modern period*, promoted a secular worldview. Drawing on Neoplatonism in general, the church ingested into its understanding of Christianity a two-tiered perspective on the world. During this period, the typical European inclined increasingly towards efficiency, task orientation, achievement and punctuality. The importance of philosophy and science encouraged analytical thinking. In general (and according to the logic of an ideal type), the modern period produced people with a rules-based conscience profile. Thus, the statement "I feel guilty" can, after several centuries of rules-based modernity, even convey a feeling of shame.

In the second half of the twentieth century, a current emerged which, depending on the particular science and perspective, is termed *postmodern*, hypermodern, ultramodern or late modern. The debate around the interpretation of this new current continues. In the opinion of philosophers and sociologists, it has to do with a radicalization, an acceleration or a crisis of modernity. Their preferred term is late modernity. On the other hand, psychologists and anthropologists detect a profound change as the postmodern has superseded the modern current.

Luc Ferry observes three reactions to this crisis of modernism, which could be perceived as three currents of postmodernism:[29] (1) a *return to the pre-modern tradition* (from a theological perspective, this would be the "orthodox"

---

28. In the field of painting, Romanticism lasted until the end of the nineteenth century, and for music even into the early twentieth century.

29. Luc Ferry, *Homo æstheticus: L'invention du goût à l'âge démocratique* (Paris: Grasset, 1990), 311–19.

response with which one could associate a section of the evangelical movement); (2) an attempt at *deconstruction* (e.g. Jacques Derrida and Thomas Altizer),[30] and (3) an attempt at *reconstruction* (from the point of view of theology and the church, one could include here process theology and the missional church movement).[31] With regard to the stance taken by the evangelicals in response to this crisis, the French religious sociologists Jean-Pierre Bastian, Françoise Champion and Kathy Rousselet make the following interesting observation:

> The evangelical focus . . . appears to be a paradox: it consists of a polarized response to a certain kind of cultural modernity and to the homogenising of globalization, while at the same time harmonising perfectly with the new forms of communication which enable their worldwide development and which indeed form one of the most important factors of that homogenization.[32]

Thus, the postmodern currents reveal themselves in a great variety of ways. First, we must affirm that the concepts of modernism and postmodernism are complex and vague. But we must also bear in mind that during a cultural change, elements of continuity and discontinuity exist side by side. If we have this in mind, we should not be surprised that the researchers have a variety of perspectives. A focus on achievement, efficacy and punctuality, and an emphasis on individualism and analytic thinking reveal a rules-based conscience. At the same time, anthropologists and sociologists have observed a shift from a rules-based conscience among the pre-war and post-war generations to an increasingly relational conscience among today's generations and the deconstruction of the "grand narratives" (cf. section 5.3.5).[33] Theologians talk about a crisis of truth.[34] On one hand, one would be forced to speak of the continuity of features of rules-based modernism, and, on the other hand, of a new era with a relational conscience. But even during modernity, the typical profile of persons in Europe consisted of a blend of both orientations.

---

30. E.g. Jacques Derrida, *Dissemination* (London and New York: Continuum, 1981); Jacques Derrida, *Margins of Philosophy* (Brighton: Harvester Press, 1982); Thomas J. J. Altizer, *Living the Death of God: A Theological Memoir* (Albany: State University of New York Press, 2006).

31. Process theology contradicts the classical view that God is unchanging by insisting that God is in some respects temporal. The missional church movement insists on the missional dimension of the church. Its advocates work on the involvement of churches in local evangelism.

32. Jean-Pierre Bastian, Françoise Champion and Kathy Rousselet, ed., *La globalisation du religieux* (Paris: Harmattan, 2001), 16.

33. E.g. Jean-François Lyotard, *The Postmodern Condition: A Report on Knowledge* (Minneapolis: University of Minnesota Press, 1985).

34. E.g. David F. Wells, *No Place for Truth* (Grand Rapids: Eerdmans, 1993) and *Above All Earthly Pow'rs: Christ in a Postmodern World* (Grand Rapids: Eerdmans, 2005).

In the next two tables, I have attempted to reduce the complexity of the current debate to a simplified typological appreciation of the modern and postmodern periods. In Table 21, I compare them as opposing currents.

Table 21: Typological Analysis of Modernism and Postmodernism

Modernism (rules-based)	Postmodernism (relational)
Fragmented worldview	Holistic worldview
Priority of intellect, masculinity, work	Priority of emotions, femininity, relationships
	Anti-authoritarianism
	Pluralism, relativism, tolerance

In Table 22, I have listed the main features of postmodernism as a countercurrent to modernism according to the chief contribution and emphasis of the scientific disciplines.

Table 22: Features of Postmodernism by Scientific Discipline

Postmodern Features	Science
Pluralism, relativism, tolerance	Philosophy
Generation X and later ones, anti-authoritarianism	Sociology
Holistic worldview, relational conscience	Cultural anthropology

Before concluding this section, I need to comment on the difference between "modern" and "postmodern" theories, which I described in the introduction to the three basic concepts (personality, culture, religion) in the second chapter (cf. section 2.1). Whereas functionalism and structuralism have their origin in modern thinking, constructivism can be ascribed to postmodernism. Four models of worldview (the layers model, the five soteriological concepts, time orientation and mana) are predicated on "modern" concepts (functionalist and structuralist ones). The model of conscience orientation, whether rules-based or relational, brings the two approaches, modern and postmodern, together by blending the structuralist and the poststructuralist perspective and going beyond it.

5.3.4 Globalization and Hybridity

During the second half of the twentieth century, coinciding with late modernity (or postmodernity), the phenomenon of globalization emerged. The latter brought a continually increasing global interconnectivity, which was interpreted in two ways: in terms of homogenization and fragmentation.

Theories of homogenization proceed on the assumption that globalization makes cultures more and more similar. In describing this phenomenon, George Ritzer introduced the term "McDonaldization" of society.[35] In the same vein, there is talk of the "gospel of McD, Disney and Facebook" as a way of describing the unifying of thought and the cult of efficiency and profitability, of show business, and the importance of external appearances. In the Christian context, international and transnational services offer their strategies to the whole world. For example, the proponents of Campus for Christ claim that their "four spiritual laws" are applicable as tools for worldwide witness. Centres of theological and liturgical production such as Hillsong and Bethel, world bestsellers such as *The Shack* and *Moments with Jesus*,[36] and preachers such as Joel Osteen, Joyce Meyer and others can influence believers throughout the world. On the other hand, the fact that they write and preach from an affluent Western perspective has not encouraged theological thought about suffering and the capacity to endure.

Theories of fragmentation point out that globalization strengthens differences, tensions and intercultural conflicts, leading to an identity crisis. Samuel Huntington's *The Clash of Civilizations* is perhaps the best-known example of such a perspective.[37] Among many theological observers, especially Western ones, the rise of so-called contextual theologies has also caused the fear of a fragmentation of theology into several regional theologies, which would ultimately lack the necessary universality of a message the all-embracing import of which one wishes to maintain.

Globalization is leading to a breakup of societies, further encouraged by the influx of migrants. This not only increases the mixture, but also the tendency towards relational orientation, for migrants from the South and East live and act mostly in a relational way. In sociological terms, this intermingling within the context of globalization can be described as a hybridity of cultural and religious phenomena, which can trigger an identity crisis.

---

35. George Ritzer, *The McDonaldization of Society* (Thousand Oaks, CA: Pine Forge, 1993).

36. William P. Young, *The Shack* (London: Hodder & Stoughton, 2007); Bill Johnson, Eugene Luning et al., *The Moments with Jesus Encounter Bible: 20 Immersive Stories from the Four Gospels* (Bethel, CA: Destiny Image Publishers, 2021).

37. Samuel P. Huntington, *The Clash of Civilizations and the Remaking of World Order* (New York: Simon & Schuster, 1996).

5.3.5 The Generations of the Twentieth and Twenty-First Centuries in the West

With regard to the twentieth and twenty-first centuries, sociology perceives a sequence of different generations, first in American society, and then also elsewhere.[38] When the theory of generations claims that there are differences between the generations – a fact which is contested – it must be noted that within any generation there is considerable diversity. This means that we actually note differences between the average values of various generations. It is generally true that individuals develop independently in contemporary fragmented societies and shape their own values and goals; so these must be individually analyzed. The classification and characterization of the generations can vary from author to author and can diverge considerably and increasingly towards contemporary generations. In Table 23, I am presenting a simplified classification of generations, and in Table 24 places the changes in their context.[39]

Table 23: Chronology of Generations in the West

Name	Alternative Names	Year of Birth
Pre-war generation	Boosters	1925–1945
Post-war generation	Baby boomers	1946–1965
Generation X	Busters	1966–1980
Generation Y	Millennials	1981–1995
Generation Z	Zoomers	1996–2010
Generation Alpha		2011–2025

---

38. Cf. Douglas Coupland, *Generation X: Tales for an Accelerate Culture* (New York: St. Martin's Press, 1991); William Strauss and Neil G. Howe, *Generations: The History of America's Future, 1584 to 2069* (New York: Quill, 1992); Kath Donovan and Ruth Myors, "A Generational Perspective into the Future," in *Too Valuable to Lose: Exploring the Causes and Cures of Missionary Attrition*, ed. William D. Taylor (Pasadena: William Carey Library, 1997), 41–73; Gary L. McIntosh, *Make Room for the Boom . . . or Bust: Six Church Models for Reaching Three Generations* (Grand Rapids: Revell, 1997); Marc McCrindle and Emily Wolfinger, *The ABC of XYZ: Understanding the Global Generations* (Sydney: University of New South Wales Press, 2011), https://mccrindle.com.au; James E. White, *Meet Generation Z: Understanding and Reaching the New Post-Christian World* (Grand Rapids: Baker, 2017); Jolene Erlacher and Katy White, *Mobilizing Gen Z: Challenges and Opportunities for the Global Age of Missions* (Pasadena: William Carey Library, 2022).

39. McCrindle and Wolfinger, *The ABC of XYZ*.

In-Depth Analysis of Personality, Culture and Religion 157

Table 24: Changes in the Western Context

Generation	Events	Technology	Cars	Music	Toys
Pre-war generation (1925–1945)	World War II (1939–1945)	Radio	Model T Ford (1927)	Record player (1948)	Roller skates
Post-war generation (1946–1965)	Moon landing (1969)	Television (1956)	Ford Mustang (1964)	Audio cassette (1962)	Frisbee
Generation X (1966–1980)	Stock market crash (1987)	Computer IBM (1981)	Opel Rekord (1978)	Walkman (1979)	Rubix cube
Generation Y (1981–1995)	September 11, 2001	Internet email SMS	Toyota Prius (1987)	DVD (1995) iPod (2001)	BMX bike
Generation Z (1996–2010)	Global financial crisis (2008)	Laptop Google Facebook Twitter	Tesla Model S (2012)	Spotify (2006)	Folding scooter
Generation Alpha (2011–2025)	Trump Brexit (2016)	Instagram Meta	Autonomous vehicles (2020)	Smart speakers (2020)	Fidget spinner

Below, I reproduce the characteristics of the generations in a simplified way and conclude with a typological analysis of their worldviews and conscience orientations.

The pre-war generation (born 1925–1945; boosters):
- Attainment of peace and security;
- Improvement of living conditions;
- Work is more important than family;
- Loyalty and stability;
- Prefers working individually to being in a team;
- The chief means of communication is the telephone;
- Mostly task-oriented individualists; conscience is distinctly rules-based;
- The last generation to fully reflect the modern era.

The post-war generation (born 1946–1965; baby boomers):
- Belief in technology and the future;
- Idealists: ecology, world peace, focus on the Majority World;
- Tolerant of abortion and homosexuality;
- Intolerant of inefficiency and incompetence;
- Questioning of authority, morality and tradition;
- Work is still more important than family (*workaholics*); in work they are team-oriented and career-conscious, with a structured way of working;
- Basic values: health, idealism, creativity;
- The chief means of communication is the phone, later e-mail;
- Generally rules-based with some relational orientation;
- Positioned between the modern and postmodern approaches.

Generation X (born 1966–1980; busters):
- Initially it was the unknown generation (X);
- Focus on fun ("fun generation") and events;
- Friends and family are more important than work;
- Vital importance of communication; especially e-mail and mobile phone;
- One has to be "cool"; cult of the body;
- Pluralism, relativism, tolerance;
- Basic values: "soft individualism" (independence combined with interdependence), search for meaning;
- In the workplace: independent, flexible, focused on results, technologically savvy, sharing power and responsibility, interested in work-life balance;
- Anti-authoritarian;
- The first generation to be mainly relational (pleasure, family, communication) and less rules-based (individualism, direct communication, anti-authoritarian attitude). Having had little confrontation with norms during socialization, members of generation X may be deficient in conscience development ("lacking feelings of shame and guilt");
- Generation X is therefore wholeheartedly representative of postmodernism as the counter-current to modernism.

Millennials (born 1981–1995):
- Also referred to as generation Y;
- The characteristics of generation X are more strongly apparent among millennials: focus on pleasure and events, priority of friends and family, great importance of communication (the smartphone), being "cool," selfies, cult of the body;
- Millennials have grown up with the smartphone and social media and are therefore more technology savvy (digital natives) and capable of multi-tasking;
- Millennials tend to be autonomous, while remaining mutually dependent in their peer group ("soft individualism," generation I and we). They have an open attitude to spiritual matters, while remaining unattached in regard to religion and politics (maybe generation). They are pragmatic, ecological and open towards multi-ethnic communities;
- Basic values: networking, teamwork, self-realization;
- Work must be fun: demand for a private life, but more work-life blend than work-life balance;
- Chief means of communication: smartphone, web 2.0;
- Millennials could be characterized by the following key words, which partly reveal inner paradoxes: free, sharing, digital, option, procrastination ("postponeitis");
- Millennials tend to be even more relational than generation X. Their lack of conscience development can be more marked than in generation X (a conscience "without feelings of shame or guilt"), partly because they have grown up in families where both parents worked and had little time for them.

The characteristics of the two following generations are still very incomplete and tentative, because of lack of hindsight and lack of studies with sufficient large cohorts, they are not yet defined well enough.

Generation Z (born 1996–2010; zoomers):
- They are the first generation to grow up in a globalized world, that means in the "everything, everywhere, all at once" mentality;
- Demanding, impatient, and conscious of health and ecological issues; self-realization is the priority;
- The zoomers tend to be even more relational than generation Y. Their deficits in conscience development can also be more marked than in generation Y.

Generation Alpha (born 2011–2025):
- They are the first generation born entirely during the twenty-first century; they are fully in the digital age;
- Even more relational than generation Z. The deficits in conscience development can be more marked than in generation Z.

In the field of spirituality, we can make similar observations. The spiritual life shifts from a strict rules-based discipline towards a rather chaotic life of faith. In Table 25, I summarize the contours of the spirituality of consecutive generations.

Table 25: Spirituality in Western Generations

	Spirituality and Pastoral Care	Motivation for a Commitment	Length of Commitment
Pre-war generation (1925–1945)	Discipline: "no Bible, no breakfast"; is pastoral care necessary? I have the Lord.	Call of God; do what God has prepared for us	Do God's will; commitment for a lifetime
Post-war generation (1946–1965)	Battle for regular meditation: "I have a lot to do"; pastoral care may help	Help underprivileged persons; work according to my gifts	Reserve a time for God; choose a particular project (job description)
Generation X (1966–1980)	Thirst for deeper spiritual life; pastoral care is necessary	Information on the task to be accomplished; work according to my gifts	Reserve a time for God; choose a particular project (job description)
Generation Y Millennials (1981–1995)	Thirst for deeper spiritual life; pastoral care is necessary	Information on life conditions; help people	Reserve a time for God; choose a particular people
Generation Z (1996–2010) & Generation Alpha (2011–2025)	Thirst for deeper spiritual life; pastoral care is necessary	Realise my potential	Reserve a time for God; choose a particular people

Pastoral care becomes increasingly vital for survival. Decision making for a commitment develops from a call of God towards an altruistic relational motivation, the perspective therefore moving from the vertical towards the horizontal. The duration of the commitment is shortened from generation to generation. In the field of employment, especially non-governmental organizations and mission societies, short-term commitments have been created.

Table 26 summarizes the main features of the members of these generations as well as the generational characteristics.

Table 26: Main Features of Western Generations

Generation	Main Features	Generational Characteristic
Pre-war generation (1925–1945)	Individualist workers (workaholics)	Last generation of modernity
Post-war generation (1946–1965)	Idealists: ecology, world peace, focus on Majority World	Post-1968 generation
Generation X (1966–1980)	Team workers, fun generation, work-life balance	First generation of postmodernity
Generation Y, Millennials (1981–1995)	multi-tasking, generation me and we, maybe generation, work-life blend	First generation of digital natives
Generation Z (1996–2010)	Everything, everywhere, all at once	First entirely global generation
Generation Alpha (2011–2025)		First generation to be entirely born in the twenty-first century

During the twentieth century, we can observe a development away from a rules-based conscience towards an increasingly relational conscience. At the same time, there has been a transition from a two-tiered worldview to a holistic one. As a consequence of the growing hybridity of societies in the context of globalization, an analysis of each individual in a society is necessary in order not to fall into the trap of undue generalization. This means that the generalizations concerning the generations, which I have set out in this section and summarized schematically in Table 27, should be interpreted with caution. They do nevertheless offer a general explanatory framework.

Table 27: Worldviews of Western Generations

Generation	Two-tiered Worldview	Holistic Worldview	Rules-based Conscience	Relational Conscience
Pre-war generation (1925–1945)	+++		+++	
Post-war generation (1946–1965)	++	+	++	++
Generation X (1966–1980)	+	++	+	++
Generation Y (1981–1995)	+	+++		+++
Generation Z (1996–2010)		++++		++++
Generation Alpha (2011–2025)		+++++		+++++

5.3.6 An Encounter on the Bus

To illustrate possible differences between generations, here is an everyday event:[40] An elderly man on his way to work sits down on a bus beside a teenager who has placed his feet on the nice new upholstery. After a moment's reflection, the elderly man attempts to influence the young person to behave according to the norms. "You have put your feet on the upholstery!" is shrugged off with "So what!" The point that his shoes might have dog dirt on them, and that this could be bad not only for the upholstery but also for the next passenger, is met with the response, "My shoes are clean." Continuing with softened voice, so that no one else could hear, the man then asks, "Do you also do that at home?" and receives the answer, "My parents are for it! Okay?" The man decides to take a drastic but effective measure. He addresses the other passengers, saying: "Just look at that. This young man ..." And already the feet are down and stay there. Why? Rules-based attempts by a rules-based functioning elderly man are of no avail. The relational conscience only responds when exposed and threatened with loss of face.

---

40. Cf. Lothar Käser, "Angewandte Anthropologie in Deutschland aus der Sicht von Afrikanern und Asiaten," *Evangelikale Missiologie* 17.3 (2001): 91–94, 94.

5.3.7 Being a Single Woman in Egypt

To conclude this reflection on the characteristics of different societies, both historically and in the present, here is the experience of Heike Tiedeck as a single woman in Egypt, in her own words:[41]

> I spent a year in England studying Arabic and Theology. This involved an intensive course at a language school in Cairo. Together with a fellow woman student, I looked for somewhere to stay for two months. We found lodgings in the house of a family. The elderly owner lived below with his wife and adult unmarried daughter, and we were above. We were now his daughters, said the old man when we moved in, and we were pleased with that.
>
> At the beginning of our studies, the language school organized a party, beginning at 9 o'clock in the evening. We only needed to cross a big road to get there. The next day the old man paid us a visit, wanting to know where we had been off to the previous evening. We told him, while realizing from that moment on that we were being watched.
>
> Somewhat later, I received a telephone call from one of the women teachers at the school. This was before there were any mobile phones. She rang the number of the family, who informed us that the call was for us, so that we could then lift the receiver. I spoke English with the teacher. Hardly had the call ended when the old man appeared again, asking why I had received a call from an Egyptian man. My reaction was one of incomprehension. Apparently, the teacher, who had a somewhat deeper voice, had introduced herself in Arabic when she rang and asked to speak with me. Since I, unlike my fellow student, was not yet married, I was now under special surveillance.
>
> The third occasion brought me to tears. I had a female acquaintance in Cairo and wanted to visit her. So I had to phone her. In the house where she lived, there was only the one house phone, answered by the caretaker. So I had to explain in Arabic that I wanted to speak to this particular person. When I got back from the visit, I was berated by the old man. He had listened in to my telephone conversation with the caretaker and once again drawn his (wrong) conclusions. Fortunately, the acquaintance

---

41. Tiedeck, *Kulturen verstehen lernen*, 37–38.

phoned again later and explained the situation, so my reputation was saved.

That was Heike Tiedeck's experience as a single woman in a relational, Muslim, and hierarchically organized society where it was not customary for single women to live outside the family. She was immediately put under the guardianship of her landlord and monitored, the purpose being to avoid any loss of honour and any damage to the reputation of the family.

5.4 Religions

This section discusses the influence of religions on the behaviour of individuals and societies. Worldview is once again the obvious starting point. I will first consider the cultural and religious system lying at the root of all other cultural and religious systems: animism. I will then look at the worldviews and identities associated with the religions, with reference to the layers model of the order of creation and the conscience orientation.[42]

5.4.1 Animism

I regard animism as the cultural and religious system underlying the development of all other religions. I have indeed already mentioned this, in chapter 4 (cf. sections 4.1.3.3 and 4.1.7.2). Among other things, we find indications of this in many commonalities between animism and other religions, e.g. purity regulations, sacrifices, representations of deities, and the mediators between the visible and invisible world. This biblical reference is also relevant: "Formerly in Israel, anyone who went to inquire of God would say, 'Come, let us go to the seer'; for the one who is now called a prophet was formerly called a seer" (1 Sam 9:9). The seers, diviners and necromancers are the mediators with the invisible world in animism. Moreover, the Bible and cultural anthropology agree that religions are human products, "works made by human hands" (e.g. Ps 115:4). From this, we can assume that the different versions of animism began to develop after the fall.

In this section, I will first examine the advantages and disadvantages of the different terms employed in referring to animism, before dealing with some definitions and classifications. I will then describe the animist worldview and

---

42. Cf. Hannes Wiher, *What Do You Believe? Learning to Understand Religions* (Carlisle: Langham Global Library, forthcoming).

its concept of a person. I base my development largely on Lothar Käser's book on animism.[43]

5.4.1.1 Terminology

The expression used most frequently in the English-speaking world for animism is *traditional ethnic religions*. The allusion is to so-called traditional societies, formerly preliterate, today often marginal. The problem with this description is that traditional religions are not just an ancient phenomenon from the past but remain very apparent in contemporary societies.

The scientific community has generally retained the term *animism*. It derives from the Latin *anima, animus*, which in the Roman world indicated a personal spirit being that is believed to accompany a person's body throughout life. Its presence is important for maintaining the vital functions of the body, and it survives the death of the body. Indeed, the concept of the "soul" is central to traditional religions. However, the problem with this term is that animism comprises far more than a concept of the "soul." It is a worldview and a comprehensive cultural and religious system.

In evangelical circles, there is often talk about the occult. The term is derived from the Latin *occultus* "hidden." Hence, it alludes to phenomena which are hidden from the (superficial) knowledge of the West and which are studied today by the sciences of parapsychology and anomalistics.[44] Indeed, animist people groups have a much more detailed and profound awareness of these things than Western populations.

The terms *esotericism* (from the Greek *esoteros* "within, the inner") and New Age are, in my opinion, Western designations for animism. The New Age is an expression which came into use towards the end of the twentieth century to sum up various currents of esotericism. It alludes to the Age of Aquarius, in which humanity will supposedly recognize its psychic and spiritual potential and its inner and universal peace. Both currents are characterized by an inner turnaround expressed in an individual, multifaceted and syncretistic spirituality.

---

43. Lothar Käser, *Animism: A Cognitive Approach* (Nuremberg: VTR, 2014).

44. The term was coined in 1980 by the anthropologist Robert W. Wescott. This links him with Thomas Kuhn, who regards as anomalies results of observations which seem to contradict earlier theoretical notions and assumptions about the world. Robert W. Wescott, *Introducing Anomalistics: A New Field of Interdisciplinary Study* (Deerfield Beach: Kronos, 1980); Thomas S. Kuhn, *The Structure of Scientific Revolutions* (Chicago: University of Chicago Press, 1962) and *The History of Science* (London: Routledge, 1977).

5.4.1.2 Definition and Classification

Animism can be viewed as a set of strategies offering answers to people's questions and solutions to the problems of human existence. It features a belief in the existence and effectiveness of spirit beings which manifest themselves in human or animal form and command knowledge and abilities beyond human capacity. These beings are not merely spirits (in the narrower sense of the word), but also the "souls" of persons, animals and objects. Animism is more than a religion: it comprises a worldview with conceptions pertaining to the natural sciences (physics, chemistry, botany and medicine), social sciences (psychology, sociology), humanities (philosophy), and theology. Animism is also more than a belief in demons. We have ample evidence that animist systems have existed for thousands of years. If they were completely demonic, they would have been destroyed a long time ago.

There are tens of thousands of variations of animism, but two main types can be distinguished. In type one, found among nomadic groups (hunters and gatherers), there is no veneration of ancestors. For them, after death, the soul becomes an evil spirit being. The mediator with the invisible world is the shaman, who goes into a state of ecstasy and *sends* his soul out in order to make contact with his spirit aids. This kind of animism is predominant in North and South America and Asia.

Type two, found among settled groups (peasant farmers), does include veneration of ancestors. According to their view, after death, the soul becomes a benevolent spirit being and continues to be a member of the family (an ancestor). The mediator with the invisible world is the medium, who goes into a trance and *is visited* by the spirits of the ancestors. This type of animism is present in Africa and Europe. In India and China, there is a blend with both shamans and the veneration of ancestors, on account of the immigration of nomadic groups.

5.4.1.3 The Animist Worldview

In animist understanding, the world consists of (1) material beings and objects and (2) spirit beings and objects. The latter are invisible, except in dreams and trances. They are called *spirit doubles.* This means that mountains, rivers, waterfalls, trees, villages, persons, animals, statues and masks all possess their own spirit double. These two "worlds" are separated neither geographically nor in time, and they are profoundly dependent on each other. However, spirit beings have more power and more significance. That is why they are venerated. Hence, there is a hierarchical ordering. People seek harmony with spirit beings as well as with the dead (the ancestors in type two described above), often through gifts and blood sacrifices. Animist systems are therefore predominantly relational and holistic cultural and religious systems.

5.4.1.4 The Animist Concept of the Person

Historically Europeans, drawing on Greek ideas, have distinguished two ways of thinking about the composition of the person: body and soul (*bipartite*) and body, soul and spirit (*tripartite*). Animist cultures, on the basis of their worldview, have a different concept of the person: the body is accompanied by its spirit double. In the literature, the latter is also called the "free soul" or "dream ego," because during a dream it leaves the body for the purpose of its own undertakings. If the spirit double is away from the body for a long time, the latter becomes tired, then ill, then comatose, and eventually dies. This happens particularly if a specialist in accessing the invisible world (a shaman or a medium) puts the spirit double out of action.

Animist cultures locate the seat of the emotions, intellect and character (abbreviated SEIC[45]) in one of the large organs (heart, liver, bowels, etc.) of the body and also in the SEIC of the spirit double. In many cultures, the heart is the location. Among the Greeks, it was also the bowels and the midriff (diaphragm). This is why Jesus, when moved with compassion, uses the Greek word for having a bowel movement (*splanchnizomai*, e.g. Matt 14:14). Among North American First Nations, the scalp was removed and burned if one wished to destroy the "soul" definitively, together with the body. The ancient Egyptians, for whom the perspective of eternal life was very important (as seen in the pyramids), considered burning bodies alive as the corresponding method for people's complete elimination, including their memory. According to the animist conception, the body is accompanied by three spirit beings, or in a sense by three "souls": its SEIC, located e.g. in the heart, and its spirit double, furnished with its own SEIC. So the composition of the person could be described as "quadripartitite."

It is evident that in the course of mission history the terms for spirit doubles were changed through contact with Christianity into SEICs, the seat of a person's moral character. This can be observed through the Greek terms (*psychē, pneuma*), the Latin ones (*animus, anima, spiritus*), and also the Indo-Germanic ones. For example, the German word *Seele* (soul) is composed of *See* (lake) and the particle *l*, indicating affiliation. Among the animist Goths, the term referred to water spirits (spirits of the dead). Through Christianization the term became a SEIC, indicating the invisible part of the body, or in other

---

45. SEIC is an acronym for the Seat of the Emotions, Intellect and Character.

words a "soul." The origin of this transformation lies in the translation of the Bible into Gothic by the missionary Ulfilas (Gothic Wulfila "little wolf"), who rendered the Greek word *psychē* with the Gothic *saiwalō*, the predecessor of the English word *soul* and the German *Seele*.[46]

In retrospect, it is clear that the Europeans falsely interpreted the Greek animist notions when they classified these different terms, for they all describe the invisible part of the body and can be regarded as synonyms. The adoption of these terms for the soul by the European Indo-Germanic people groups introduced a degree of confusion into the well-ordered concepts of the soul (SEIC and spirit double) in the languages of animist people groups. Table 28 presents schematically the corresponding concepts in English, Hebrew and two languages of originally animist African peoples (Malinke and Kikongo).

Table 28: Classification of Terms for Soul in Four Languages

Function	English	Hebrew	Malinke	Kikongo
Seat of the emotions	soul	*leb*	*sondomē*	*ntima, moyo*
Seat of the intellect	mind	*leb*	*sondomē*	*ntima, moyo*
Seat of the character	?	*leb*	*sondomē*	*ntima, moyo*
Immortal part of the person (spirit double)	soul	*ruah*	*nii*	*mfumu kutu*
Spirit being	spirit	*ruah*	*nii*	*mfumu kutu*

In Hebrew, Malinke and Kikongo, the SEIC is located mainly in the heart (*leb, sondomē* and *ntima* respectively). The immortal part of the person (the spirit double) and a spirit being are described with the same term: *ruah, nii* and *mfumu kutu* respectively. In the Kikongo language, the situation is somewhat more complicated. The Bakongo people live along the estuary of the Congo River. During the five hundred years since their first encounter with Christianity, the word for spirit double, *moyo* "breath," has changed into a SEIC, approximating to *ntima* "heart." The term for another spirit double, *mfumu kutu*, literally "chief of the ear," has for the most part disappeared during those five hundred years. With regard to most of the other regions, the length of time since the first in-depth contact with Christianity has been less than one hundred and twenty years. According to Käser, at least five generations, or

---

46. Cf. Hans-Peter Hasenfratz, *Die Seele: Einführung in ein religiöses Grundphänomen* (Zürich: Theologischer Verlag, 1986), 88–93.

about one hundred and twenty-five years, are required for the transformation of the notions of the soul.

5.4.2 Religions and Their Worldviews

Having presented animism as a foundational cultural and religious system, I now turn to the religions in terms of their underlying worldviews. Table 29 presents the religions in relation to the layers model and their conscience orientation.

I begin with religions which have a *holistic worldview*. These are the closest to animism, with very similar relational systems. This means that as in animism, cultural and religious elements are interwoven in their structures. In the holistic worldview, the universe is an integrated whole. Examples of holistic cultural and religious systems are Hinduism (which succeeded Indian Brahmanism) and Shintoism in Japan. We can assume that within their living environment they developed from animism.[47] Daoism and Confucianism, Chinese philosophies which grew out of Chinese animism,[48] likewise can be classified as holistic worldviews. Finally, we must also mention Chinese (Mahayana) and Tibetan (Vajrayana) Buddhism and the folk religions.[49]

---

47. However, Hinduism also has a philosophical component.

48. According to Luc Ferry, "Philosophy is always the secularization of a religion." Thus, Daoism and Confucianism would be a secularization of the Chinese religions (with a significant animist component). Theravada Buddhism would be a secularization of Hinduism, just as Platonist and Aristotelian Greek philosophy would represent a secularization of Greek animism. Ferry, *La tentation du christianisme*, 100.

49. A folk religion is a blend of an institutional religion and animism.

Table 29: Religions and Their Worldviews

	Relational Conscience		Rules-based Conscience	
	Holistic Worldview	**Hebrew Worldview**	**Two-tiered Worldview**	**Secular Worldview**
Layers of Creation		God		*Invisible aspect excluded*
	Supreme being		Spirit	
	Spirit beings Ancestors	Spirit beings Angels	*Middle sphere excluded*	
	Humans Animals Plants Matter	**Humans** Animals Plants Matter	**Humans** Animals Plants Matter	**Humans** Animals Plants Matter
Religions & Philosophies	Animism Hinduism Shintoism Daoism Confucianism Chinese and Tibetan Buddhism Folk Religions	Judaism Christianity Islam	Plato	Aristotle European Enlightenment Sri Lankan and Thai Buddhism

The *Hebrew worldview* also emerged from a holistic (animist) worldview. We can find evidence for this in Genesis, Exodus and Deuteronomy. These books affirm that God is the creator of the universe. But as opposed to animist deities, the biblical God is distinct from his creation, and is therefore "holy" (cf. Gen 1–2; Deut 19:2). Islam as a reform movement of Judaism and Christianity still orders the building blocks of creation in the same way as the Hebrew worldview. However, in other aspects of their worldview, such as regarding the five soteriological concepts, there are clearly significant differences between the Islamic and the biblical worldview. In the layers model of creation, the Hebrew worldview reflects the aspect of the biblical worldview which takes account of the structuring of creation. Together with the holistic worldview, the Hebrew perspective belongs to the relational worldviews. As already mentioned, beyond being essentially holistic, the biblical worldview also contains some important dichotomies, e.g. creator and creation, body and soul, light and darkness, etc.

The *two-tiered worldview* separates the material and visible world from the immaterial and invisible one. Plato's philosophy provides an example. It represents a fragmented perspective on the world and is predominantly rules-based. In medieval Roman Catholic Europe, influenced by Neoplatonism, the "middle sphere" was blocked out of the worldview.[50] This is the sphere which the spirit beings (including the ancestors) are believed to inhabit and which, in the animist worldview, is responsible for diseases and misfortunes. Hence, in the animist worldview, this sphere determines daily life, and as such it also influences the folk religions.

The philosophy of the Enlightenment, which is the source of the *secular worldview*, went a step further, blocking out everything invisible in the world. It only takes account of what can be observed and measured. Hence, it is also very much a fragmented worldview. The main ideas of Enlightenment philosophy are correlated with Aristotelian philosophy. In Asia, representatives of a secular worldview reflect the original philosophies of Confucius and Buddha. The latter corresponds to Sri Lankan and Thai (Theravada) Buddhism. They follow the original teaching of the Buddha, which is in principle a materialist philosophy. Later, both philosophies adapted themselves to the holistic Chinese worldview. During this process, Theravada Buddhism morphed into the so-called Buddhism of the Great Vehicle (*mahayana*), by integrating various elements of Chinese animism, Confucianism and Daoism.

Clearly, persons who convert from Hinduism or from a secular society to the Christian or Islamic faith cannot change their worldview overnight. Sustained instruction is required until the imprinting acquired in early childhood can be transformed. Also, several of these ideal types of worldviews can be present in one and the same person. As a Christian, I have a Hebraic worldview in relation to the layers model. But through my socialization in a European society and through my education, I have incorporated some two-tiered and secular elements into my worldview. These diverse worldviews are influential in different situations of my daily life: when I am ill, I am inclined to take medicine, a decision prompted by my secular worldview. But because of my biblical worldview, I am also impelled to pray. My two-tiered worldview allows me to continue working, although I know that I ought to take it easy.

As Table 29 shows, most religions express a holistic worldview. With regard to conscience orientation, holistic worldviews focus on relationship and harmony. Hence, the way we encounter animists and adherents of Asian

---

50. Paul G. Hiebert, "The Flaw of the Excluded Middle," *Missiology: An International Review* 10.1 (1982): 35–47; Hiebert et al., *Understanding Folk Religion*, 89–91.

religions needs to be similarly oriented: relational, holistic, and looking for harmony.

The worldviews of the folk religions, which are a blend of an institutional religion and animism, are determined primarily by their animist aspects, for according to the animist worldview disease and misfortune are caused by spirit beings. Since most believers throughout the world belong to these forms of folk religions, they have a holistic worldview.[51] As well as being holistic and anthropocentric, the animist worldview has, with regard to the five soteriological concepts, a socially defined concept of sin and a concept of salvation in terms of prosperity. Concerning conscience orientation, the animist worldview is relational and person oriented, focused on acquiring status, holistic in thought, with an "and-and" logic. This kind of reasoning has no difficulty combining contradictory matters – for example practising two religions simultaneously both of which demand total allegiance. That is why animists and adherents of folk religions have no problem with patterns of behaviour which an "either-or" logic would classify as syncretistic.

With regard to the conscience orientation of religions, some are almost exclusively relational, some maintain a balance between being relational and rules-based, and some are rules-based. In presenting the religions in this way, I always think in terms of Weberian ideal types.

5.4.2.1 Relational Religions

Religions in this group include animism, folk religions and Indian religions. The last of those contains Hinduism, to some extent a formalized Indian animism. However, it also contains a philosophical component, the *brahman-atman* philosophy, based on cosmic unity and harmony, which is developed in the songs of the Bhagavad-Gita. The relational religions of Eastern Asia include Shintoism, to some extent Japanese animism, and the Chinese religions. In the Chinese category are Daoism, which teaches cosmic harmony, and Confucianism, which is a theory of social harmony. Both religions began as philosophies, a secularization of Chinese animism, and then adapted to the Chinese worldview, which is relational and holistic. At the beginning of the Christian era, Buddhism arrived in China and developed the so-called Great Vehicle (*mahayana*), which absorbed the relational and holistic Chinese worldview. As a typical expression of such a worldview, it values inner harmony.

---

51. Cf. Hiebert et al., *Understanding Folk Religion*.

5.4.2.2 Balanced Relational and Rules-Based Religions

In chapter 3, we saw that the Bible offers a balanced conscience orientation, both relational and rules-based. Hence Judaism, and Christianity (as a reform movement of Judaism) have a relational and rules-based focus. This is also true of Islam as a reform movement of Judaism and Christianity. Sri Lankan and Thai Theravada Buddhism, as a reform movement of Indian Brahmanism, remain relational, but as a protest movement of Brahmanism they have moved towards being rules-based. Since Theravada Buddhism has largely disregarded the invisible aspects of the universe, it maintains its link with animism in order to complete its fragmented worldview. This folk expression of Theravada Buddhism is represented by the Hindu statues integrated into the temples of Sri Lankan Buddhism, and similarly by the "spirit houses" erected next to human dwellings in Thailand.

5.4.2.3 Rules-Based Philosophies and Religions

The philosophies and religions underlying two-tiered and secular worldviews (those of Plato, Aristotle and Sri Lankan Buddhism), have given rise to rules-based conscience orientations. This is especially true of the philosophy of the European Enlightenment.[52]

5.4.3 An Offering for the Smallpox Goddess

I conclude this brief reflection on religions with a story from South India at the time of a smallpox epidemic.[53] The drugs administered by the doctor in a government hospital seemed to have no effect on the progression of the disease. After the death of several children, the elders of Muchintala, a small village to the south of Hyderabad, called a diviner, hoping that he could discover the cause of the epidemic. In his opinion, Misamma, the smallpox goddess, who lived in a rock under a tree near the village, was dissatisfied because at the last festival five years ago only two goats were sacrificed instead of a water buffalo. Moreover, she expected a festival every three to four years.

When the elders heard that, they immediately initiated a collection to raise funds for a proper sacrifice. In due course, their messengers came to Venkayya and his brothers, who had converted to Christianity three years ago. Venkayya told the messengers that as a Christian he could not contribute to the village

---

52. Cf. Wiher, *What Do You Believe?*

53. Cf. Paul G. Hiebert and Frances F. Hiebert, *Case Studies in Missions* (Grand Rapids: Baker, 1987), 126–28.

offering. The elders, who all belonged to a high caste, were enraged when they heard of the disobedience of Venkayya and his brothers, who belonged to no caste and were thus untouchables. They summoned the resisters and explained that they had nothing against them for praying to the God of the Christians, that everyone was allowed to worship their god. Misamma, they said, was not a deity of the heavens like Rama, Allah or the God of the Christians. She was an earth spirit and lived in a rock. Even the Muslims would contribute to the offering.

When Venkayya insisted that he and his brothers could not contribute to the offering, the elders criticized his disobedience and his lack of solidarity and accused him of becoming a danger to the village. The following day the envoys of the elders prevented Venkayya's wife from drawing drinking water and water to irrigate the rice fields. They also denied her access to the shops so she could not buy anything.

Finally, Venkayya's daughter also caught smallpox. What was he to do now? The missionary in the next village, to whom they turned for advice, also insisted on not contributing to the offering. But did he understand the situation Venkayya and his brothers were in? Could they not ask God to heal the girl and at the same time pay the contribution for the village offering? Wasn't the contribution more like a village tax than an offering to a goddess? Venkayya had many questions. From the perspective of an outsider, one can well imagine that the missionary, probably rules-based, could have difficulty in understanding the effects the relational and hierarchical environment of Hinduism, with its emphasis on solidarity, could have on the life of a Christian. If you were in Venkayya's place, what would you decide to do?

5.5 Analysis of the Cultures and Religions of the World

Having considered people and their communication, societies and religions, I now attempt an analysis of the world's cultures and religions in order to provide us with an overview, and because I wish to create a general orientation framework for individual analysis. I believe this analysis can be useful despite the previously expressed limitations of generalizations.

Readers will note that these different analytical grids are useful not only in an obvious context of intercultural mission, but also in the world of work or even in the functioning of a local church since in these contexts also an increasing mix of subcultures and influences is taking place, notably through the internet.

In general, I proceed from deeper to more superficial levels. I begin by looking at the deepest layers of each worldview, using the model of conscience orientation. First, I examine the religions involved, beginning with the religious system underlying them all, animism, and its variants (Esotericism, New Age), followed by the institutional religions (Hinduism, Buddhism, Judaism, Islam, Christianity). I turn next to the particular historical epochs (modernity, postmodernity, globalization with its hybridity). As a second step, I employ cognitive (more superficial) models, namely the five soteriological concepts, the layers model of creation and time orientation. As a third step, I then proceed to the level of the societal sphere or even the individual. According to the particular situation, the sequence can be adapted.

To begin with, I analyze the general conscience orientation of a world region and combine this with religion. In Africa, animism is the basis of societies and cultures. African societies are thus predominantly relational and have a holistic worldview. Depending on the region, Islam or Christianity is the dominant religion. Generally speaking, these two religions have adapted to the relational basis, often in the form of a folk religion, by accepting animist elements. In South Asia, Hinduism is the foundation of society, and in Southeast Asia, it is local animism together with Buddhism. All these are relational religions, with the exception that Theravada Buddhism has a strong rules-based component. As we have already noted, Theravada Buddhism had to be complemented with an animist component because of the holistic cultural foundation. In China, the blend of animism, Daoism, Confucianism and Mahayana Buddhism forms the foundation of society and culture, also a relational worldview. In Japan, Shintoism and the Japanese expression of Mahayana Buddhism also create a relational and holistic basis for culture.

All these reflections can be modified in the next step, in which I turn to the historical periods and worldview currents. In today's world, with industrialization during the modern period, cultures have become more secularized and thus rules-based (with a focus on efficiency, achievement, punctuality and analytic thinking). For example, we can see this development in India, Singapore and China. With postmodernism, understood as a counter-current to modernism, cultures have become more strongly relational. This second phenomenon emerges most clearly in North America and Western Europe. Hence, professional specialists and intellectuals in most parts of the world work in an environment which developed in the modern era and is therefore focused on rules, whereas traditional milieus remain relational. For example, a banker in Singapore may be working in a professional environment based mainly on rules, while his behaviour in family life is permeated with relational traditions. The same is true of Western youth: the workplace is rules-based but private life is often relational. Africa itself continues to have a relational focus in both the private sphere and the workplace.

In the highly developed and fragmented societies, the analysis must be on an individual basis, because the manifold influences of socialization, of the immediate environment and the Internet can shape individual personality profiles in quite different ways.

5.6 Leadership

The next two sections are concerned with two important aspects of social and church life: leadership and conflict resolution.

5.6.1 Leadership and Conscience Orientation

In terms of conscience orientation and mana, three types of leaders and a particular type of subordinate under them can be distinguished.

Firstly, there is the *relational leader*, of which there are two sub-types. The first of these strives for honour, prestige and power. Such leaders can be found everywhere, but especially in hierarchical societies such as India with its caste system. These leaders exercise their office in an authoritarian way, as can be currently observed in China, India, Russia and Turkey. The second subtype of leaders looks for harmony. They strive for consensus and pursue a mutual approach in reaching a decision.

The *rules-based leader* desires to act correctly and effectively. Such leaders consult their co-workers and the experts. They can be found in egalitarian societies such as those of English, German and Scandinavian speaking Europe and in North America. They cultivate a democratic style of leadership.

A third type of leader could be described as *animist*. Through their initiation into the invisible world, they have acquired a special power to which the ordinary members of society have no access. They are bearers of mana in such a way as to make them unassailable and inviolable. Regardless of whether they appear to be good leaders or not, no one will be able to overthrow them, unless it is someone with more mana at his command or with the help of greater power from the invisible word. Their behaviour, whether as a benevolent or malevolent dictator, depends on their character. Since the concept of mana is focused on honour, prestige, authority, charisma and power, such leaders have a relational conscience and therefore correspond in a certain way to the first type of relational leader.

Usually, these three types of leaders interact with subordinates who have their own particular conscience orientation. If the personality types of superiors and subordinates converge, we can expect harmonious collaboration, but if they diverge, the relationships are likely to be less harmonious.

Among subordinate co-workers, there may be some who have been socialized by an *anti-authoritarian upbringing*. Their conscience either is relational or has developed little during socialization and is therefore functionally deficient, neither rules-based nor relational. Such a conscience will sense neither shame nor guilt following violation of a norm. There are great numbers of such individuals in large cities throughout the world. They are difficult to lead.

5.6.2 Leadership and Western Generations

In the evolution of the leadership style over the generations, we observe, on one hand, a progression from a very marked hierarchy to a flat hierarchy. The former corresponds to a relational culture, the latter to a rules-based system. On the other hand, we see a development from a leadership style with a strict control to an even more relational one. This evolution is also reflected in the perception of the ideal leader. Whereas in the pre-war generation, it is the commander at the top of the hierarchy, in the Generation Alpha we find a friend integrated into the team activity. This second development expresses an accentuating relational system. We note therefore a crossed evolution of the conscience orientations: on one hand, a change from a relational leadership style to a rules-based one, and, on the other hand, an accentuation of a relational style. Here we are confronted with a blend (a hybridity) which is typical for globalization, as we already have observed it in the phenomenon of "soft individualism" in contemporary generations. I summarize these findings in Table 30.[54]

---

54. McCrindle and Wolfinger, *The ABC of XYZ*.

Table 30: Leadership Style and Western Generations

Generation	Leadership Style	Ideal Leader
Pre-war generation (1925–1945)	Controlling	Commander
Post-war generation (1946–1965)	Directing	Thinker
Generation X (1966–1980)	Coordinating	Doer
Generation Y (1981–1995)	Guiding	Supporter
Generation Z (1996–2010)	Empowering	Collaborator
Generation Alpha (2011–2025)	Inspiring	Co-creator

5.6.3 Decisions

In social environments where people's consciences are relational, decisions are typically made in groups. For example, it means that if someone wants to convert to a different faith, that person cannot make the decision alone. There is an obligation to consult the family – especially the head of the family, the uncles and older brothers. In environments where the conscience is rules-based, there are no limits on individual decisions, including conversions. Leaders also make their decisions individually or collectively according to the prevailing conscience orientation.

5.6.4 Attitudes to Planning

When it comes to planning a project, an educational pathway, or one's own life, the method of procedure is determined by one's time orientation. Persons with a past orientation have a limited capacity for planning future events. For example, a chemist with this kind of focus orders a drug only when the stocks are empty. By contrast, a person with a future orientation has a greater ability to anticipate future events and crises. Such a chemist orders a drug as soon as the supply reaches a critical point.

5.6.5 Negotiations

Conscience orientation also affects the style of diplomatic or business negotiations. In rules-based environments, technical skill is most important. In relational circles, status and relationships are more important than competence and expertise. This is particularly true in the world of diplomacy.

Issues of protocol play no part in rules-based circles as long as the relevant expertise is ensured. In relational environments, things are quite different. Here protocol has priority: who speaks first and who speaks last? In relational environments these orderings are strictly established. Normally, the person at the top of the hierarchy has the last word and sums up the various positions of the previous speakers.

5.6.6 The Role of Written Agreements

In societies with a preference for an oral approach, consisting mainly of relational persons, written agreements are at first glance less important than the persons taking part and the oral negotiations. The written agreements become important, indeed very important, when they summarize the preceding oral negotiations. In rules-based environments, where members can often read and write, written agreements record the regulations agreed upon in negotiations and confirm them as valid in law.

5.7 Dealing with Conflicts

Within any social environment, ways of understanding and dealing with conflicts depend on the conscience orientation.

5.7.1 Perception of Conflicts

In rules-based contexts, the human phenomenon of conflict is regarded as perfectly normal. When it arises, it is brought into the open and openly discussed. In a relational and hence shame-oriented social environment, conflict creates feelings of shame and disharmony and must therefore be kept hidden. Table 31 sums up how conflict is perceived in terms of conscience orientation.

Table 31: Perception of Conflict According to Conscience Orientation

Rules-Based Conscience	Relational Conscience
Conflict is a normal phenomenon in human relationships	Conflict disrupts harmony in relationships and is to be avoided
Conflict is brought into the open and openly discussed	Conflict is hidden and covered up

5.7.2 Causes of Conflicts

Different types of personality, styles of communication and leadership as well as priorities in life can lead to conflicts. These have already been discussed above (cf. sections 4.1.1, 4.2.2, 4.6). With regard to priorities and goals in life, the focus and the concerns given to different values depend on the conscience orientation. In relational environments, harmony in relationships, respect, honour, power, affluence and well-being are of particular importance. By contrast, in rules-based environments, truth, right and justice take priority in terms of goals and values (see Figure 9).

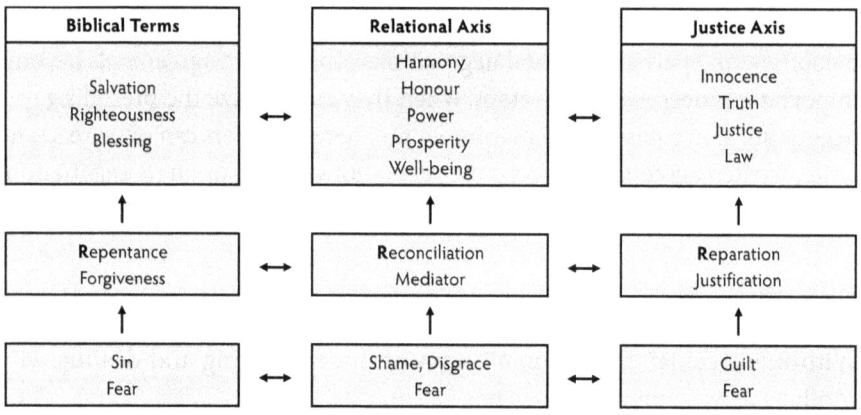

Figure 9: Causes of Conflict and Conceptions of Forgiveness

The conception of sin and salvation and the expectation of forgiveness are different in the two conscience orientations. While the attention in a rules-based environment is centred on the repair of the fault (of the sin), in a relational context, it is rather the reconciliation between individuals and families that is in focus. Thus, European penal codes insist on reparation through a fine or a prison sentence. In contrast, in relational societies, reconciliation is sought through family reunions. The Bible, for its part, places particular emphasis on changing thought and behavior (repentance, in Greek *metanoia*). According to the biblical model, we will therefore adopt a balanced approach to forgiveness through repentance, reconciliation and reparation (the 3 Rs).

5.7.3 Styles of Conflict Resolution

Ways of dealing with conflicts likewise depend on the conscience orientation. In a relational environment, mediation between the parties in a dispute is predominant; in a rules-based social environment, confrontation is in focus. In a relational environment, it is expected that those on a socially lower level should initiate a solution. On the other hand, we observe in the Bible that God as the superior one generally leads the way in solving the problems between humanity and himself. He takes the initiative: "Adam, where are you?" (Gen 3:9); Cain, "why are you angry? Why is your face downcast?" (Gen 4:6). Afterwards, God sends the patriarchs and the prophets as mediators: Noah, Abraham, Samuel, Isaiah and Jeremiah. They convey a message which is at the same time a warning and a call to reconciliation with God. When the time is fulfilled (Gal 4:4), God sends his Son, Jesus Christ, a perfect mediator (1 Tim 2:5), the "chief shepherd" (1 Pet 5:4; cf. John 10:11–14). For his part, Jesus entrusts the ministry of reconciliation to us, and we have the following message: "Be reconciled to God" (cf. 2 Cor 5:18–20). Beyond the Christian ministry of reconciliation, authorities in general, particularly religious authorities (the pastor, the priest, the imam and the shaman), are common mediators in society and in the religious community, on account of their pre-eminent role.

With regard to the styles of dealing with conflicts, this is mostly conveyed by parents to their children, and usually unconsciously. They, too, are a function of conscience orientation. In Table 32 presents the conflict management styles schematically, together with analogies from the animal world.[55]

Table 32: Styles in Dealing with Conflicts

	You lose	You win
I lose	*Avoiding* (the passive turtle)	*Accommodating* (the lovable teddy bear)
I win	*Competing* (the aggressive shark)	*Collaborating* (the wise owl)
Both of us win and lose to some extent: *Compromising* (the wily fox)		

Among the styles mentioned in Table 32, "avoiding," "accommodating" and "competing" are typical of relational persons. Conflict is to be avoided, because it signifies the shame of disharmony, which should not be. Moreover, the paralysis of shame can block proper action. The moment I realized that I tended to avoid all conflicts as a team leader, that I failed to initiate solutions, and that I thus contributed to aggravating problems, I had a very bad conscience.

---

55. Donald C. Palmer, *Managing Conflict Creatively: A Guide for Missionaries and Christian Workers* (Pasadena: William Carey, 1990), 26–31.

Of course, I did not choose this style consciously. It derives from my deep relational orientation (cf. section 4.1.1).

Usually, the more dominant person in a relationship prevails over the weaker person. In a marriage it is typically the husband, though not always. Alternatively, the weaker person accommodates to the decisions of the dominant person. The former always loses out. Usually that means women and children. Making compromises is the style of rules-based persons. One has to be able to negotiate with some degree of emotional distance to find the way to equal gain and loss. One often speaks of a *win-win* situation, meaning that both parties gain to some degree. But the ideal is collaboration, in which both win completely. This also requires a degree of emotional harmony between the parties.

5.8 Summary

In this chapter, I have examined the worldviews of persons, societies, cultures and religions, together with two important elements of social and church life: leadership and conflict management. In analyzing people's worldviews, I have used the same models as I applied in analyzing societies, their layers and spheres, cultures and religions, with the reservations that a transfer of a model from one entity to a more complex one requires. I have established that among the models proposed for analyzing worldviews the model of conscience orientation, being located on the most fundamental level of worldview, is the most fruitful for analyzing people. In analyzing the worldviews, I have observed that most people groups seem to operate with a holistic and relational worldview, on account of their culture and religion. This is more and more the case as the younger generations of the West become increasingly relational. However, through the globalization of systems of education, science and economics, intellectuals, scientists and experts throughout the world must come to terms with a rules-based professional environment developed in the context of Western modernity. This has brought about a blending of worldviews, giving birth to a cultural and religious hybridity. As a consequence, the analysis of worldviews must necessarily be conducted at the individual level. For this reason, generalizations about whole societies and their layers and spheres are only attempts to offer grids of interpretation which must be supplemented through individual empirical analysis.

For Further Reading

European Values Study, https://europeanvaluesstudy.eu.

Lingenfelter, Sherwood G., and Marvin K. Mayers. *Ministering Cross-Culturally: An Incarnation Model for Personal Relationships.* Grand Rapids: Baker, 1986, 2003, 2016.

Wiher, Hannes. "Worldview and Oral Preference Learners and Leaders." In *Beyond Literate Western Practices: Continuing Conversations in Orality and Theological Education*, ed. Samuel E. Chiang and Grant Lovejoy, 109–25. Hong Kong: Capstone Enterprises, 2014.

Wiher, Hannes. *Shame and Guilt: A Key to Cross-Cultural Ministry.* Bonn: Culture and Science Publications, 2003.

World Values Survey, https://www.worldvaluessurvey.org/wvs.jsp.

6

Conclusion

In this book, I have proceeded from the hypothesis that persons, communication between them, and the ways in which societies, cultures and religions function are expressions of the underlying worldviews. In analyzing cultures, I have therefore made use of an enormous simplification, which could be termed an "abbreviation." This is necessary because none of us has the time required to study in depth all the various academic disciplines involved in the research of personalities, societies, cultures and religions. We have realized that a deeper understanding of the worldviews and identities of our conversation partners enables us to approach them with more love, competency and effectiveness, through communication tailored to those partners. This sensitivity to different worldviews is apparent in the recorded communications of Jesus Christ.

I have established that the God of the Bible who created humankind desires that his creatures should live and act in a balanced way on both the relational and rules-based axis. This enables them to maintain relationships permeated by love and respect, and to live according to the rules which the creator has given us in the Bible as a benchmark. I have shown that the work of theologians is strongly pervaded by their worldview, of which they themselves remain largely unaware. The same can be said of the thought and behaviour patterns of believers. In the past, this has led to conflicts between different Christian branches, between religions and theological positions, the causes of which we can understand today. Worldviews also exert an influence on church life, which in most cases reflects the prevailing currents of the particular society to which the church belongs. In this way, its various forms of expression become more understandable.

I have also demonstrated that today the majority of the world's population is predominantly relational, on account of their adherence to animism, a folk religion or another relational religion, or owing to their socialization in an environment subject to few rules. However, this generalization is not without risk. Through globalization in recent decades, societies have become fragmented. Hence, an individual analysis is more necessary than ever. Our personality profile enables us to become aware of our cultural and theological "glasses," lenses and filters. This should be supplemented by an in-depth study of the profile of our conversation partners.

I believe that with the help of the models I have presented, we can understand all persons, societies, cultures and religions throughout the world. Indeed, the single model of conscience orientation presented here will already enable us to analyze them very effectively and deeply. Using all five models, we will possess a set of tools for not only analyzing them but also helping us to improve our relationships with them and orienting our communication of the good news in a way which is faithful to Scripture and relevant for our conversation partners.

Appendices

Appendix 1

Individuals and Their "Cultural Skin Layers"

During the conversion and discipleship process, we have to reach not only into the centre of a personality (the "name," worldview and identity), but also the "cultural skin layers." Here is a list of these layers as conceived by Hans Bürki.[1]

Name (Self, Identity)

The biblical expression for a person's individuality is the name. Under the influence of sin, individuals lost their name. They have become anonymous; they no longer know who they are. The defining act of redemption is that God calls us by our name (Isa 43:1; Gen 17:5; 32:28–30; Matt 16:18; Mark 3:16; John 21:15–17; Rev 2:17). The call and the revelation of God's name are often two sides of the same event (Exod 3:4, 14; cf. 1 Cor 15:10).

Affective Layer (Imitation, Intuition, Initiative)

Whenever we are communicating with someone, we can't avoid opening ourselves up and revealing who we are. Everything about ourselves which we allow to be seen, we sense as a threat to our identity. This means that every intimate relationship is emotionally loaded. This vulnerable inner nucleus of our being is protected by an emotional layer. It becomes hardened by sin and shame. God's redemptive work consists in changing these defensive feelings into joyful openness. Shame is turned into honour.

---

1. Hans Bürki, "Évangile et culture," in *Évangile, culture et idéologies*, ed. René Padilla, Hans Bürki and Samuel Escobar (Lausanne: Presses bibliques universitaires, 1977), 13–50.

Protective Layer (Mask, Character)

Individuals develop their secret life plan when quite young and are determined to defend it. They are convinced that this life plan and its associated defence mechanisms represent their true identity and that they are essential for their development. But living with a mask, even if coated with a Christian veneer, prevents them from freely embracing initiatives during their lives.

Intellectual Layer

Evangelism based on feelings and evangelism which only invokes the will and reason are both equally one-sided. It is not sufficient to accept a series of biblical doctrines and seek to apply them. Even the way one thinks and the power of the will are determined by the particular culture. Therefore, theology and ethics must likewise be related to context.

Physical Layer (Face, Body, Senses, Clothes)

This layer protects or expresses, conceals or exposes. The liberation and transformation of the body, previously exploited through egocentric ambition, and the individual's reconciliation with it lead to psychosomatic healing. Asceticism is of no use for controlling bodily needs. Cultural models in this area need to be critically scrutinized whether they are of a repressive kind or promote liberality. Jesus opens our eyes in this matter (Matt 6:22, 25, 29–30; Mark 10:13–16; Luke 7:38–39, 44–46).

Linguistic Layer (Conceals or Reveals)

Language forms the mind, structures the senses, and imprints the individual's perception. By the same token, words reveal the personality of the individual (Matt 12:34–37; Jas 3:5–8).

Family and Friendship Layers (Privileged Relationships)

Since the family plays a dominant role in the moulding of the individual, it is inevitable that the psychological and social umbilical cord will be severed. This operation is often very painful (Gen 2:24; Luke 2:35; 9:23; 14:26; 1 Pet 1:18). A person is released from the family in order to be given back to it.

Sociocultural Layer

To be of service to one's birthplace, one's forebears or one's ethnic affiliation, one must first be freed from them. This abandonment consists in loosing ourselves from the fetters with which each individual holds us captive. Consistent with this liberation, the church is called to be a new community of freed people.

Cosmic Layer (Space/Time)

Man is both part of and ruler of creation. However, in this capacity, man is also subject to death. The experience of new birth throws a primordial light on birth, death and resurrection. The gospel awakens between people and their environment a new relationship of love, suffering and empathy for the whole of creation.

Transcendental Layer (Light/Darkness)

Man is naturally religious and has shaped numerous religious systems. This religiosity needs to be liberated and purified by the gospel in order to bring to light the difference between religion and life in Christ.

Appendix 2

Typologies of Peoples and Cultures

Typology According to Mary Douglas

Drawing on cultural surveys by cultural anthropologists in various cultures, Mary Douglas developed a typology using four types of culture, classified on the basis of structure and community.[1]

Table 33: Mary Douglas' Typology

	Weak Community	Strong Community
Weak Structure	*Individuating Culture*	*Interrelating Culture*
Strong Structure	*Institutionalizing Culture*	*Hierarching Culture*

Table 34: Mary Douglas' Characteristics of Culture Types

Cultural Type	Structure/Community	Characteristics
Individuating	Weak Structure Weak Community	Individual identity Individual decisions Fosters creativity and innovation Values independence and autonomy
Institutionalizing	Strong Structure Weak Community	Identity from following rules and submitting to authority Focus on individual's role Values submission

---

1. Mary Douglas, *Risk and Blame: Essays in Cultural Theory* (London: Routledge, 1992).

Cultural Type	Structure/Community	Characteristics
Interrelating	Weak Structure Strong Community	Collective identity based on dialogue and interaction Values equality
Hierarching	Strong Structure Strong Community	Collective identity based on submitting to hierarchy Discourages creativity and innovation Values a hierarchical community

Mary Douglas' typology, compiled according to the structure and community within cultures, is reminiscent, by analogy, of conscience orientation with its division into rules and relationships. It is of interest for those living in an intercultural environment.

Typology According to Hofstede

Based on his analysis of the business world since the 1960s, Geert Hofstede has developed six dimensions of cultural orientation which are widespread internationally in commercial circles.[2]

---

2. Geert H. Hofstede, *Culture's Consequences: International Differences in Work-related Values* (Beverly Hills: Sage Publications, 1980); *Cultures and Organizations: Software of the Mind* (New York: McGraw-Hill, 1991, 2005).

Table 35: Hofstede's Typology

Low power distance Equal distribution of power, flat hierarchy	*High power distance* Unequal distribution of power, steep hierarchy
Individualism Primacy of the individual	*Collectivism* Primacy of the group
Masculinity Emphasis on competition	*Femininity* Readiness for cooperation
High uncertainty avoidance Avoidance of the unexpected and of ambiguities	*Low uncertainty avoidance* Acceptance of the unexpected and of ambiguities
Low long-term orientation Little regard for tradition; High acceptance of change	*High long-term orientation* High regard for tradition; Small acceptance of change
Restraint Strongly regulated social behaviour	*Indulgence* Little regulation of social behaviour

This typology would appear to be of significant use for the business world and its international teams. It also has implications for dealing with conflicts.

Typology According to Meyer

Another typology, which Erin Meyer also developed for the business world, distinguishes eight parameters for classifying persons and cultures worldwide. The parameters measure whether we *communicate* or *evaluate* directly or indirectly, whether we persuade through principles (why?) or applications (how?), whether we lead democratically or hierarchically, whether we decide by consensus or according to rank, whether our trust rests on the accomplishment of tasks or on persons, whether we disagree contentiously or modestly, and whether we plan and schedule in a strictly fixed or flexible way.[3]

---
3. Erin Meyer, *The Culture Map: Decoding How People Think, Lead, and Get Things Done across Cultures* (New York: PublicAffairs, 2014).

Table 36: Meyer's Typology

Direct communication	Indirect communication
Evaluation through direct feedback	Evaluation through indirect feedback
Persuasion through principles (why?)	Persuasion through applications (how?)
Democratic leadership	Hierarchical leadership
Decision through consensus	Decision according to rank
Task-oriented trust	Person-orientated trust
Contentious discussion	Modest discussion
Strictly fixed planning	Flexible planning

Meyer's typology would appear to fit our needs much better, since it comprises communication, evaluation, styles of persuasion and leadership.

Typology According to Weber

A fourth typology, developed by Christian Weber for missionary service, establishes five areas with cultural imprint:[4]

Table 37: Weber's Typology

Thought Patterns	rational	occult
Time Orientation	punctuality	event
Communication Style	direct	indirect
System of Ordering	democratic	feudal
Form of Creativity	organized	spontaneous

Weber's typology approximates even more closely our requirements for an intercultural approach to mission. The areas of time orientation, communication style, system of ordering and form of creativity seem very meaningful.

---

4. Christian Weber, *Wie andere Kulturen die Bibel sehen* (Zürich: TVZ, Mission 21, 2020), 22–23, 26–28.

Typology According to Lingenfelter and Mayers

A fifth typology with basic values was developed by the two missiologists Sherwood Lingenfelter and Marvin Mayers on the basis of their observations in the world of mission. Their typology is composed of six pairs of basic values.[5]

Table 38: Lingenfelter and Mayers' Typology

Time orientation	Event orientation
Dichotomistic thinking	Holistic thinking
Crisis orientation	Non-crisis orientation
Task orientation	Person orientation
Status focus	Achievement focus
Willingness to expose vulnerability	Concealment of vulnerability

This typology of Lingenfelter and Mayers, developed in the world of mission and resting on the basic values of persons and cultures, seems to me even better suited to our requirements for an intercultural missional approach.

---

5. Sherwood G. Lingenfelter and Marvin K. Mayers, *Ministering Cross-Culturally: An Incarnation Model for Personal Relationships* (Grand Rapids: Baker, 1986, 2003, 2016), https://books.google.com.

Appendix 3

Typology of Personality According to Conscience Orientation

Rules-Based Personality	Relational Personality
The person strives for what is right	The person strives for harmony and honour
Partial attribution of failure: "What I did is wrong"	Total attribution of failure: "I am bad"
Guilt after infringement	Shame after discovery
Peace when the error is atoned for	Peace when harmony and honour are restored
Individualism	**Collectivism**
Exclusive attitude	Inclusive attitude
Individual independence	Dependence on the group
Initiative is encouraged	Initiative is suppressed
Personal effectiveness is more important than the group	Harmonious relationships have priority
Competition, confrontation	Cooperation, harmony
Personal rights are important	Obligations towards the group are important
Acquisition for oneself, materialism	Sharing, generosity, simplicity of lifestyle
Decisions made individually, no wasting of time on discussions	Decisions made with group consensus
Direct communication	Indirect communication
Candidness, openness, incorruptibility, resolution, perseverance – individual virtues (relational persons can feel these virtues to be brutal or impolite)	Humility, flexibility, readiness to compromise (rules-based persons can understand these virtues as obliquity)
Independence and autonomy are appreciated	Friendship, readiness to help, patience and hospitality are appreciated

Individual Identity	Group Identity
Identity through individual awareness	Identity through group awareness
Personal identity is defined in terms of personal achievements	Personal identity is defined by group status, age, ancestry, title, rank
Security through the feeling of correct attitude towards norms, rules and goals	Security through manifold relationships and adherence to the group and to society
Time Orientation	**Event Orientation**
Life is determined by time schedules	Life is determined by events
Punctuality and a fixed programme are what matters	Events are not determined by time
Quantitative concept of time	Qualitative concept of time
Task Orientation	**Person Orientation**
Satisfaction through attaining personal goals	Satisfaction through integrating into a group
Completing tasks is more important than relationships	Relationships are more important than completing a task
Search for friends with similar goals	Search for friends who are group-oriented
Acceptance of isolation in order to achieve personal goals	Shunning of isolation, sacrificing personal goals for the sake of relationships
Achievement Focus	**Status Focus**
Achievement, wealth and success determine the worth of a person	Age, descent, rank and position determine a person's value
Search for friends with similar achievements, independent of descent	Search for friends with the same status and the same descent
All have the same rights and opportunities	Rights and opportunities both depend on status
Egalitarian society	Hierarchical society

Analytic Thinking	**Holistic Thinking**
Judgements are right/wrong, black/white	Judgements are open-ended
Either-or reasoning	Both-and reasoning
Fragmented perception: a character trait or an action is taken into account separately	Holistic, integrated perception: evaluation of the whole person and all circumstances
Abstract thinking	Concrete thinking
Detached perception of objects (science)	Personal involvement with the object
Information and experiences are classified systematically	Information and experiences remain clearly unclassified, details (events, characterizations) independent
Analytical conclusions	Analogical conclusions (analogy)
Learning through explanation	Learning through imitation
Courage to Fail	**Fear of Losing Face**
Ready to accept failure	Save face, avoid failure
Prepared to try new things	Remain within safe boundaries
Admission of guilt, weakness and failure	Denial of mistakes, withdrawal in order to hide weakness
Open to constructive criticism	Criticism is understood as an attack
Addresses personal matters openly	Addresses personal matters vaguely
In relationships truthfulness is more important than harmony	In relationships harmony is more important than truthfulness

Appendix 4

Questionnaire and Personality Profile[1]

Please examine to what extent each of the following forty-eight statements expresses your personal opinion or attitude towards life. If the statement does not apply to you at all, put the number 1 in the relevant space. If it is very applicable, indicate 7. If you only partly agree, enter a number between 1 and 7. All fields should be completed with a number from 1 to 7.

Questions

___ 1. I would not like to work for a big company, because I would not be able to retain the overall grasp of the whole.

___ 2. I enjoy meeting with friends to discuss just about everything.

___ 3. I avoid setting goals, out of fear that I would not attain them.

___ 4. My view of myself is more important than the judgement of others.

___ 5. I don't think about the future. I take things as they come.

___ 6. For me an issue is either right or wrong, black or white. I don't like it when people debate "grey zones." That looks more like compromise than truth.

___ 7. In making decisions, I think there could be several correct possibilities.

___ 8. When I set a goal for myself, I put all my energy into reaching it, even if other matters get neglected.

___ 9. I am always one of the first to try something new.

___ 10. I prefer to mix with people like myself (people belonging to my social status).

---

1. Adapted from Lingenfelter and Mayers, *Ministering Cross-Culturally*, 17–24.

___11. I consider time to be a very precious commodity.

___12. If my car needs a repair, I prefer to take it to the specialist centre rather than to my neighbour who also carries out small repairs in his garage. I know you can always depend on the professionals.

___13. I enjoy having onlookers. It spurs me on to improve my achievements.

___14. Before I buy a car, I find out about it in the specialist magazines and also consult friends and relatives.

___15. My desk is always tidy and my work plan organized. Every object has its place.

___16. I attend courses and read textbooks in order to continue my education.

___17. I would accept a more attractive position in a distant town, even if it meant losing close contact with friends and family.

___18. I find it difficult to socialize with people who are professionally above me.

___19. I always wear a watch. I hate being late.

___20. I can't stand people treating me like a stereotype.

___21. In general I don't worry about what might possibly happen. If a real problem crops up there is always time to sort it out.

___22. If I have to wait somewhere, I often initiate a conversation with strangers.

___23. It embarrasses me to arrive late. I would rather stay away from an event than enter after it has begun.

___24. When I hear about a particularly interesting event, I try to alter my schedule so that I can take part in it.

___25. I plan my day and my week. I get annoyed if my programme – my routine – is disrupted.

___26. In a discussion, I take part only after I have heard all the arguments.

___27. I agree with the familiar maxim, "The end justifies the means."

___28. Now and again I like to break out of my routine and try something unusual. It keeps life interesting.

___29. When I'm working on a project, I usually keep at it till it is finished; other things have to wait.

___30. At my local pub there are certain preferred dishes which I always order.

___31. There is no work so urgent that I couldn't abandon and thus disappoint my friends by not going to a barbecue party.

___32. I always respect the authority of my superiors, even if in my view they're wrong.

___33. I believe our language has a standard grammar and that everyone should express themselves according to the rules.

___34. I sometimes alter cooking book recipes a little in order to introduce some change to the menu.

___35. In discussions I stick to my point of view, even if I become aware that it is wrong. I find it hard to admit my mistake.

___36. One can't rest on the successes of the past. One should prove oneself afresh each day.

___37. When I start at a new workplace, I make a special effort to impress my colleagues.

___38. When I introduce people, I include their occupation and title, as well as their name.

___39. I discuss my problems with others, and accept advice gladly.

___40. I avoid games at which I am not very skilled.

___41. When I meet acquaintances, I always exchange a few words, even if I'm in a great hurry.

___42. For next year, and for the next five years, I have set certain goals for myself which I would like to achieve.

___43. I like working on several projects simultaneously. It means I can select whatever I fancy at that particular moment.

___44. Whenever I am making a large purchase, I buy the first best offer without having previously compared prices in different shops.

___45. I love art. When looking at works of art, I try to imagine what the artist wants to express.

___46. I don't like discussing topics which lead to no definite outcome.

___47. I don't like being ruled by the appointment schedule. I prefer to tackle spontaneously whatever needs to be done.

___48. When I am in charge of an event, I make sure that it begins and ends on time.

Analysis of the Answers

To determine your personal profile, enter below your answers to each of the statements of the questionnaire. (For example, if your answer to statement 1 was 5, put 5 in the first field on the line next to "holistic thinking"). Add the five numbers in each line and divide the total by five in order to discover your number of points for each basic value.

	Basic Value	Score					Total	Average
1.	Punctuality orientation	11	19	23	25	48		
2.	Event orientation	5	24	29	31	47		
3.	Analytic thinking	6	11	15	33	46		
4.	Holistic thinking	1	5	20	26	45		
5.	Crisis orientation	6	12	16	30	44		
6.	Serenity	7	9	21	34	43		
7.	Task orientation	8	12	17	27	42		
8.	Person orientation	2	13	22	31	41		
9.	Status focus	10	18	32	33	38		
10.	Achievement focus	4	14	20	36	37		
11.	Fear of losing face	3	23	32	35	40		
12.	Courage to fail	9	13	28	34	39		

To learn your conscience orientation, add the score on the following basic values and divide the total by 5:

Rules orientation: 1 + 3 + 7 + 10 + 12 = ___ : 5 = ___

Relational orientation: 2 + 4 + 8 + 9 + 11 = ___ : 5 = ___

Personal Profile

Now take your average for all these basic values and identify the point of intersection of these average values in the appropriate grids. This point indicates your fundamental tendency.

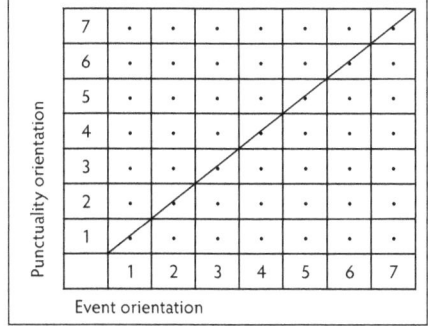
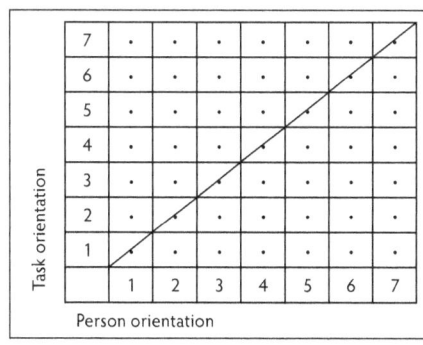
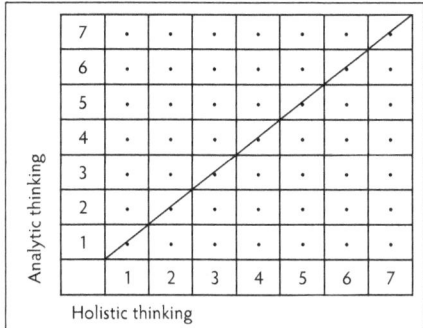
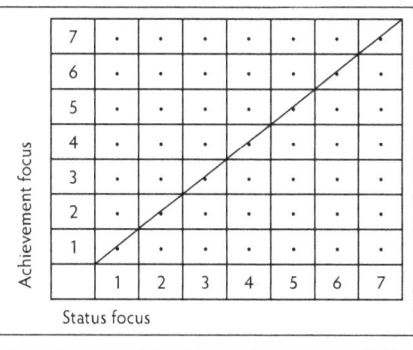
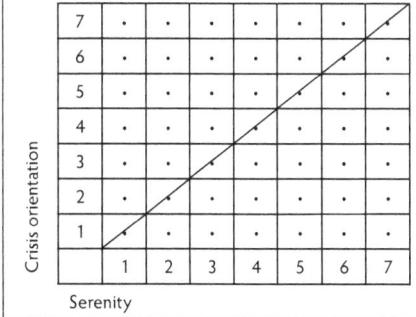
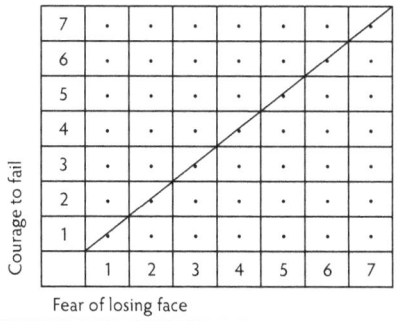

The personal profile of basic values is a rough representation of the motivations lying behind the actions of individuals within their culture. Each graph portrays the opposing tension of the character traits, but not in terms of opposites. The values ultimately indicate the relative strength of each of these character traits when it comes to making a decision during interaction with others. A result of (2/6) for someone on the first grid (2 for event orientation and 6 for punctuality orientation) indicates that time is exerting much more force on the decisions and actions of this person than the duty of successfully completing the events in which the person is taking part. A result of (2/2) would mean that neither had significant influence.

When results tend towards different conscience orientations (rules based and relational), the personal profile indicates a mixed personality made up of some dominant basic values on the rules axis and others on the relational axis. In this way, every person is a unique mixture of basic values with a specific personality profile.

The personal profile and the scores do not say anything about which basic values have been acquired during early childhood and which ones later on. When a value has been imprinted in early socialization onto a personality, it will influence its behaviour strongly and it will be difficult to change the character trait. Values that have been acquired during adult life will be easier to modify. This implies that the personality profile of the two parents have a strong impact on the personal profile of their children. This basic orientation will direct behaviour most of life unless worked on intentionally.

Appendix 5

The Five Soteriological Concepts and Chronological Bible Teaching

The five soteriological concepts are normally taught by telling Bible stories, ideally in chronological order. Chronological Bible teaching is the natural framework for a comparative study between the soteriological concepts of the Bible and those of the interested individual in the process of discipleship. It is therefore a suitable method for intercultural communication of the gospel. It is important to teach the five soteriological concepts before and after the new creation in the form of stories. Here are some selected guidelines with regard to these five concepts.

1. The Concept of God

- God is the creator (Gen 1:1). As creator he is greater than all other beings (including all spirit beings such as demons and ancestors). In Hebrew this means that he is holy (Lev 19:2).
- The creation was good (Gen 1:31); God is good (by contrast, fate in Islam, Hinduism and Buddhism is both good and bad).
- God desires to be the exclusive and ever-present partner of man (Gen 17:1; 28:16–17).

2. The Concept of Man

- Human beings are made in the image of God (Gen 1:26–27) with a conscience, free will and responsibility (in contrast to Islam, Hinduism and Buddhism).
- Human beings are created male and female (Gen 1:27). The woman is "the helper" and counterpart (*'ezer kenēgedo*, Gen 2:18). Hence there is equality between men and women (in contrast to animism, Islam, Hinduism and Buddhism).

- Man is granted honour and power from God: he is God's representative. It is his task to cultivate and preserve the creation (Gen 2:15) and name every living creature (Gen 2:19–20).

3. The Concept of Evil

- Evil entered the world through Satan at one time in history (Gen 3:1). Evil is thus not ontologically pre-existing. Neither does evil come from God in the form of fate (cf. Islam).
- At the beginning, Satan was an angel of God who later fell. Satan is separated from God on account of his hubris (Isa 14:12–17; Ezek 28:11–19; Rev 12:9; 20:10).
- A portion of the angels follow Satan (Rev 12:4). Those are the demons.

4. The Concept of Sin[1]

- Man decided to become autonomous (Gen 2:17). Sin is "to miss the goal" (Hebrew *hata'*, Greek *hamartia*); the solution is to turn around and turn to God (Hebrew *shub* "to turn around," Greek *metanoia* "change of mind and of behaviour"). Sin is about becoming one's own lord, whereas God desires to be Lord. Sin does not wait to appear on the scene until the violation of the norm is publicly revealed, as is the case with the relational conscience and animism.
- God discovers the sin (Gen 3:8). Shame enters the world (Gen 3:7, 10). Man is driven out of paradise (Gen 3:23): he suffers in his work (Gen 3:17–19) and rules over his wife, who suffers pain in childbirth (Gen 3:16).
- The consequence of sin is that man loses harmony, honour, and innocence (Rom 3:23), and that death enters the world (Rom 5:12; 6:23).

---

1. In this presentation, the concepts of evil and sin are separated, according to the reasoning of Genesis 3. Evil entered the world through Satan; by giving in to Satan's temptation, people decided to deviate from God's commands.

5. The Concept of Salvation

- We cannot merit our salvation, but salvation comes through the intervention of *the Saviour* (*the mediator*: 1 Tim 2:4–5) (as in animism, where the ancestors are the mediators, in folk religions, and in Mahayana Buddhism, where the bodhisattvas are the mediators; in contrast to Islam, Hinduism, and Hinayana Buddhism; however, Muhammad, Rama, and Krishna are also some sort of mediators).
- We cannot manipulate the invisible world to get salvation (in contrast to the prosperity gospel and dominion theology).
- Jesus Christ's mediation and *blood sacrifice* restore harmony and righteousness through forgiveness (Rom 3:23), as in animism and the folk religions, in contrast to Hinduism and Buddhism.

The two lines of salvation (mediation and blood sacrifice) are presented on the basis of the following stories.

Who is the Saviour? Forgiveness comes through the intervention of the mediator (1 Tim 2:4–5):

- The son of the woman will strike the head of the serpent (Gen 3:15).
- The ark rescues the faithful remnant of mankind, Noah's family (Gen 6–9).
- Joseph saves Jacob's family through his suffering (Gen 37–48).
- Moses rescues the people of Israel through suffering (Exodus to Deuteronomy).
- The Lord will raise up a prophet like Moses from among the people of Israel (Deut 18:15).
- A king like David (a son of David) will save the people (2 Sam 7:16).
- A virgin will bear a son named Immanuel (Isa 7:14).
- A shoot shall come out from the stump of Jesse (a son of David) and will reign (Isa 11:1).
- The suffering servant of the Lord will save the people (Isa 42:1–9, etc.).
- The Son of Man will reign (Dan 7:13).
- Jesus Christ is the son of David (Matt 1:1), the son of the woman (Luke 1:26–38), the Son of Man (Matt 9:6; 12:40; 16:27) and the suffering Servant of the Lord (Luke 4:18–19; John 13), and he saves the world.

Who is the blood sacrifice? The blood sacrifice of Jesus Christ restores harmony and justice (Rom 3:23). In the Bible, blood is the bearer of life (Lev 14:11; Heb 9:22). Hence the blood sacrifice is the mediator of forgiveness leading to restoration of life (in fullness).

- God provides the skin of an animal offered as an atoning sacrifice to "cover" the shame (Gen 3:21; cf. Heb 9:22).
- Abel's blood sacrifice is accepted whereas Cain's good works are rejected (Gen 4).
- Abraham's son is replaced by a ram. God will provide a lamb (Gen 22).
- The Passover lamb must be without blemish (Exod 12).
- Sin and guilt offerings are required for the forgiveness of sins (Lev 4–5).
- The sacrifices on the Day of Atonement are designated for the High Priest and for the people (Lev 16).
- The guilt sacrifice of the servant of God is offered for many (Isa 52:13–53:12; Mark 10:45).
- Jesus Christ is the son of Abraham (Matt 1:1), the Lamb of God (John 1:29) and the suffering servant of the Lord (Matt 26–27).

Sources in Relation to the Context

For the modern, Western context: Cross, John R. *The Stranger on the Road to Emmaus* (Olds, Canada: GoodSeed, 1996), https://www.goodseed.com.

For the Hinduist, Buddhist and postmodern context: Cross, John R. *By This Name* (Olds, Canada: GoodSeed, 2007), https://www.goodseed.com.

For the Animist and Muslim context: Cross, John R. *All that the Prophets Have Spoken*. Olds, Canada: GoodSeed, 1999, https://www.goodseed.com; McIlwain, Trevor. *Building on Firm Foundations: Guidelines for Evangelism and Teaching Believers*. 9 vol. Sanford: New Tribes Mission, 1987.

Bibliography

Adeyemo, Tokunboh, ed. *The Africa Bible Commentary: A One-Volume Commentary Written by 70 African Scholars.* Nairobi: Word Alive, 2006.
Altizer, Thomas J. J. *Living the Death of God: A Theological Memoir.* Albany: State University of New York Press, 2006.
Anselm of Canterbury. *Cur Deus homo?* London and Sydney: Griffith, Farran, Okeden & Welsh, 1890. https://archives.org.
Augsburger, David W. *Pastoral Counselling across Cultures.* Philadelphia: Westminster, 1986.
Augsburger, David W. *Conflict Mediation across Cultures: Pathways and Patterns.* Louisville: John Knox, 1992.
Augustine. *De Doctrina Christiana.* Corpus Christianorum 1. Paris: Brepols, 1982.
Austin, John L. *How to Do Things with Words.* London: Oxford University Press, 1955.
Barth, Karl. *Church Dogmatics, vol. 3: The Doctrine of Creation.* London: T&T Clark, 1936, 2009.
Bastian, Jean-Pierre, Françoise Champion, and Kathy Rousselet, ed. *La globalisation du religieux.* Paris: Harmattan, 2001.
Bavinck, Johan H. "Elenctics." In *An Introduction to the Science of Missions.* Grand Rapids: Baker, 1960, 221–75.
Bediako, Kwame. *Theology and Identity: The Impact of Culture upon Christian Thought in the Second Century and in Modern Africa.* Oxford: Regnum Books, 1992.
Bediako, Kwame. *Jesus in Africa: The Christian Gospel in African History and Experience.* Minneapolis: Fortress, 2000.
Bediako, Kwame. "Scripture as the Hermeneutic of Culture and Tradition." *Journal of African Christian Thought* 4, 1 (2001): 2–11.
Berger, Peter L. *The Sacred Canopy: Elements of a Sociological Theory of Religion.* Garden City: Doubleday, 1967.
Berger, Peter L., and Thomas Luckmann. *The Social Construction of Reality: A Treatise in the Sociology of Knowledge.* Oxford: Oxford University Press, 1967.
Berne, Eric. *Games People Play: The Psychology of Human Relationships.* Harmondsworth: Penguin Books, 1968.
Berne, Eric. *What Do You Say After You Say Hello? The Psychology of Human Destiny.* New York: Bantam, 1972.
Beyerhaus, Peter. "Theologisches Verstehen nichtchristlicher Religionen." *Kerygma und Dogma* 35, 2 (1989): 106–27.
Bockmühl, Klaus. *Hören auf den Gott der redet.* Giessen: ABC-Team, 1990.
Bosch, David J. "Evangelism: Theological Currents and Cross-Currents Today." *International Bulletin of Missionary Research* 3 (1987): 98–103.

Bosch, David J. *Transforming Mission: Paradigm Shifts in Theology of Mission.* Maryknoll: Orbis, 1991.

Bürki, Hans. "Évangile et culture." In *Évangile, culture et idéologies*, ed. René Padilla, Hans Bürki, and Samuel Escobar, 13–50. Lausanne: Presses bibliques universitaires, 1977.

Calvin, John. *Institutes of the Christian Religion.* Grand Rapids: Eerdmans, 2009.

Carter, Rita. *Mapping the Mind.* London: Weidenfeld & Nicolson, 1998; rev. ed.: Berkeley: University of California Press, 2010.

Chiang, Samuel E. "Editor's Note." *Orality Journal* 1, 1 (2012): 8. https://orality.net/resources.

Chiang, Samuel E. "Three Worlds Converged: Living in an Oral, Literate, and Digital Culture." In *Worship and Mission for the Global Church: An Ethnodoxology Handbook*, ed. James R. Krabill, 179–83. Pasadena: William Carey Library, 2012. https://orality.net/resources.

Chiang, Samuel E., and Grant Lovejoy, ed. *Beyond Literate Western Models: Contextualizing Theological Education in Oral Contexts.* Hong Kong: Capstone Enterprises, 2013. https://orality.net/resources.

Chiang, Samuel E., and Grant Lovejoy, ed. *Beyond Literate Western Practices: Continuing Conversations in Orality and Theological Education.* Hong Kong: Capstone Enterprises, 2014. https://orality.net/resources.

Chiang, Samuel E., and Grant Lovejoy, ed. *Beyond Literate Western Practices: Honor and Shame and the Assessment of Orality Preference.* Hong Kong: Capstone Enterprises, 2015. https://orality.net/resources.

Cobb, John B. Jr. "Beyond Pluralism." In *Christian Uniqueness Reconsidered: The Myth of Pluralistic Theology of Religions*, ed. Gavin D'Costa, 81–95. Maryknoll: Orbis, 1990.

Codrington, Robert H. *The Melanesians: Studies in Their Anthropology and Folklore.* New York: Clarendon Press, 1891.

Constantineanu, Corneliu, and Peter Penner, ed. *Central and Eastern European Bible Commentary.* Carlisle: Langham Global Library, 2023.

Coupland, Douglas. *Generation X: Tales for an Accelerate Culture.* New York: St. Martin's Press, 1991.

Cross, John R. *The Stranger on the Road to Emmaus.* Olds, Canada: GoodSeed, 1996. https://www.goodseed.com.

Cross, John R. *All that the Prophets Have Spoken.* Olds, Canada: GoodSeed, 1999. https://www.goodseed.com.

Cross, John R. *By This Name.* Olds, Canada: GoodSeed, 2007. https://www.goodseed.com.

Deci, Edward L., and Richard Ryan, *Intrinsic Motivation and Self-Determination in Human Behavior.* New York: Plenum, 1985.

Derrida, Jacques. *Dissemination.* London and New York: Continuum, 1981.

Derrida, Jacques. *Margins of Philosophy.* Brighton: Harvester Press, 1982.

DeSilva, David A. *Despising Shame: Honor Discourse and Community Maintenance in the Epistle to the Hebrews.* Atlanta: Scholars Press, 1995.

DeSilva, David A. *Honor, Patronage, Kinship and Purity: Unlocking New Testament Culture.* Downers Grove: InterVarsity Press, 2000.

Donovan, Kath, and Ruth Myors. "A Generational Perspective into the Future." In *Too Valuable to Lose: Exploring the Causes and Cures of Missionary Attrition*, ed. William D. Taylor, 41–73. Pasadena: William Carey Library, 1997.

Dooyeweerd, Herman. *Roots of Western Culture: Pagan, Secular and Christian Options.* Toronto: Wedge, 1979.

Douglas, Mary. *Purity and Danger.* London: Routledge & Kegan Paul, 1966.

Douglas, Mary. *Risk and Blame: Essays in Cultural Theory.* London: Routledge, 1992.

Douglas, Mary. *Leviticus as Literature.* Oxford: Oxford University Press, 1999.

Edgar, William. *Created and Creating: A Biblical Theology of Culture.* Downers Grove: InterVarsity Press, 2017.

Engelsviken, Tormod. "Mission, Evangelism and Evangelization: From the Perspective of the Lausanne Movement." *International Review of Mission* 96, 382/383 (2007): 204–9.

Erlacher, Jolene, and Katy White. *Mobilizing Gen Z: Challenges and Opportunities for the Global Age of Missions.* Pasadena: William Carey Library, 2022.

Ferry, Luc. *Homo æstheticus: L'invention du goût à l'âge démocratique.* Paris: Grasset, 1990.

Ferry, Luc, and Lucien Jerphagnon. *La tentation du christianisme.* Paris: Grasset, 2009.

Flanders, Christopher, and Werner Mischke, ed. *Honor, Shame, and the Gospel: Reframing Our Message and Ministry.* Pasadena: William Carey Library, 2020.

Flemming, Dean E. *Contextualization in the New Testament: Patterns for Theology and Mission.* Leicester: Inter-Varsity Press, 2005.

Geertz, Clifford. *The Interpretation of Culture.* New York: Basic Books, 1973.

Georges, Jayson, and Mark D. Baker. *Ministering in Honor-Shame Cultures: Biblical Foundations and Practical Essentials.* Downers Grove: InterVarsity Press 2016.

Gilliland, Dean S. "The Incarnation as Matrix for Appropriate Theologies." In *Appropriate Christianity*, ed. Charles H. Kraft, 493–520. Pasadena: William Carey Library, 2005.

Green, Daniel, and Mel Lawrenz. *Encountering Shame and Guilt: Resources for Strategic Pastoral Counselling.* Grand Rapids: Baker, 1994.

Hempelmann, Heinzpeter. *Prämodern, Modern, Postmodern: Warum "ticken" Menschen so unterschiedlich? Basismentalitäten und ihre Bedeutung für Mission, Gemeindearbeit und Kirchenleitung.* Neukirchen-Vluyn: Neukirchener Verlagsgesellschaft, 2013.

Hesselgrave, David J. *Communicating Christ Cross-Culturally.* Grand Rapids: Zondervan, 1980.

Hesselgrave, David J. *Paradigms in Conflict: 10 Key Questions in Christian Missions Today.* Grand Rapids: Kregel, 2005.

Hiebert, Paul G. "The Flaw of the Excluded Middle." *Missiology: An International Review* 10, 1 (1982): 35–47.

Hiebert, Paul G. "Critical Contextualization," *Missiology* 12 (1984): 287–96. Reprints: *Anthropological Insights for Missionaries*. Grand Rapids: Baker, 1985, 171–92; *International Bulletin of Missionary Research* 11, 3 (1987): 104–12.

Hiebert, Paul G. *Anthropological Insights for Missionaries*. Grand Rapids: Baker, 1985.

Hiebert, Paul G. *Anthropological Reflections on Missiological Issues*. Grand Rapids: Baker, 1994.

Hiebert, Paul G. *Missiological Implications of Epistemological Shifts: Affirming Truth in a Modern/Postmodern World*. Harrisburg: International Trinity Press, 1999.

Hiebert, Paul G. *Transforming Worldviews: An Anthropological Understanding of How People Change*. Grand Rapids: Baker, 2008.

Hiebert, Paul G., and Frances F. Hiebert. *Case Studies in Missions*. Grand Rapids: Baker, 1987.

Hiebert, Paul G., R. Daniel Shaw, and Tite Tiénou. *Understanding Folk Religion: A Christian Response to Popular Beliefs and Practices*. Grand Rapids: Baker, 1999.

Hofstede, Geert H. *Culture's Consequences: International Differences in Work-related Values*. Beverly Hills: Sage Publications, 1980.

Hofstede, Geert H. *Cultures and Organizations: Software of the Mind*. New York: McGraw-Hill, 1991, 2005.

Huntington, Samuel P. *The Clash of Civilizations and the Remaking of World Order*. New York: Simon & Schuster, 1996.

Kant, Immanuel. *Critique of Judgment*. Indianapolis: Hackett, 1986.

Käser, Lothar. "Angewandte Anthropologie in Deutschland aus der Sicht von Afrikanern und Asiaten." *Evangelikale Missiologie* 17, 3 (2001): 91–94.

Käser, Lothar. *Foreign Cultures: A Cognitive Approach*. Nuremberg: VTR, 2014.

Käser, Lothar. *Animism: A Cognitive Approach*. Nuremberg: VTR, 2014.

Kato, Byang H. *Theological Pitfalls in Africa*. Nairobi: Evangel, 1975.

Kearney, Michael. *Worldview*. Novato: Chandler and Sharp, 1984.

Krabill, James R., ed. *Worship and Mission for the Global Church: An Ethnodoxology Handbook*. Pasadena: William Carey Library, 2012.

Kraft, Charles H. *Christianity in Culture: A Study in Dynamic Biblical Theologizing in Cross-Cultural Perspective*. Maryknoll: Orbis, 1979, 2005.

Kraft, Charles H. *Worldview for Christian Witness*. Pasadena: William Carey Library, 2008.

Kuhn, Thomas S. *The Structure of Scientific Revolutions*. Chicago: University of Chicago Press, 1962.

Kuhn, Thomas S. *The History of Science*. London: Routledge, 1977.

Lausanne Movement. "Lausanne Covenant (1974)." https://lausanne.org/content/covenant/lausanne-covenant.

Lausanne Movement. "Theological Implications of Radical Discipleship." In *Let the Earth Hear His Voice: Official Reference Volume, Papers and Responses*.

International Congress on World Evangelization Lausanne, ed. James D. Douglas, 1294–96. Minneapolis: World Wide Publications, 1975.

Lausanne Movement. *Willowbank Report: Consultation on Gospel and Culture (1978)*. Lausanne Occasional Paper no. 2. https://lausanne.org/content/lop/lop-2.

Lausanne Movement. "Grand Rapids Declaration on Evangelism and Social Responsibility (1982)." Lausanne Occasional Paper no. 21. https://lausanne.org/content/lop/lop-21.

Lausanne Movement. "Manila Manifesto (1989)." https://lausanne.org/content/manifesto/the-manila-manifesto.

Lausanne Movement. "Cape Town Commitment (2010)." https://lausanne.org/content/ctc/ctcommitment.

Lausanne Theology Working Group. "Statement on the Prosperity Gospel." *Evangelical Review of Theology* 34, 2 (2010): 99–102.

Lewis, Michael. *Shame: The Exposed Self*. New York: Macmillan, 1992.

Lingenfelter, Sherwood G. *Transforming Culture: A Challenge for Christian Mission*. Grand Rapids: Baker, 1992.

Lingenfelter, Sherwood G., and Marvin K. Mayers. *Ministering Cross-Culturally: An Incarnation Model for Personal Relationships*. Grand Rapids: Baker, 1986, 2003, 2016. https://books.google.com.

Lovejoy, Grant, ed. *Making Disciples of Oral Learners*. Lausanne Occasional Paper no. 54. Lima, NY, Bangalore: Lausanne Committee on World Evangelization and International Orality Network, 2005. https://orality.net/resources/docs/Making_Disciples_of_Oral_Learners-1264691848.pdf.

Lyotard, Jean-François. *The Postmodern Condition: A Report on Knowledge*. Minneapolis: University of Minnesota Press, 1985.

Madinger, Charles. "Coming to Terms with Orality: A Holistic Model." *Missiology* 38, 2 (2010): 201–13.

Malina, Bruce J., and Richard L. Rohrbaugh. *Social-Science Commentary on the Synoptic Gospels*. Minneapolis: Fortress, 1992.

Maslow, Abraham H. *Motivation and Personality*. New York: Harper & Row, 1970.

Mbiti, John S. *New Testament Eschatology in an African Background*. London: SPCK, 1969.

Mbiti, John S. *African Religions and Philosophy*. London: Heinemann, 1969.

McCrindle, Marc, and Emily Wolfinger. *The ABC of XYZ: Understanding the Global Generations*. Sydney: University of New South Wales Press, 2011. https://mccrindle.com.au.

McIlwain, Trevor. *Building on Firm Foundations: Guidelines for Evangelism and Teaching Believers*. 9 vol. Sanford: New Tribes Mission, 1987.

McIntosh, Gary L. *Make Room for the Boom ... or Bust: Six Church Models for Reaching Three Generations*. Grand Rapids: Revell, 1997.

Meyer, Erin. *The Culture Map: Decoding How People Think, Lead, and Get Things Done across Cultures*. New York: PublicAffairs, 2014.

Micah Network. "Declaration on Integral Mission (2001)." https://live-micah-global.pantheonsite.io/wp-content/uploads/2020/10/integral_mission_declaration_en.pdf.

Moon, Jay. "I Love to Learn, But I Don't Like to Read: The Rise of Secondary Oral Learning." *Orality Journal* 2, 2 (2013): 55–65.

Müller, Klaus W. *Das Gewissen in Kultur und Religion: Scham- und Schuld-orientierung als empirisches Phänomen des Über-Ich/Ich-Ideal. Lehrbuch Elenktik*. Nuremberg: VTR, 2009.

Müller, Klaus W. *Conscience – The Moral Law Within: Formation and Function of Super-Ego/Ego-Ideal, Shame and Guilt within Society, Culture and Religion. Handbook Elenctics*. Nuremberg: VTR, 2024.

Naugle, David K. *Worldview: The History of a Concept*. Grand Rapids: Eerdmans, 2001.

Neyrey, Jerome H., ed. *The Social World of Luke-Acts: Models for Interpretation*. Peabody: Hendrickson, 1991.

Neyrey, Jerome H., ed. *Honor and Shame in the Gospel of Matthew*. Louisville: John Knox, 1998.

Ng, Edmund. *Shame-informed Counselling and Psychotherapy: Eastern and Western Perspectives*. London: Routledge, 2020.

Nida, Eugene A. *Customs and Cultures: Anthropology for Christian Missions*. New York: Harper & Row, 1954.

Nyirongo, Leonard. *The Gods of Africa or the God of the Bible? The Snares of African Traditional Religion in Biblical Perspective*. Potchefstroom: University of Potchefstroom, 1997.

Palmer, Donald C. *Managing Conflict Creatively: A Guide for Missionaries and Christian Workers*. Pasadena: William Carey, 1990.

Penner, Peter F., ed. *The Word and Its Mission. Slavic Bible Commentary: A Contextual and Relevant Commentary for Eurasia*. Minneapolis: Fortress, 2017.

Peskett, Howard, and Vinoth Ramachandra. *The Message of Mission*. Downers Grove: InterVarsity Press, 2003.

Pew Research Center. "Religious Landscape Study." https://www.pewforum.org/religious-landscape-study.

Polanyi, Michael. *Personal Knowledge: Towards a Post-Critical Philosophy*. Chicago: University of Chicago Press, 1960.

Priest, Robert J. "Missionary Elenctics: Conscience and Culture." *Missiology* 22 (1994): 291–306.

The Holy Quran. Text, Translation and Commentary by Abdullah Yusuf Ali. Doha: Publications of Presidency of Islamic Courts and Affairs, State of Qatar, 1946.

Redfield, Robert. *The Primitive World and its Transformations*. Harmondsworth: Penguin, 1968.

Richards, E. Randolph, and Brandon J. O'Brien. *Misreading Scripture with Western Eyes: Removing Cultural Blinders to Better Understand the Bible*. Downers Grove: InterVarsity Press, 2012.

Richards, E. Randolph, and Richard James. *Misreading Scripture with Individualist Eyes: Patronage, Honor, and Shame in the Biblical World.* Downers Grove: InterVarsity Press, 2020.
Ricœur, Paul. *Oneself as Another.* Chicago: University of Chicago Press, 1992.
Ridderbos, Herman. *Paul: An Outline of His Theology.* Trans. John R. de Witt. Grand Rapids: Eerdmans, 1975.
Ritzer, George. *The McDonaldization of Society.* Thousand Oaks, CA: Pine Forge, 1993.
Rohrbaugh, Richard L., ed. *The Social Sciences and New Testament Interpretation.* Peabody: Hendrickson, 1996.
Russell, James C. *The Germanization of Early Medieval Christianity: A Socio-historical Approach to Religious Transformation.* New York: Oxford University Press, 1994.
Ryan, Richard, and Edward L. Deci. *Self-Determination Theory: Basic Psychological Needs in Motivation, Development, and Wellness.* New York: Guilford Publishing, 2017.
Ryken, Philip Graham. *What Is the Christian Worldview?* Phillipsburg: P&R Publishing, 2006.
Rynkievich, Michael A. *Soul, Self, and Society: A Postmodern Anthropology for Mission in a Postcolonial World.* Eugene: Cascade, 2011.
Shaw, R. Daniel. "The Context of Text: Transculturation and Bible Translation." In *The Word among Us*, ed. Dean S. Gilliland, 141–59. Dallas: Word, 1989.
Silzer, Sheryl Takagi. *Biblical Multicultural Teams: Applying Biblical Truth to Cultural Differences.* Pasadena: William Carey Library, 2014.
Smith, James K. A. *Desiring the Kingdom: Worship, Worldview, and Cultural Formation.* Cultural Liturgies Series 1. Grand Rapids: Baker Academic, 2009.
Sperber, Dan, and Deirdre Wilson. *Relevance: Communication and Cognition.* Oxford: Blackwell, 1986.
Spiro, Melford E. *Children of the Kibbutz.* Cambridge: Harvard University Press, 1958.
Spiro, Melford E. "Social Systems, Personality, and Functional Analysis." In *Studying Personality Cross-Culturally*, ed. Bert Kaplan, 93–128. New York: Harper & Row, 1961.
Stott, John R. W. *The Contemporary Christian: Applying God's Word in Today's World.* Leicester: Inter-Varsity Press, 1992.
Strauss, William, and Neil G. Howe. *Generations: The History of America's Future, 1584 to 2069.* New York: Quill, 1992.
Sundermeier, Theo. *Den Fremden verstehen: Eine praktische Hermeneutik.* Göttingen: Vandenhoeck und Ruprecht, 1996.
Taber, Clyde. "Contextualizing the Gospel in a Visual World." *Orality Journal* 2, 1 (2013). https://orality.net.
Tennent, Timothy C. *Invitation to World Missions: A Trinitarian Missiology for the Twenty-first Century.* Grand Rapids: Kregel, 2010.
Tiedeck, Heike. *Kulturen verstehen lernen: Wie interkulturelle Begegnungen gelingen können.* Nuremberg: VTR, 2018.

Treier, Daniel J. "Person." In *Evangelical Dictionary of Theology*, ed. Daniel J. Treier and Walter A. Elwell. Grand Rapids: Baker Academic, 2017.

Van Rheenen, Gailyn. "Animism, Secularism and Theism: Developing a Tripartite Model for Understanding World Cultures." *International Journal of Frontier Missions* 10, 4 (October 1993): 169–71.

Von Rad, Gerhard. *Old Testament Theology, vol. 2: The Theology of Israel's Prophetic Traditions.* Edinburgh: Oliver and Boyd, 1965; Westminster: John Knox Press, 2001.

Waardenburg, Jacques. *Classical Approaches to the Study of Religion: Aims, Methods, and Theories of Research. Introduction and Anthology.* 2nd ed. Berlin and Boston: De Gruyter, 2017.

Walls, Andrew F. "Converts or Proselytes? The Crisis over Conversion in the Early Church." *International Bulletin of Missionary Research* 28, no. 1 (2004): 2–6.

Watzlawick, Paul et al. *Pragmatics of Human Communication: A Study of Interactional Patterns, Pathologies, and Paradoxes.* New York: W. W. Norton & Co., 1967.

Weaver, Warren, and Claude E. Shannon. *The Mathematical Theory of Communication.* Urbana: University of Illinois, 1963.

Weber, Christian. *Wie andere Kulturen die Bibel sehen.* Zürich: TVZ, mission 21, 2020.

Weber, Max. *The Protestant Ethic and the Spirit of Capitalism*, ed. Richard Svedberg. Los Angeles: Roxbury, 1905, 1996.

Weber, Max. *Gesammelte Aufsätze zur Wissenschaftslehre.* Tübingen: J.C.B. Mohr, 1922.

Wells, David F. *No Place for Truth.* Grand Rapids: Eerdmans, 1993.

Wells, David F. *Above All Earthly Pow'rs: Christ in a Postmodern World.* Grand Rapids: Eerdmans, 2005.

Wescott, Robert W. *Introducing Anomalistics: A New Field of Interdisciplinary Study.* Deerfield Beach: Kronos, 1980.

White, James E. *Meet Generation Z: Understanding and Reaching the New Post-Christian World.* Grand Rapids: Baker, 2017.

Wiher, Hannes. *Shame and Guilt: A Key to Cross-Cultural Ministry.* Bonn: Culture and Science Publications, 2003.

Wiher, Hannes. "Worldview and Oral Preference Learners and Leaders." In *Beyond Literate Western Practices: Continuing Conversations in Orality and Theological Education*, ed. Samuel E. Chiang and Grant Lovejoy, 109–25. Hong Kong: Capstone Enterprises, 2014.

Wiher, Hannes. *Holistic Mission: An Historical and Theological Study of Its Development, 1966-2011.* WEA World of Theology Series 25. Bonn: Culture and Science Publications, 2022.

Wiher, Hannes. *Sharing the Good News: Evangelism in the Light of Scripture, Mission and Communication Science.* Nuremberg: VTR Publications, 2024.

Wiher, Hannes. *What Do You Believe? Learning to Understand Religions.* Carlisle: Langham Global Library, forthcoming.

Winter, Ralph. "Is It Possible? Global Cross-Cultural Mission Collaboration, 1910 to 2010." *Mission Frontiers* 31.1 (2009).

Wintle, Brian et al., ed. *South Asia Bible Commentary: A One-Volume Commentary on the Whole Bible*. Grand Rapids: Zondervan, 2015.

Wolff, Hans Walter. *Anthropology of the Old Testament*. Trans. Margaret Kohl. Mifflintown: Sigler Press, 1996.

Wright, Christopher J. H. *The Mission of God: Unlocking God's Narrative*. Downers Grove: InterVarsity Press, 2006.

Wright, N. T. *The New Testament and the People of God*. Minneapolis: Fortress, 1992.

Wrogemann, Henning. *Intercultural Theology, vol. 1: Intercultural Hermeneutics*. Trans. Karl E. Böhmer. Downers Grove: IVP Academic, 2016.

Wrogemann, Henning. *Intercultural Theology, vol. 2: Theologies of Mission*. Trans. Karl E. Böhmer. Downers Grove: IVP Academic, 2018.

Wu, Jackson. *Reading Romans with Eastern Eyes: Honor and Shame in Paul's Message and Mission*. Downers Grove: InterVarsity Press, 2019.

Wu, Jackson, and Ryan Jensen. *Seeking God's Face: Practical Reflections on Honor and Shame in Scripture*. Pasadena: William Carey Library, 2022.

Index of Names

A
Alderfer, Clayton 101
Altizer, Thomas J. J. 153
Ambrose of Milan 3
Anselm of Canterbury 104, 109
Augsburger, David W. 127
Augustine of Hippo 3, 35, 37, 110
Austin, John L. 63, 143

B
Balaam 93-94
Barth, Karl 37
Bastian, Jean-Pierre 153
Bediako, Kwame 46, 69-70, 103-4
Benedict, Ruth 20
Berger, Peter L. 31
Beyerhaus, Peter 15
Boas, Franz 20
Bockmühl, Klaus 139
Bosch, David J. 121-22
Briggs Myers, Isabel 12
Bürki, Hans 14, 189

C
Calvin, John 23, 35, 70, 105
Campus for Christ 155
Carter, Rita 142
Champion, Françoise 153
Chiang, Samuel E. 139, 141, 183
Clemens of Alexandria 70
Codrington, Robert 62
Comte, Auguste 20
Cook Briggs, Katherine 12
Coupland, Douglas 156
Cross, John R. 82, 212

D
Deci, Edward L. 101
Derrida, Jacques 153

DeSilva, David A. 79
Donovan, Kath 156
Dooyeweerd, Herman 32, 36
Douglas, Mary 91, 193-94
Durkheim, Émile 20

E
Edgar, William 16
Engelsviken, Tormod 121-22
Erlacher, Jolene 156
Escobar, Samuel 14, 189
Eusebius of Caesarea 46

F
Ferry, Luc 98, 152, 169
Flanders, Christopher 79
Flemming, Dean E. 37
Foucault, Michel 21
Freud, Sigmund 13, 55

G
Geertz, Clifford 31
Georges, Jayson 79, 133
Gilliland, Dean S. 16, 118
Green, Daniel 126-27

H
Hasenfratz, Hans-Peter 168
Hegel, Georg Friedrich 20
Hesselgrave, David J. 18, 116, 123
Hiebert, Paul G. 4-5, 32, 34, 36-37, 41, 44, 68, 76, 150, 171-73
Hofstede, Geert H. 194-95
Howe, Neil G. 156
Huntington, Samuel P. 155

I
Idowu, Bolaji 70

J
James, Richard 117
Jerphagnon, Lucien 98
Jung, Carl Gustav 12–13
Justin Martyr 70

K
Käsemann, Ernst 111
Käser, Lothar 1, 17, 26, 30, 32, 34, 36, 43, 62–63, 162, 165, 168
Kato, Byang H. 60, 70
Kearney, Michael 39–40
King Saul 93
Krabill, James R. 140–41
Kraft, Charles H. 16, 32, 34, 36, 92
Kroeber, Alfred 20

L
Lawrenz, Mel 126–27
Lewis, Michael 55–56, 80
Lingenfelter, Sherwood G. 59–60, 136–37, 142, 148, 183, 197, 203
Lovejoy, Grant 139–41, 183
Luckmann, Thomas L. 31
Lyotard, Jean-François 153

M
Madinger, Charles 140–41
Malina, Bruce J. 79
Malinowski, Bronislaw 20
Maslow, Abraham H. 101
Max-Neef, Manfred 101
Mayers, Marvin K. 59–60, 136–37, 142, 183, 197, 203
Mbiti, John S. 43, 46, 60, 70
McCrindle, Mark 156, 177
McIlwain, Trevor 212
McIntosh, Gary L. 156
Mead, Margaret 20
Meyer, Erin 195–96
Meyer, Joyce 155
Mischke, Werner 79
Mulago, Vincent 70
Müller, Klaus W. 1, 36, 79
Myors, Ruth 156

N
Naugle, David K. 32–38, 40
Neyrey, Jerome H. 79
Ng, Edmund 127
Nyirongo, Lenard 60

O
O'Brien, Brandon J. 117, 133
Origen of Alexandria 46
Osteen, Joel 155

P
Padilla, C. René 14, 189
Palmer, Donald C. 181
Priest, Robert J. 90, 128, 212

R
Radcliffe-Brown, Alfred R. 20
Redfield, Robert 40
Ricci, Matteo 46
Richards, E. Randolph 117, 133
Ricœur, Paul 69
Ridderbos, Herman 29, 98
Ritzer, George 155
Rohrbaugh, Richard L. 79
Rousselet, Kathy 153
Russell, James C. 151
Ryan, Richard 79, 101
Ryken, Philip G. 32, 36, 102–3

S
Samuel 14, 139, 141, 155, 181, 183, 189
Shannon, Claude E. 143
Shaw, R. Daniel 44, 118
Silzer, Sheryl Takagi 18
Smith, James K. A. 36
Sperber, Dan 143
Spiro, Melford E. 51–54, 141, 148
Stott, John R. W. 17, 117, 121–22
Strauss, William 156
Stuhlmacher, Peter 111
Sundermeier, Theo 71–72

T
Taber, Clyde 140

Tatian 70
Taylor, William D. 156
Tennent, Timothy C. 16
Tertullian 70
Tiedeck, Heike 138, 148, 163–64

U
Ulfilas 168

V
Von Rad, Gerhard 60

W
Waardenburg, Jacques 26
Walls, Andrew F. 98
Watzlawick, Paul 144
Weaver, Warren 143
Weber, Christian 196
Weber, Max 20, 32, 151
Wells, David F. 153
White, James E. 156
White, Katy 156
Wiher, Hannes 1, 17, 27, 47, 63, 91, 93, 124, 131–33, 137, 141, 146, 164, 173, 183
Wilson, Deirdre 143
Wolff, Hans Walter 29, 60
Wright, Christopher J. H. 24, 89
Wright, N. T. 140
Wrogemann, Henning 21

Index of Subjects

A
achievement focus 136, 149, 197, 200, 206
action 21, 52, 63, 86, 121, 167, 181, 201
amulet 63
analogue communication 142
analytic thinking 107, 136, 142, 149, 201, 206
ancestor 166
ancient Near East 61, 124, 146, 151
and-and logic 76
anima 13, 165, 167
animism 85, 164–66, 169, 171–73, 175, 185, 209–11
anomalistics 165
antagonistic approach 132
anti-authoritarianism 154
antiquity 13
apologetics 38, 106
apophatic theology 107
attachment figures 51–52
autonomy 125, 136–37, 193, 199

B
baby boomers 156, 158
baraka 62, 65
baroque 149, 152
basic values 31, 34, 136, 197, 208
Bethel 155
biblical interpretation 120, 133
Big Five 12
BIOS 19, 22, 35
black box 13, 35, 39, 48
bounded set 149–50
Brahmanism 169, 173
Buddhism 46, 64, 85, 169–73, 175, 209, 211

C
cannibalism 63
Cape Town Commitment 123
centred set 149
character 37–38, 46, 69, 102, 110, 167–68, 176, 201, 208
Christ as victor 107, 109
Christ-centred shalom 108
coherence 35, 37–39
collectivism 136, 195, 199
compassion 87, 167
conflict 4, 76, 123, 127, 145–46, 176, 179–82
conflict resolution 146, 176, 180
Confucianism 85, 169–72, 175
congregationalist model 125
conscience orientation 40, 49, 53–54, 57, 59, 62, 68, 70, 73, 75, 77, 87, 93, 102, 104–5, 109–10, 112, 114, 119–20, 127–28, 131–33, 135–36, 140–42, 145–46, 149–52, 154, 164, 169, 171–73, 175–82, 186, 194
constructivism 8, 154
contextualization 46, 119–20
conversion 53, 66, 68, 73–76, 102–3, 105, 128, 189
counselling 125, 127–28, 133
courage to fail 136, 201, 206
covenant formula 89, 112, 115
creation 24–25, 37, 40, 46, 61, 67, 73, 75, 77, 102, 139, 149, 164, 170, 175, 191, 209–10
critical contextualization 68
critical realism 4
critical realist theology 4
cultural anthropology 1, 7, 21, 33, 47, 62, 77, 164
cultural identity 69, 76, 105

cultural layers 74
cultural mandate 21
cultural skin layers 73, 77, 189
cultural triangle 117–18

D
dabar 63, 66
Daoism 86, 169–72, 175
deconstruction 153
deep structures 2, 8, 13, 53, 66, 70, 72, 77, 133
defence mechanisms 190
demonic imprint 21, 103
diachronic 5, 37
dialogue 93, 109, 121, 132, 194
diffusionism 20–21
digital communication 142
digital orality 141
direct communication 199
discourse theory 21
divine imprint 47
dogmatic theology 107
dominion theology 211

E
efficiency 71, 149–50, 152, 155, 175
egalitarian society 149, 200
ego ideal 54–55
either-or logic 76
empirical psychology 12–13, 39
Enlightenment 4, 25, 33, 152, 170–71, 173
episcopal model 124–25
epistemology 4, 33
esotericism 165
essentialism 7, 136
ethnodoxology 140–41
Ethnodoxology Network 140
evangelism 45, 74, 120–23, 128, 139, 145, 153, 190
event orientation 60, 136, 197, 200, 206
event speech 131–32
evolutionism 20–21
extraversion 12

F
fall 21, 37, 57, 102, 104, 117, 164
fear of losing face 136, 201, 206
fear of the Lord 88
fetish 63
five soteriological concepts 40, 46–47, 57, 73, 75, 77, 102, 107, 154, 170, 172, 175, 209
folk religions 169, 171–72, 211
forgiveness 45, 47, 49–51, 57–58, 69, 85, 88, 90–92, 104, 107, 109, 127, 149–50, 180, 211–12
fragmentation 21, 155
functionalism 7, 20–21, 154

G
Generation
 Generation Alpha 156–57, 160–62, 177–78
 Generation X 154, 156–58, 160–62, 178
 Generation Y 156, 160–62, 178
 Generation Z 156–57, 159–62, 178
Germanic peoples 151
glasses 19, 22, 31, 35, 118, 186
globalization 111, 149, 153–55, 161, 175, 177, 182, 186
Grand Rapids Declaration 121
group identity 149, 200

H
health and wealth gospel 61–62
Hebrew worldview 41, 46–47, 75, 89, 102, 170
hēsēd 87, 108, 113
hierarchical society 149, 200
Hillsong 155
Hinduism 46, 64, 85, 169–72, 174–75, 209, 211
historicism 33
history 1, 3, 7, 20, 24, 35, 37–38, 67, 72, 77, 102, 104, 107, 109, 125, 148, 167
holistic thinking 107, 136, 142, 149, 197, 201, 206

holistic worldview 41, 162, 170
hybridity 155, 161, 175, 177, 182

I
iceberg 19, 22
ideal type 54, 152
identification 55, 127
identity "in Christ" 67, 69
inaugurated eschatology 61, 108
in-depth approach 2, 5
indirect communication 199
individualism 136, 195, 199
input 12, 35
interconnectivity 155
intercultural communication 91, 101, 127–28, 209
International Orality Network 139–40
introversion 12
ipséité 69

J
justification 58, 105, 107, 109–10, 124, 151

K
karma 46, 64
kataphatic theology 107
kerygmatic approach 132

L
late modernity 111, 149, 152, 154
Lausanne Covenant 121
Lausanne Movement 17, 120–23, 139, 145
layers model 40, 46, 61, 73, 77, 102, 149–50, 154, 164, 169–71, 175
leader 124, 176–77, 181
leadership 71, 124–25, 127, 133, 135–36, 141, 147, 176–77, 180, 182, 196
lens 19, 117–18, 186
levirate 93
lifestyle 54, 73, 199
living dead 149

M
mana 40, 62–66, 73, 77, 89, 91, 154, 176
Manila Manifesto 121
McDonaldization 155
meaning 25, 33, 55, 62, 67, 74, 76, 87, 101, 107–8, 110–11, 118–20, 158, 182
mediation 58
mediator 50, 70–71, 88, 91–92, 105, 146, 149, 166, 181, 211–12
medieval Christianity 151
Mediterranean 109, 114, 124–25, 146, 151
mêmeté 69
metacommunication 144
middle sphere 171
millennials 156, 159–61
missional church movement 153
mission studies 3
modalism 16
modernism 8, 152–54, 158, 175
modernity 8, 37–38, 145, 149, 152–53, 161, 175, 182
Myers Briggs Type Indicator 12
mystery cults 36

N
narrative identity 69–70
narrative theology 107
negotiations 178–79
Neoplatonism 151–52, 171
New Age 165, 175
new creation 61, 74–75
non-verbal communication 123, 128, 131–32, 145–46

O
OCEAN 12
onion 19, 22
output 12, 35

P
paradoxical communication 144
people orientation 136

persona 13
personality profile 54, 186, 208
person orientation 197, 200, 206
perspectivism 33
persuasion 196
philosophy 1–3, 18, 32–33, 36–39, 46, 77, 152, 166, 169, 171–73
plausibility structures 34
pluralism 26, 154, 158
postmodernism 8, 152–54, 158, 175
postmodernity 8, 145, 149, 154, 161, 175
poststructuralist 8, 154
post-war generation 156–58, 160–62, 178
power dynamics 8
power encounter 106–7, 132
preparation for the gospel 46
presbyterian model 124–25
pre-war generation 156–57, 160–62, 178
priesthood of all believers 125
process theology 153
proclamation 45, 120–23, 132
prosperity gospel 211
psychoanalysis 13, 39, 51, 54, 126–27
psychology 1, 3, 13, 32, 47, 68, 77, 148, 150, 166
punctuality orientation 60, 136, 206
purity 41, 85, 90–91, 164

R
realized eschatology 61, 108
receptor-oriented communication 92
reconciliation 49, 58, 88, 92, 111, 149–50, 180–81, 190
reconstruction 153
redemption 37, 67, 92, 102, 109, 189
Reformation 110–11, 125, 139, 149, 151–52
relational approach 104, 106, 109, 111–12, 124, 132, 144
relational encounter 132
relational personality 136, 199
relational society 149

relational theology 107
relativism 20–21, 33, 154, 158
religious experiences 25
religious studies 1, 3, 25, 77
Renaissance 149, 151–52
reparation 50, 58, 88, 110, 127, 149–50, 180
repentance 58, 88, 109, 180
righteousness 74, 87, 92, 108, 110–11, 113–15, 120, 180, 211
romanticism 33, 149, 152
rules-based ethics 112
rules-based personality 136, 199
rules-based society 149–50
rules-based theology 107

S
satisfaction theory 104, 107, 109
Scholasticism 13
secular worldview 41, 170
SEIC 167–68
semiotic 20–21, 33
Septuagint 86, 119
shaman 166–67, 181
Shema sentences 131
Shintoism 85, 169–70, 172, 175
social responsibility 121, 145
sociology 1, 3, 7, 33, 77, 156, 166
soul 13, 38, 87, 112, 165–70
spirit beings 40, 45, 166–67, 171–72, 209
spirit double 91, 166–68
spirituality 160, 165
spiritual warfare 65, 107
split-level Christianity 76–77
status focus 136, 149, 197, 200, 206
strategic pastoral counselling 126–27
structuralism 7, 154
subjectivism 33
superego 13, 54–55
supernatural 62, 65
synchronic 5
syncretism 76
systematic theology 107

T

talisman 63
task orientation 136, 197, 200, 206
temperament 12
theocentric covenant ethics 115
theocentric relational ethics 112
theology of the word 106
theories of fragmentation 155
theories of homogenization 155
The Shack 155
three horizons 117, 119
time orientation 40, 59, 77, 154, 196–97, 200
transactional analysis 13
transculturation 118
tree 18–19, 22, 173
tri-polar perspective on religions 47
truth encounter 106–7, 132
two-tiered worldview 41, 162, 170

U

unified identity 68, 76

V

verbal communication 131, 142
vicarious atoning sacrifice 107, 110

W

Willowbank Report 17
woman in Endor 93
word (in action) 66

Langham Literature and its imprints are a ministry of Langham Partnership.

Langham Partnership is a global fellowship working in pursuit of the vision God entrusted to its founder John Stott –

> *to facilitate the growth of the church in maturity and Christ-likeness through raising the standards of biblical preaching and teaching.*

Our vision is to see churches in the Majority World equipped for mission and growing to maturity in Christ through the ministry of pastors and leaders who believe, teach and live by the word of God.

Our mission is to strengthen the ministry of the word of God through:
- nurturing national movements for biblical preaching
- fostering the creation and distribution of evangelical literature
- enhancing evangelical theological education

especially in countries where churches are under-resourced.

Our ministry

Langham Preaching partners with national leaders to nurture indigenous biblical preaching movements for pastors and lay preachers all around the world. With the support of a team of trainers from many countries, a multi-level programme of seminars provides practical training, and is followed by a programme for training local facilitators. Local preachers' groups and national and regional networks ensure continuity and ongoing development, seeking to build vigorous movements committed to Bible exposition.

Langham Literature provides Majority World preachers, scholars and seminary libraries with evangelical books and electronic resources through publishing and distribution, grants and discounts. The programme also fosters the creation of indigenous evangelical books in many languages, through writer's grants, strengthening local evangelical publishing houses, and investment in major regional literature projects, such as one volume Bible commentaries like *The Africa Bible Commentary* and *The South Asia Bible Commentary*.

Langham Scholars provides financial support for evangelical doctoral students from the Majority World so that, when they return home, they may train pastors and other Christian leaders with sound, biblical and theological teaching. This programme equips those who equip others. Langham Scholars also works in partnership with Majority World seminaries in strengthening evangelical theological education. A growing number of Langham Scholars study in high quality doctoral programmes in the Majority World itself. As well as teaching the next generation of pastors, graduated Langham Scholars exercise significant influence through their writing and leadership.

To learn more about Langham Partnership and the work we do visit **langham.org**

www.ingramcontent.com/pod-product-compliance
Lightning Source LLC
Chambersburg PA
CBHW071429150426
43191CB00008B/1093